Məst

The Ecstatic

Məst - The Ecstatic (English)

Credits:
Cover image: Mohana Hanumatananda
Back cover painting: Kirti Khandelwal

Published by:
Gurulight
Email: info@gurulight.com
Web: www.gurulight.com

© Mohanji (Mohan Pathirisseri Kesavan).
All rights reserved.
First edition published August 2020

Məst
The Ecstatic

Mohanji

Gurulight

This Book is offered as flowers of gratitude
To the Great Masters of every path
who guided mankind to freedom from all kinds
of bindings of mind, intellect and ego, through time;
To all the kind beings who exist on earth and in other realms;
To all the wisdom and knowledge
that flows from them like an eternal river
that is consistently nourishing the seekers of each generation;
To the eternal silence that fathered
the entire dimensions of sounds of the universe,
even the frequencies of creation, sustenance and dissolution.
To the eternal mind that stays unaffected by
the creations and un-creations of the universe.
To the known and unknown Masters
of the past, present and future, in all the planes of existence, and
To the Grand Tradition that flows through
hundreds of Spiritual Gurus
forever...

FREEDOM AND ECSTASY – THE FIRST *Mast*

The Hindu scriptures suggest that time repeats itself eternally in cycles. Each cycle consists of four ages in succession with a steady decline of awareness from one age to the next. In the first age, the Golden age, all beings are in the aspect of God all the time, forever immersed in perpetual consciousness, and the operating platform is unconditional love. No confusion. No distortion. No illusion. No expectation. No evil. Perfect harmony. There is complete flexibility, complete freedom. In the second age, the Silver age, duality took birth - a 'me' separate from 'you'. Each being now had the choice to stay directly connected to consciousness or to stay separate to experience the play of Unity consciousness.

Despite the separation, one had full awareness of their direct connection to Unity consciousness but there was a danger of identifying completely with the separation and losing this awareness. The identification brings illusions, then the corresponding desires and the corresponding life. That is when karma takes birth. With each yuga, the aspect of separation intensifies until the separation becomes complete in the Bronze age (our present age), when we are totally detached from the truth. Then, the Masters come and show us who we were. Some people may understand and want to return while others may still not understand. Eventually the cycle completes, the universe is dissolved and restored to the Golden age, thus starting the next cycle.

In later ages, many saints were attempting to connect to the perpetual consciousness directly as in the Golden Age. Try as they might, they couldn't attain that state. Around that time, there appeared in the Himalayas, a man with matted hair, completely naked, spear in hand, dancing away. Just singing and dancing. He drove away, anyone who came near him out of curiosity. Most thought he was mad and ignored him. But some wondered, "How can this man be perpetually ecstatic?" Our happiness is based on conditions. This man never stays in one place. He is not worried about people, place, situations or time." His total freedom was very difficult to understand. They followed him everywhere. He didn't care. He lived in complete abandon. His happiness was not fixed on anything outside. He was in his own world. Sometimes, he would ask them to sit down and connect to their spine and then he would leave. He was not there to teach them all the time. This went on for some time. Gradually, the people who followed him became powerful. How did they progress to that awareness?

Their minds were focused entirely on him. It didn't matter what happened outside. Thus, they became him. They started having the same experiences. They detached from people, spaces, situations and time. They became eternally free. Freedom is the greatest gift a Master can give to any disciple. Freedom from people, time, space, situations, concepts and even from himself. They had no mind outside of them. Everything shifted inside. They lost awareness of the world outside, even became oblivious of their own body. After an eternity of contemplation, the ecstatic murmur from deep within drowned all the external sounds. The intensity of the internal murmur sucked in – all the senses, mind, intellect and ego. It was like a huge whirlpool. Everything fell into it and got dissolved. They danced without moving. The inner dance! The dance of beingness! The dance of ecstasy and bliss, dissolution and complete oneness. They were HOME.

This is the story of the first *Mast*. They called him Shiva, which means "the liberated". If you understand this story well, you will see how the Tradition began - from complete pathlessness. There is no path to latch onto. What happens then? You are liberated - 100% freedom. What is the core of the whole teaching? Be yourself. Be natural. Be you. This is what Shiva tells people. If you choose to be yourself, you will be very powerful. If you understand yourself, you understand the whole of creation. This is what Shiva represents - the whole consciousness represented inside. He exists through all the ages but we have lost the power to see him. He remains as a reminder of your lost glory. You are the whole consciousness. Go within. Be in ecstasy with yourself. Become You! Become *Mast*!

समस्ताः लोकाः सुखिनो भवन्तु
Samastha Loka Sukhino Bhavanthu
(May all the beings in all the worlds be happy)

ॐ शान्तिः शान्तिः शान्तिः
Aum Shanti Shanti Shanti
(Peace, peace, and peace be everywhere!)

DEDICATION

With deep gratitude, I surrender this book, my humble contribution, as flowers offered at the feet of our Grand Tradition of absolute freedom and ultimate liberation; all the great masters which Time provided to the thirsty minds; great guides and selfless beings who walked ahead of us, are with us and will be with us, and who led us, lead us and are still leading us.

Liberation is our very nature. We are always liberated. Our mind-matter (mind, intellect and ego, the processors of our system) does not make us feel it that way because they are associated with our identifications – our possessions and positions. Since we spontaneously associate ourselves with our incarnations and things outside of us, we remain bound to the usual "me and mine" feelings. Since we do not feel our liberated state, we have methods and means to make us feel and experience our true nature of liberated existence. A *Mast* is a walking expression of complete liberation. Atmananda is liberation personified.

The Tradition of liberation has no beginning nor end. It flows eternally. There is no room for ownership or ego. All are part of the grand design. All are integral. All are significant. All are insignificant, too, in the grand canvass of existence. All exist and do not exist. The Grand Tradition flows eternally. This is where we belong; this is our real family. There are no boundaries. Tradition has no barriers – no gender, caste, colour, creed, country, culture or customs. One Father (the supreme unbound consciousness) and various aspects and expressions of that One Father. Ignorance alienates us, while understanding and awareness unite us. Man, minus ego is GOD.

I bow down to all the children of this rich Tradition of supreme unconditionality. I bow down to this rich Tradition built and cemented with FAITH and SUPREME LOVE. Every thought, every word and every action are offered as sacred water of Mother Ganga at the feet of the great Tradition of Supreme Masters. This soul and body, time and space, are all gifts of the Tradition. What can I offer you, my Tradition, which is not already yours? I surrender my seeming knowledge at the feet of the Tradition of liberation. I surrender my ignorance too, at the feet of the Tradition. I simply do not exist, except as a representation of the great Tradition.

All knowledge is useful for somebody. All words have value to somebody. All are valuable in the universe. All are creations. All are expressions. There is no wastage in the world. Nothing is wasted. When you look at the world through eyes of respect and gratitude, all that you can see is unbound beauty and indescribable joy of diversity. The complexity of creation is unfathomable too. When you understand the consciousness of Atmananda, you will sink into this feeling of emptiness from ego and unending gratitude towards every aspect of existence within us and outside us.

I bow and surrender everything to the Light of Wisdom eternally flown to us by the Tradition of great Masters of the grand universe.

ACKNOWLEDGEMENTS

I thank all those people who trusted me and stood by me through different terrains of life. I respect their integrity, consistency, trust, and faith in me, and the unconditional love that they maintained despite the ebbs and flows of life. I thank them, especially for not expecting much from me, and for accepting my weaknesses and strengths as an ordinary human being. I am grateful to them for not judging me. I thank them for accepting my numerous flaws, terrestrial deficiencies, naiveties, and gently guiding and saving me from the treacherous paths of life. I thank them for not putting me on a pedestal and not expecting too much from me.

I am not separate from those who love me. Neither am I separate from those who hate me. I am happy to be part of their lives. I enjoy their presence and proximity. The same goes with those who like me or dislike me, accept me or reject me, trust me or distrust me. The world is an interesting medley of numerous melodies. The best thing to do is to listen to what is being played, like when you tune in to your neighbourhood radio broadcasting station. You can avoid listening to it by switching it off. But if you choose to stay in touch with society, what streams through it needs to be accepted and heard, whether you like it or not. Not tuning in is considered escapism, denial, and even stagnation in life. Hence, it is not recommended.

I would like to express my gratitude to all those who supported me energetically and physically in the creation of these stories.

Especially, I thank the great Tradition of Liberation. I am not sufficient or significant. I am the most insignificant. The Tradition of Liberation flows eternally. There have been many before us, and many will walk after us too. We all are passing through this earth with our bodies today. We have no more significance besides the fact that we are alive at this point. We cannot take anything from here anywhere, but we can experience anything we want while being here. That also depends on our capacity, or availability of the senses and most importantly, availability of the mind.

I make it a point to practice insignificance, and this helps me detach from temptations of terrestrial accolades and glories. Hence, I am sure this work is not my best and not even mine, *per se*. Some words that travelled through my mind found their way into this document. It became a book. If you like it, it would be gratifying to know. If you do not enjoy it, my sincere apologies for having wasted your time. I always remain a servant of the Tradition of Liberation.

I would like to thank my wife, Devi Mohan, and daughter, Mila Mohan, for their eternal patience for my eccentric lifestyle. I would like to thank my parents for their unfailing and unstinting support over all these years. I would like to thank Rajesh Kamath for the time and patience to compile, structure and present my thoughts and words into this book. I express my sincere gratitude to Sunita Kripalani for patiently editing the language of this book. I also thank Rajeshwari Menon Prakash and Sathya Shivakumar for their contributions in the making of this book.

With all my love,
Mohanji

IN SEARCH OF THE PRECIOUS

We belong to a grand tradition of non-violence, selflessness, compassion, kindness, unconditional love, sharing and caring. We are its children, as well as its torchbearers. But we live in a world of make-believe and pretence. We pretend to be happy with our momentary pleasures and to be what we are not. Humans are slaves of circumstances, with our whole existence mortgaged to uncertain yet compelling comfort zones. Every moment, we live our karmic inevitability and helplessness as incarnations, totally ignorant. Even though we possess the potential for a liberated existence, all the while, we internally resist everything that happens! We even express our incomprehension of the true meaning of liberation through strange behavioural choices such as smoking, drugs, alcohol, a variety of indulgences, wild and destructive habits and actions, restlessness, and many other things; things that we consider as our freedom of choice deluding as the existence of liberation. All this is helplessly binding us more and more to earth. Most of us feign happiness until death. Some pretend for a short period that they are happy before they quickly realise that nothing transitory can give permanent happiness. Everyone pretends. In our times, people are looking for quick remedies and instant *nirvana*. I wonder, "Is that possible?"

At some point in their life, some people realise that there is a much deeper version to our mundane existence. They attain the strength and will to explore that possibility. They might be considered as abnormal, eccentric or even anti-social. Minds fail to understand them. Minds misunderstand them. Through constant self enquiry, they stabilise their awareness within themselves. Separating themselves from the world of noises, they swim in the ocean of the unfathomable Divine. Unchangeable and inaccessible to the senses and mind. The world of noises and the world of mind may consider them as madmen as well. Sometimes, they are ridiculed or maybe even crucified but they remain unaffected by the world of noises, needing nothing from it. These are the pure, priceless diamonds of every generation.

One such precious diamond lived around four centuries ago, a wandering monk by the name of *Baba*[1] Atmananda Chaitanya. He was referred to as *Rasta*[2] *Baba* (the *Baba* on the road), for Atmananda was always 'on the road'. He neither cared about disclosing his identity or mundane details such as his date and place of birth nor about his name and stature. Many people thought that the *Baba* was a madman because he contradicted himself several times, confused everyone, didn't bother about food or clothing, and was invariably always wandering. Some mornings, people would find him sweeping the road. If someone gave him money, he would buy food and distribute it amongst the poor and hungry – children, old people, and stray animals. Consumed by this activity, there were many days when Atmananda simply did not eat.

He seldom stayed at one place for more than three nights and, irrespective of the weather, he kept travelling. Many people followed him and accompanied him on his seemingly aimless journeys – some out of curiosity, others out of faith, believing him to be a true Master. He accepted no disciples, never initiated anyone to any paths of spiritual pursuit, but took care of all those

---
[1] *Fatherly figure. Used as a mark of respect.*
[2] *Road. In this context, one who lives on the road*

who dared to live with him. He lived his life with sheer abandon, and people who connected to his consciousness spontaneously or choicelessly became flexible because of his lack of pattern. Extreme flexibility is a sign of high spiritual stability. The more flexible you are in the world, the more spiritual you are. This was exactly the message he was giving to the world.

Atmananda was a *Mast* – one who is fully and completely settled within himself. One who has nothing to do with the external world and remains totally unbound to materials, people, positions, and possessions; one who has all the powers, but hardly cares to use them or display them, for they need nothing from the earth.

A *Mast* exists in perfect freedom, not the freedom that we talk about – the choices between material possessions, positions, and emotions. Perfect freedom is total freedom from existence itself – living inaction, no ownership, no desires, no likes or dislikes. We are no doubt free to make our choices, free to choose what we eat, whether to be married or not, to possess something material or not: this is what we believe to be true freedom. But all this is relative freedom. Existence in perfect freedom is when we need nothing from here when we give no importance to our lives, positions, and possessions when we are ready to give everything possible to the world without expecting anything in return. No situation, person, material or state evokes any emotion in a *Mast*. He lives the stillness of the all-pervading Supreme Consciousness and remains unruffled by all events of life.

In this pretentious world of possessions and positions, the methods of Atmananda Chaitanya and many such saints of our grand Tradition of liberation may not make much sense to people with minds. We usually hold on to our insecurities, phobias, fears, prejudices, concepts, anxieties, and ego. We would rather walk the familiar path of certainty than the ever-uncertain path of pathlessness to supreme liberation. This is our usual attitude. Only a few see the light because liberation from the birth and death cycle is not everyone's concern, let alone priority. Most choose the darkness of ignorance because, in this darkness of relative existence, they can easily hide lifetimes of repetitive patterns. We can hide our true nature under the cloak of darkness as well, and ease into the masks of life. Those who relish their cowardly nature may even justify it to feel safe and sane. They chant, "Light is sorrow, darkness is bliss!" Are we amongst those cowards who refuse to face themselves? Think well. And brace yourself to read further, for this is the story of practical education by a surreal saint, for an unlikely student!

FREEDOM AND ECSTASY – THE FIRST *Mas̱t* vii

DEDICATION...x

ACKNOWLEDGEMENTS xii

IN SEARCH OF THE PRECIOUS xiv

SECTION 1: FRUITS OF TRADITION 1
- Chapter 1: A Seeker Is Born 2
- Chapter 2: A Seeker Is Made 11
- Chapter 3: The Humble Disciple 20
- Chapter 4: The Glorious Master 26
- Chapter 5: The Golden Path 34
- Chapter 6: Pearls Of Wisdom 42
- Chapter 7: A Tale Of Two Friends 61
- Chapter 8: The Farewell 66
- Chapter 9: The Homecoming....................................... 72

SECTION 2 : ATMANANDA'S MEMOIRS 84
- Chapter 1: Causes And Effects 85
- Chapter 2: A Siddha Of The Himalayas 102
- Chapter 3: The Farmer's Son 108
- Chapter 4: Atmananda And The Thief 112
- Chapter 5: At Home With A Tiger And A Snake.................... 117
- Chapter 6: A Day In The Life Of Atmananda 124
- Chapter 7: Different Strokes.. 134

Section 3: Atmananda's Odyssey 152
Chapter 1: A Strange Tryst With A Begging Bowl 153
Chapter 2: Sweetmeats To Liberation 166
Chapter 3: Aghora Babaji And Rama Shastri 172
Chapter 4: The Akshaya Patra (Inexhaustible Vessel) 180
Chapter 5: Divine Designs Of Life... 189
Chapter 6: Hotter Than The Raging Sun 195
Chapter 7: Born Of Fire.. 206

Section 4: The Eternal Wings Of A Grand Tradition 211
Chapter 1: An Encounter With An Ageless Saint Of The Himalayas 212
Chapter 2: The Inevitable Journey To The Himalayas 221
Chapter 3: Go To The North. Do Not Look Back................... 225
Chapter 4: The Journey To Liberation.. 235
Chapter 5: The Master Seeketh The Seeker 242

Section 5: Atmananda Leaves…   …Atmananda Lives 248
Chapter 1: Glimpses Of The Avadhoota.................................... 249
Chapter 2: Manu Breaks His 'Silence'... 255
Chapter 3: Preparing For The Exit 259
Chapter 4: The Final Goodbye 263
Chapter 5: A Naga Baba's Account 267
Chapter 6: Presence From The Beyond....................................... 271
Chapter 7: Watch And Witness The Cows 277

SECTION 6: TEACHINGS OF ATMANAND **284**
    CHAPTER 1: MEMORIES OF A WANDERING MONK 285
    CHAPTER 2: A DREAM OF REVELATIONS 289
    CHAPTER 3: VISIONS OF THE DARK SIDE 302
    CHAPTER 4: CHHAYA VAIRI AND THE GOODNESS FACTOR 313
    CHAPTER 5: EXPENSIVE IGNORANCE 319
    CHAPTER 6: THE PEAK OF EMPTINESS... 323
    CHAPTER 7: THE PATH OF THE PATHLESS 326
    CHAPTER 8: RULES OF THE TRADITION.. 337
    CHAPTER 9: QUOTES FROM ATMANANDA 339
GLOSSARY..347

SECTION 1

Fruits of Tradition

*"Tradition never leaves the hand of the true seeker.
Gurus transcend oceans of existence to be with a true seeker.
This is the promise of the Tradition
where eligibility is the only factor."*

CHAPTER 1

A SEEKER IS BORN

A few centuries ago, a humble, saintly priest by the name of Vishnu Sharman lived in a village in present-day Maharashtra, with his wife Savithri Devi and their only son Vamadeva. Vamadeva was a quiet, brilliant boy and both the parents were proud of him. Given the boy's keen intelligence, Vishnu Sharman wanted Vamadeva to gain scholarship in the scriptures and become a priest so he would do well in life. Like other young village children, the young boy was sent for part time lessons to the old village temple where the young priest, Trivikrama, taught them during his free time, after completing his morning worship and chores. The short lessons were mostly chanting Vedic *mantras* with the correct intonation. Trivikrama would also share stories from the scriptures and of the great Masters, both past and present.

One of his favorite topics was *Maharishi*[3] Shantananda, a great Master from Varanasi. Rarely a day would pass without Trivikrama speaking about *Maharishi* Shantananda with awe and reverence. He said that it is a matter of great fortune to have a Master of such high stature, which is bestowed only on one with countless lifetimes of good deeds. He reiterated that *Maharishi* Shantananda was one of the greatest Masters of their time and was recognised as a *Maharishi*.

---

[3] *a great sage*

Each day, Vamadeva's desire to have *Maharishi* Shantananda as his Master, grew stronger and stronger until he made a firm decision that he would not accept anyone else.

When Vamadeva turned eight, it was time for his formal education. One evening, when the family discussed this over dinner, Vamadeva expressed his intense desire to his father. "I want to go to Varanasi to train under *Maharishi* Shantananda," he said. Vishnu Sharman was taken aback. "How did the lad know about this great Master from faraway Varanasi?", he wondered. Sensing his father's surprise, Vamadeva quickly added, "Trivikrama, our temple priest mentioned about *Maharishi* Shantananda who lives in Varanasi."

Vishnu Sharman asked Vamadeva, "Do you know how far Varanasi is? It takes more than a month of exhausting travel from our village to reach there. Hence, if you choose to go there, it will not be possible for you to visit us. It is also not easy for us to travel up and down. The *Maharishi* wants students to focus fully on their education, without any distractions. When parents come, they sometimes get emotional and cry which affects not just their child but others as well. Hence, he permits visits only in case of emergencies or if it is absolutely necessary. We may not see each other through all the years of your apprenticeship. Do you understand that? Are you aware of what you're asking for? Wouldn't you rather learn somewhere close so we can meet each other often? If you are close by, we can get your favorite food from home and anything else you would like to have. You can also visit us whenever you miss home or your mother's cooking. Maybe you don't have to leave home and can travel daily from here." Vamadeva refused to budge.

Vishnu Sharman continued, "Trivikrama must have told you the difficulty, nay impossibility, of getting accepted by *Maharishi*

Shantananda as a student? He hardly takes any students and is known to reject aspiring students for a trifle. The *Maharishi* is a great sage and can understand just by their mere presence, if someone is a worthy student. Hence, he doesn't even look or talk to candidates seeking acceptance. Most are discarded after a mere glance, some without even a look. He just shakes his head and goes away. Do you understand how demoralising such a rejection can be? There are many accomplished teachers closer to home. One of them would surely appeal to you." The child was unrelenting.

Vishnu Sharman persisted, "The *Maharishi* is a chronic introvert known for his silence. He rarely speaks and seldom gives any oral instructions or teachings. It takes an extremely mature, observant and keen mind to witness and understand the subtle movements, moods and mannerisms of the Master and translate that subtle language into realisation. Do you know how difficult that is, for even the learned and the wise? How will you manage? You are a mere child of eight. With his non-engaging manner of teaching, you need to know what to get from him and how to take it out. Do you even know what you can or want to learn from him? Imagine going through all the years of training and not have anything to show for it. You will feel like a complete failure. We respect your wishes and don't want to go against it. But this is impossible and risky. Please heed our advice and reconsider your decision. We want only the best for you."

Whatever Vishnu Sharman and Savithri Devi said fell upon deaf ears. Even though they tried their utmost to dissuade him, Vamadeva persisted that he would only submit himself to the tutorship of Shantananda. Though his parents could not understand the reason for his persistence, they respected their son's decision and did not want to force their opinion on him. The child was keen, but his parents were troubled by the prospect of not seeing their son for all the years of his apprenticeship and the potential of ruining his education and life, should he be rejected or choose to quit. They would have preferred him to train nearby under a more conventional but accomplished teacher, so they could visit their son whenever they wished to see him. They also felt it their duty to make Vamadeva aware of the ill consequences of his decision. However, none of their arguments could deter Vamadeva from going to Varanasi to seek an audience with Shantananda. They reluctantly agreed to fulfil the desire of their only son.

After a long journey of several weeks of travelling on foot, bullock cart rides, and spending nights in various private homes, shelters, and inns, Vishnu Sharman and Vamadeva reached the city of Varanasi. Throughout the trip, Vamadeva was silent and contemplative, while his father talked incessantly, afraid that he would not get such a chance again in life. Vishnu Sharman was secretly hoping and praying that Shantananda would reject his son or that Vamadeva would change his mind about living and studying with the Master at Varanasi, especially after the long, grueling travel. He was convinced that he was only going to Varanasi to show Vamadeva around and then bring him back.

After reaching the holy city, they rested for a few days, visited the Lord Kashi Vishwanath temple that every Hindu is supposed to visit at least once in his lifetime, bathed in the Ganga, and drank the sacred water to their heart's content. They made enquiries about Shantananda and how they could meet him. They got to know that every morning at 3 a.m., the Master came to bathe at the ghats[4] with his disciples, irrespective of the weather. They were advised

---

[4] *A flight of steps leading down to a river*

to meet him after he had his dips to avoid interrupting his morning rituals. They had dinner and then spent the night in an open area close to the ghats along with the many sadhus (renunciate monks) who were resting under the trees. They got up early in the morning and bathed in the river since it is inauspicious to meet a great Master without completing one's ablutions. After their ablutions, they reached the ghats an hour earlier and sat down by the side of the steps, eagerly awaiting Shantananda's arrival. The soothing, soft light of the full moon gently illuminated the surroundings and the waters of the Ganga.

At 3 a.m., as anticipated, they saw Maharishi Shantananda in the distance walking towards the ghat, with three of his disciples. He was handsome and majestic with his long flowing white beard. His long white flowing dress shimmering in the moonlight gave him an angelic appearance. He was six feet tall, elegant, and moved with a stately gait – graceful and enchanting. Every step was measured, mindful and taken with purpose. He was stillness in motion. With a copper pot in one hand and a fresh pair of white clothes draped over his shoulders, he walked down the steps of the ghat to reach the river. He took the clothes off his shoulders and placed them on the steps of the ghat. Except for his loin cloth, he took off his clothes, dipped them in the river and started to wash them. His disciples requested him to allow them to wash his clothes but he declined with a slow, gentle nod of his head.

While his disciples were chanting loudly, Shantananda chanted silently and incessantly, visible only through the soft and gentle movement of his lips. They remembered the locals' advice not to disturb his morning rituals. They had been told that he would be chanting all the time in the morning as part of his daily worship, right from the walk till he took his bath. After he had finished washing his clothes, he then slowly entered the river and stood quietly in silent prayer, unperturbed like a statue amidst the freezing waters. He took time to immerse himself very slowly and stayed underwater for a very long time, as if he didn't need to breathe, before eventually emerging from the waters just as slowly. It was almost as if he was in a meditation. After taking a few such dips, he slowly stepped out of the river, changed his clothes and retraced his movements back up the steps of the ghat with his disciples closely following behind.

Vamadeva and Vishnu Sharman beckoned closer, bowed their heads and greeted him with folded hands. Maharishi Shantananda paused. They prostrated at his feet and then stood in front of him. His face was an ocean of calm, and he looked like someone who had crossed the barriers of desires. His intense but peaceful eyes were deep pools of wisdom. He looked at them and without uttering a word, questioned them with barely a flicker of his eyes as if asking, "Who? Why? What do you want?" Vamadeva stepped forward, bowed his head and spoke, "Maha Guro, I seek your discipleship."

Maharishi Shantananda glanced at the young boy. His eyes seemed to penetrate the young boy's constitution, piercing through the visible into the invisible. There was a slight movement on his elegant face, perhaps the dawn of a faint smile, maybe a recognition from another life, or maybe due to what he saw in Vamadeva. Maharishi Shantananda was a man of few words. He observed silence and spoke only when it was extremely essential to communicate through words. He inclined his head forward and asked the boy in a very deep, booming voice:

– *Name?*
– This param buddhu (most ignorant) is called Vamadeva, respected Master!

― *What do you seek?*
― Make me see my brightness so I can merge with the brightness, respected Master!

― *The path is right here within you, why not walk?*
― I am param buddhu. I don't know the way, respected Master

― *Final destination?*
― My Self, the Supreme Self, respected Master

― *Where shall you walk from? (read: Where will you start? When can you start?)*
― At your Lotus Feet. (read: Right here! Right now!)

Saying thus, he prostrated again at Shantananda's feet

Maharishi Shantananda smiled and merely said, "Walk" (read: Come with me). Saying thus, he turned to walk the steps of the *ghat* and return to his *gurukul*[5]. Vamadeva had passed his test and was accepted! The eight-year-old truly surprised his father who looked in disbelief and wondered how his son had acquired this crisp subtle knowledge without having formally learnt anything thus far! So far, his only education had been the part-time chanting lessons from the local temple priest, Trivikrama. He was impressed by his son's effortless and confident response to the Master's cryptic questions; Vamadeva was mature and wise beyond his years. Vamadeva's destination was obvious and extremely clear.

While Vishnu Sharman was deeply impressed by the depth of his

---

[5] *A residential school system where students live as part of the Master's family and serve and learn under him*

son's knowledge at such a young age, he also feared that he would never understand his son. Vishnu Sharman did not fully understand their conversation. He only guessed a part of it and as a result, a deep fear engulfed him. A premonition that he was about to lose his son forever. "Is this the beginning of a path of renunciation for Vamadeva?" he wondered. "He is seeking silence. Will he leave everything and become a monk?" Like any other parent, he wished to see his son get a good education, marry a girl from a reputed family, have children, settle down, and lead a regular life. He could see his dreams being shattered right before his eyes. On receiving the Master's assent, young Vamadeva was overjoyed but calm. He immediately followed *Maharishi* Shantananda and his disciples. Then suddenly remembering his father's presence, he turned his head and gave his father a meaningful nod that indicated both gratitude and farewell and left with them. That was it.

Vishnu Sharman felt his heart wrench. His first thought was to follow them. But he stopped since he had not received any sign or invitation from the Master. *Maharishi* Shantananda didn't say a word to Vishnu Sharman and had merely cast a glance at him and looked in his eyes. Probably that was Shantananda's only acknowledgment of Vishnu Sharman's presence. There was no discussion on where he was taking Vamadeva, or how long the boy was expected to stay with him for his education. There were no demands from the Master either. There was just no conversation. With no sign from the Master, he felt it was inappropriate for him to go. He sat under a banyan tree by the *ghats*. He was completely confused. So many unanswered questions assaulted his mind. "When will I see my boy again? Will I ever see him again? What will I tell his mother?"

The confusion gradually gave way to despondency. He felt that he had lost his precious son, as though Vamadeva had died. He then got up and walked to the *ghat* and looked at the wet footprints on the steps, those of his son, the *Maharishi*, and the others who disappeared into the darkness, heading to the city. He felt very lonely and dejected. He sat down again and cried bitterly in the dark so no one could see his tears. His heart squeezed with the pain of his only son's departure. He grieved as though his most prized possession had been snatched from him. He then took off his clothes and plunged into the freezing, yet warm waters of Mother Ganga. He immersed himself and his sorrow in her bosom. He took many dips. When he returned to the shore, he felt better. He was calmer. Water dripping from his hair and tears in his eyes, he slowly walked towards the temple of Lord Kashi Viswanath to surrender his emotions at the Lord's feet forever.

Meanwhile, Vamadeva was unaffected and calm. He had just found his path, purpose, and destination – the very reasons for this incarnation. He was ecstatic. His Master's feet were the only reality for him. There was nowhere else to look and nothing else to see. Vamadeva walked with Shantananda and his fellow students to the *gurukul*, which was not too far from the ghats.

CHAPTER 2

A SEEKER IS MADE

Maharishi Shantananda's household consisted of himself, his wife Rukmini Devi, his son Mukunda, and a few cows and calves. The *Maharishi* had eight student disciples of different ages, and Vamadeva was the ninth. Rukmini Devi was very slim. Her walk was calm and gentle, face always looking down with her *sari*[6] drawn over it to avoid attention. A couple of copper bangles and a rudraksha mala were her only ornaments She hardly spoke, and was a devotee of Lord Ram always chanting his name inwardly. Her lean face always had an expression of one who had just come out of a deep meditation. She exuded peace and calm like her illustrious husband. She did her chores well without any sound, intrusion, scolding or confusion. In the *gurukul*, she had her place and presence and she took care of the entire household

Mukunda was older than Vamadeva by about three years and was a very quiet boy – very humble, polite and loving towards all. His face exhibited a deep contentment and always had a faint welcoming smile. If one looked at Mukunda for a while, one would feel extremely good, peaceful and stable, like "all is well with the world". Without any articulation, he created that effect. This has to be inborn; it cannot be taught. He never displayed any airs and

---

[6] Long traditional garment worn by Hindu women

almost behaved like the servant of the house. He would quietly come to eat only after others had eaten and left. Mukunda was independent, hardly speaking to his mother or father. Likewise, Shantananda seldom asked or told Mukunda anything. Mukunda was always in his own world of ecstasy and exhibited the characteristics of a great Master just like his father.

Their house was located around a kilometer from the ghats. It was walled on all the sides with a covered entrance which was almost like a small room. The entrance had a stone seat on either side for wandering monks, travellers and visitors, who frequently rested there. The students would enquire if they had eaten and if requested, deliver the food there. Those who wished to use the toilets could walk down the left side of the house. Since there were no toilets in the house, everyone including the *Maharishi* had to go outside the house to use the toilets. Past the toilets after a walled separation was the washing area where the clothes were washed. Beyond the washing area was the well which provided water for drinking, bathing, washing and so on. Beyond the well were the separate bathrooms for men and women. The facilities were compactly arranged and the well was conveniently located in the center so water could be drawn for washing, bathing and so on. Wandering monks, travellers and visitors were allowed access to the toilets, to use the bathrooms or to draw water from the well for drinking or any other purpose.

A bit further from the bathrooms was the back of the house. At one corner was a huge kitchen. Outside the kitchen, there was a small reservoir like a bathtub that was dug into the land. It was filled with water that was used by all the beings – birds, dogs, cattle and so on. The cowshed was at the other corner at the back of the house which opened into the neighboring paddy fields. There was a drain running across the left side of the house that carried the waste water in the neighboring fields. There was a pond beyond the fields. During the day, the door of the cowshed was left open so the cows could come and go at any time. At night, the door was closed to protect the calves from wild animals like jackals who were rumored to prowl in the surrounding areas. In the morning, they would go out to graze and come back in the evening. No one was required to accompany the cows unless they had to be taken to a separate field elsewhere. During the harvest season, bales of hay and water would be kept for the cows in the cowshed and the door would be kept closed.

The entrance opened into a big, open courtyard that was coated with disinfectant cow dung. Throughout the day and especially in the mornings, a variety of birds including peacocks and peahens would be ambling about in the courtyard. It was a big, tidy and well-maintained house, with rooms on the sides and the front with large verandahs on all sides. The rooms to the left were the classrooms and places for chanting, *sadhana* (spiritual practices), etc and accommodation for the students. The rooms to the right housed the granary, storage spaces and several rooms, a couple of which were used just for drying clothes. In the center of the courtyard was a *tulsi* (holy basil) plant. Shantananda slept alone and so did Rukmini Devi and they had their separate rooms. In the front, the last room to the right was Rukmini Devi's. The one to ist left was Shantananda's room and study. Unless called, no one entered Shantananda's room. Not even Rukmini Devi. The first room in the front was Mukunda's room but it was not a private room and others slept in his room as well. He did not have any special privileges as the Maharshi's son. All the rooms were airy and spacious. Fifteen students could easily sleep in one room. The verandahs were also big, neat, clean and airy with mats spread around for the students to sit and study. On rare occasions, Shantananda would sit on the verandah in front of his room and give a lecture. In the summers, the disciples and Mukunda slept on the verandah or even on the courtyard in the moonlight under the shade of the stars.

There was a white majestic bull who was called Nandi. He was fully white with not even a speck on him. Despite being huge and intimidating, he was very gentle and calm. He was never tied or leashed. Just the cowbell and a bit of ornamentation. Unlike the cows, Nandi never stayed in the cowshed and always entered via the main entrance of the house. During the day, he spent time in the courtyard, always under the window of Shantananda's room. He followed Shantananda everywhere, including his morning trip tot he ghats. Shantananda had very little interaction with Nandi except for an occasional petting which was no more than a simple touch. The students used to bathe Nandi and feed him. Rarely have people seen Nandi eat except when fed by the students. He never ate food from outside. Nandi used to leave when the light in Shantananda's room dimmed, after the window was closed at night. Except the rare times when he was seen walking outside the *gurukul*, no one knew where Nandi went in the night. More than a bull, Nandi displayed the characteristics of a faithful dog. He was almost like another disciple to Shantananda.

Every morning, a few women from the neighborhood came to assist Rukmini Devi with her household chores. However, many of the daily tasks were the responsibility of the students who actually did most of the work, including tending to the cows, seeing to their grazing, cleaning the yard and the house, sweeping and scrubbing the floor, washing the clothes, and helping in the kitchen, apart from washing their own clothes and dishes, etc. The boys took turns with the household chores. *Pranayama*[7] was an important practice that was insisted to be done by the students on a daily basis, along with silent lung breathing which would help increase their concentration. While half of the students were immersed in the practice, the others did the household work. They alternated the following day, thereby ensuring that everyone did their breathing exercises.

The *Maharishi* had a small ancestral farm a few kilometers from his home. He had inherited it from his parents and this used to be his childhood home. Since it was in the interiors and far away from the ghats, his daily morning trips to the ghats were difficult. He subsequently built and moved to his present home to be closer to the ghats. The neighboring farmers ploughed, sowed, and reaped the harvest and, in return, received a portion of the harvest while the rest was enough to sustain the *gurukul* for the year. *Maharishi* Shantananda and his disciples worked on the farm a few times a week. The *Maharishi* would work on the farm with complete focus, awareness and mindfulness. It seemed like a meditation for him. During the non-harvest season, they took the cows and calves to the farm and allowed them to graze for the day. The local king gave contributions in the form of grain, pulses and other rations as *bhiksha* (alms) to every *gurukul* in the kingdom. This coupled with the milk (and milk products) from the cows, provided additional sustenance to the *gurukul*.

Even though the *Maharishi's* household used milk, the cows and calves were always treated with utmost respect and love, and never as domesticated animals. Except for cowbells and ornaments around their necks, the cows and calves were never tied and were

---

[7] *regulate the life force*

always left free. Honoring the mother child relationship, the calves stayed with their mothers and were never separated. The cows were milked only after the calves had had their fill and only if there was excess. They never took any milk by keeping the calf away. The Ashtavakra Gita, a renowed scriptural commentary, says, "Just like the sky is not affected by the shape of the building, the soul is not affected by the shape of the body." It means that the same soul resides in the body of every being – be it a cow or a human. This was very clearly practised in the *Maharishi* household where everyone was treated as equal members of one family – be it Mukunda, the disciples, the animals, guests or visitors – with no intrusions, control or discrimination. Of the fifteen cows, only three or four were milk bearing while most were old or barren. The older cows were treated with equal respect as the younger cows, and none were ever sold or abandoned. They lived there until their natural death. Nobody would beat or harm any being. All lived together in perfect harmony.

To reduce the housework, they usually ate on disposable stitched leaf plates and seldom from the usual copper plates. These leaf plates were not washed and just thrown away. Even though the cows ate these leaf plates, the unwritten rule was that cows were not to be considered as scavengers and to be treated exactly as any human inhabitant in the household. As a matter of principle, all animals and beings were to be given food as fresh as possible. Giving of waste or leftovers as a practice was strongly discouraged in the household. Offering of food to any being was expected to be done before everyone took their meals, seldom from what was left after everybody had eaten.

There was perfect symmetry and synchronicity in the *Maharishi's gurukul* and life went on beautifully without hindrance, without any reminders or even compulsion of any kind. The entire household quietly woke up by themselves at 2:30 a.m. in the morning. They first finished their morning ablutions – brushing the teeth, cleaning their bowels, taking a bath and so on. There were no exceptions. Ensuring complete cleanliness in the morning before starting any activity was a discipline that was strictly followed in the *gurukul*. Everyone would be ready before 3:00 a.m. and quietly start their work without being told what to do.

Silence and peace reigned. Nobody argued, complained, criticised, shouted, or disturbed the tranquility of the *gurukul* and every one, irrespective of their age and position, respected each other as equals. The harmony of the *gurukul* was maintained, for the students took turns to do their chores without being told. On the rare occasions when someone forgot their duty, one of the others took over and performed the task without reminding or reprimanding the one who forgot. When the one who remembered his neglected duty later realised that someone else had completed his work for him, it became a strong, yet unspoken reminder to be even more diligent in the future. They lived an exemplary regenerative and nurturing existence. Shantananda never interfered. The communication between students simply explicitly displayed the age-old truth that when our hearts are in love, we whisper and when our hearts are separated, we shout. The real distance is the distance of hearts. Its expression is in our unconscious expressions such as whispering and shouting.

Despite the unspoken perfect discipline, there were no restrictions placed on the students. No one bothered with or judged anyone's habits. There was a senior student who had a smoking habit. He would go out of the *gurukul* and indulge. Nobody asked or cared. Everyone was free to do what they wanted with the clarity and attitude that karma would eventually take care of it. No one kept tabs on each other. It was very open and very relaxed. They were living the rules of *Sanatana Dharma*[8] - it is not for one to punish another because karma spares none for their actions.

The *gurukul* had very few visitors. Usually, the local village elders would come to seek counsel or to discuss some matter. Shantananda hardly spoke and Rukmini Devi never got involved in these matters. The visitors would usually be assisted by the students themselves. Wandering monks and travellers seeking assistance were lovingly supported by the students. Once in a while, powerful saints would come, sit near the entrance, take their meals there and leave. Their stature would be revealed by Shantananda's presence at the window to acknowledge their arrival. There would be no communication. Just eye contact. Their arrival itself was a great blessing for the household. Very rarely, a saint would come to meet Shantananda in the house. When they came, they were led to Shantananda's room and the doors were closed. There would be no sound coming from the room. Hence, there would be no indication of what was happening inside. They would then have food together. When done, they would leave as quietly as they came. There would be no demonstration. There was nothing to ask, nothing to give and nothing to talk. With their connection, their mutual presence itself was enough.

Anyone who came to the *gurukul* experienced an ocean like stillness like they were floating on water. The Master's presence and energy permeated the whole compound and to every being. The cows and calves were absolutely calm, quiet, peaceful and well mannered. They would go out, graze and come back on their own without disturbing anyone. The calves had their milk and roamed around

---

[8] Literally the eternal religion. In this context, the fundamental rules for harmonious existence

contentedly in the garden. The bull was extremely happy, calm and contented and sat like a statue. Never once was he aggressive. All the animals were almost like saints. Never was a complaint received that the *gurukul* animals had disturbed their property, ate their crops and so on.

The overwhelming stature of the Master and his presence, stability and stillness was getting translated and transferred to every being equally – be it a student, a bird or an animal. Anyone and everyone who connected to him, imbibed a part of him and became like him. The still stature of the Master was itself the education. No words were needed. Nothing else was needed. This stillness is what the *Maharishi* gave eventually. When the student was empty and ready to receive, the *Maharishi* would connect through the eyes and transfer what he had to and the student would become the Master. Then Shantananda would say, "Now you go. Don't look back. There is nothing to come back for."

They left at different times, went their own ways and settled in different places. Some left and became *parivrajakas* (spiritual wanderers) and taught wherever they went. Some retired to caves and did intense penance for the upliftment of the world. Some setup *ashrams* and had their following. Each student was empowered and sent, and was expected to do his job in his own way. There were no reunions and no followups. If they had a need, the Tradition would nurture and provide for them. If they had a question, the Tradition would provide the answer through some means. Neither did they communicate back with the *gurukul,* nor did the Master enquire after them. The Master's job was done. He raised them to his stature and set them free. No strings attached. It was now the students' job to replicate this effect wherever they went. A great example of how a school of life should be.

CHAPTER 3

THE HUMBLE DISCIPLE

When Vamadeva came to the *gurukul*, Gautama was the most senior among the *Maharishi's* students. He was probably in his early forties or late thirties. It was hard to guess his age because he shaved his head which made him look much younger. He wore a string of metal prayer beads and had a metal ear ornament on his big ears. He had a unique persona and maintained a funny, peculiar character like a comedian. He always wore white clothes. The way he walked coupled with his demeanour and shaved head, made him look like a Tao Buddhist monk. He had his own room in the *gurukul* but he allowed others to sleep there as well, seldom keeping it for himself. He preferred to sleep outside in the open verandah or sometimes even on the open courtyard. Even when it was cold.

Gautama was always very close to his Master. His total surrender and dedication towards Shantananda were so amazing that he spontaneously became a living example of how a disciple should be. Since *Maharishi* Shantananda spoke very little, Gautama was the disciple who could comprehend the silence of his Master and act upon it. He was so keenly observant and perceptive that he could decipher the Master's attention, slight facial expressions and movements and even his breath patterns. It was indeed a treat to watch Gautama translate his Master's silent communication into meaningful and appropriate expressions and actions without a word being uttered between them. The unspoken commands gave Gautama the strength to unfailingly serve the Master and his mission. It was perfect synchronisation. Gautama was the mouthpiece or the communication aspect of the silent Shantananda. Shantananda, with the spiritual stature of an Everest, and his expression, the humble and unassuming Gautama, were a beautiful combination to behold.

Gautama was always working. Never an idle moment. All types of work were the same for him – none higher or lower – be it washing clothes, tending to the cows, cleaning the floor, cooking food, instructing students, serving the Master and so on. Gautama considered work as worship. Whatever he did, he did with the same dedication and focus. That set the tone for the other students in the household. *Maharishi* Shantananda would seldom call for help. Yet, Gautama would be in the Master's room attending to his needs. There would be no communication. Hence, nobody knew what they were doing. He would stay with Shantananda in his room as long as the Master wanted.

Maharishi Shantananda did not spend much time with the students every day except during the visits to the ghats and the fire ceremony. Whatever *Maharishi* Shantananda wanted them to know, more often than not, he conveyed it through Gautama. Gautama was often asked by the Master to instruct the others. As his assistant and prime disciple, Gautama often conveyed the teacher's instructions to the other disciples on behalf of his Master. He also made time to orient them with the key teachings. More than lectures, Gautama gave gentle guidances. When he spoke, everybody attended including Mukunda. Moreover, when junior students like Vamadeva had any questions, they preferred to address them to Gautama. He had a very friendly communicative voice that put people at ease. He had his way with the students, guiding them in a way that was perfect for them – telling stories, making jokes and keeping things light amidst the total silence and perfect discipline.

In his free time, he helped Rukmini Devi with the household chores. He had great regard for Rukmini Devi, treating her with the same respect that he granted Shantananda. Again, she never called or asked for help. He would check with her to understand if anything was needed fort he household and make sure it was available. He would go in the kitchen and help with the pending work – washing or cutting the vegetables, doing the dishes, cleaning the premises, and so on. There was hardly any communication. It was knowing what needed to be done and doing it. Not telling and doing – being told what to do and doing it. Knowing and doing – the perfect attitude that one should practice in life. Gautama was a prime example of this practice in action. You would rarely see Shantananda tell him to teach something or Rukmini Devi ask him to do something. Instead, he would look, know what had to be done and do it. He never waited. Every place he was doing whatever had to be done, and doing it perfectly.

Since Shantananda preferred silence and isolation, Gautama was the de facto teacher and administrator of the *gurukul*. Despite his sheer humility, he had a natural flair for authority where he could easily discipline people and take decisions. Even though he never wore a watch, Gautama ensured that the schedule of the household was maintained with absolute perfection. He was like a clock and knew the exact timing. He woke up exactly at 2:30 a.m. and everyone around him awoke automatically, as if by an unseen nudge. It was the same with ensuring disciplined adherence to the meal times and other activities in the household. He maintained the discipline of the household by his presence and example rather than any preaching or control. Since Shantananda remained in isolation and silence, he would attend to the village elders, dignitaries and visitors who came to the *gurukul*. When he accompanied Shantananda, Gautama usually spoke, asking questions or answering on behalf of the Master because the *Maharishi* rarely spoke and mostly avoided all communication.

He even represented Shantananda for all official purposes wherever required since the *Maharishi* avoided travel. Some years ago, there was a dispute connected to Shantananda's farm. Someone had laid claims to the farm which was the primary means of sustenance for the *gurukul*. He had received a summons to appear in person before the court. Shantananda was uninterested. He said, "I am not going. Leave that property. I don't want it." Gautama interceded and requested Shantananda, "Please permit me to go to the court, represent on your behalf and sort it out." Shantananda agreed saying, "If you want to go, you may go." Gautama requested permission from the court to represent Shantananda which the judge allowed. Gautama disputed and banished the claim by providing evidence that they had been farming there since a long time.

The relevance of Gautama in the life of Vamadeva cannot be underestimated. Like the others, Vamadeva was captivated by Gautama's humility and surrender towards his Master and emulated him. Gautama was a very deep influence on all the students including Vamadeva. If *Maharishi* Shantananda was the soul of the *gurukul*, Gautama was its very life. The first sentence that Gautama uttered to Vamadeva set the tone of their relationship. He said, "Humility and gratitude in our hearts make our world wonderfully beautiful." That is the way Gautama lived. These words rang in Vamadeva's mind as an example of the right conduct in the *gurukul*, and set the foundation for his future life. Vamadeva's approach to life was modulated by observing Gautama, which moulded his mind of Vamadeva and made him <u>very</u> steady and stable.

Being young, most of the students were ignorant and had a confusion, "What is my path?". They needed direction. Based on their respective orientation, Gautama guided the students who had these doubts. Hence, his contribution in the students' life was invaluable. Alignment in the spiritual path happens only when one follows the orientation that is right for their personality and character else one will do it for the sake of doing or because of somebody else, but their heart won't be in it. It was Gautama who told Vamadeva that you must seek the path of knowledge. Vamadeva knew that the path of devotion did not appeal to him – to sit and chant, sing, and so on. Gautama guided him to follow the intellectual path and suggested him to eventually change himself into a Raja yogi. He explained to him that when he would finally become an *Avadhoota*[9], he would be connected only to Supreme Consciousness.

Gautama was very deeply respected by the students almost like a Master. Even Nandi followed Gautama wherever he went, like a bodyguard. Nandi also treated Gautama almost like Shantananda, Yet, Gautama never acknowledged their attention and remained just as a servant of the Master. He was the one who was mostly teaching, imparting knowledge, grooming and mentoring. But the manner he handled the students displayed zero ownership. He

---

[9] *Perfect Masters who have dissolved themselves in Supreme Consciousness while being in the body*

never took any favour from any disciple. He forbade students from touching his feet, a customary mark of respect to a senior or an elder. He never pushed his personal agendas. He never protrayed himself even as an *acharya* (teacher), let alone a Master. He presented himself as a simple messenger of the Master who owned nothing. His extreme humility and surrender taught the students especially Vamadeva, oft he importance of practising insignifcance as a powerful positioning and tool on the spiritual path which always keeps one well grounded. Vamadeva in later years, would lead his life similarly. He owned nothing and handled his followers similarly, without any ownership.

CHAPTER 4

THE GLORIOUS MASTER

Maharishi Shantananda, the great Master from Varanasi, was a very mysterious, powerful yet understated personality. Shantananda meant "experiencing bliss through peace". True to his name, he was *shanta* (peaceful) always, experiencing it all the time. Peace was his being, silence was his expression. It is very difficult to define him using words. He can't be put into any frame.

He had a very deep, booming voice that sounded almost like he was talking from a cave. He rarely spoke and only when extremely necessary and only what was necessary. He mostly used his eyes or facial movements to communicate. Very slight eye movements that were employed to indicate a question, an acknowledgement, an answer and so on. His interaction, be it a student, Mukunda or Rukmini Devi, would be to look in their eyes and nod. This was his only acknowledgement of another's presence, to mean he had seen them. No words were exchanged. His face appeared blank all the time as if he was always in a meditation. If someone said something, he sometimes gave no response and at other times looked at them with a blank expression. There would be no indication or response whether he had heard or understood. Sometimes, he may slightly nod in response but one would need to look very closely to notice the nod. He was stillness in motion. Whether he was sitting down, getting up, moving, turning, and so on, his movement would be minimal and agonisingly slow, with each movement being deliberate, conscious and mindful. There was an economy of movement and economy of effort involved in the movement, just enough movement as was necessary and expend only as much energy to barely complete it.

Everyone closely observed and emulated *Maharishi* Shantananda who was always calm and unshakeable. No event or activity agitated him. His very presence was powerful. His trainings were equally powerful. His method was silence and witnesshood. The teacher's silence was his strength. He taught his students witnesshood more through lack of words than through speech. With the pin drop silence and discipline, no one needed to be jumpstarted. He asked very few questions. But when questions were asked, they were powerful enough to open minds and mould one's thinking. He said very few words. But when words were uttered. They were groundbreaking words that were commands to nature. Though he seldom spoke, he demonstrated with his life.

His daily routine included a trip to the ghat in the early hours of the morning, as well as some time spent at the dhuni[10]. His disciples participated in both these activities. There was a daily fire ceremony performed at the *gurukul* by the students. On certain days, Shantananda would perform the ceremony himself. Without being told, Gautama would figure out earlier that Shantananda would do it that day and ensure that everything was kept ready. Shantananda would slowly come, sit down and conduct the ceremony. He would perform it quietly and not call anybody. However, the students would know by Gautama's involvement that Shantananda would be performing the ceremony that day and

---

[10] *An ever-burning sacred fire*

would be ready to participate as well.

Shantananda hardly instructed or interacted with the students. This was left to Gautama. Shantananda's job was to transfer when a student was ready to receive. The energy transfer was delivered to the person through eye contact. This happened when Shantananda gave talks, which were attended by all disciples. These talks were very brief and unusual and happened only a few times every year. He would connect to each person's eyes deeply and the person would feel like electricity entering his eyes. The *Maharishi* barely spoke a few sentences but it would feel like he had spoken a lot. For e.g., as he connected to a disciple, he may comment, "Oh, you have a problem waking up" or "You have trouble memorising". This seemingly innocuous comment or observation would result in an internal change in the person that would correct the stated issue completely, that was blocking their progress. He was lighting the fire inside of each one. Correction by correction, he would realign people and finally raise them to the level of his own spiritual stature – an *Avadhoota*.

Shantananda was very gentle by nature. He was quiet, very stable and saturated in peace. That was how he handled the students as well. However, his reputation in the outside world was formidable, that of a very strict, uncompromising and esoteric Master, whose tutorship was near impossible to get, whose learning required extremely high calibre and who can throw a student out anytime, sometimes even without cause. He probably allowed that image because it helped keep the crowds away. He never asked anybody to leave. People who were unable to cope with his intensity either left on their own or encountered circumstances that led to their exit. One could not even begin to describe his spiritual attainment and stature. To even feel his intensity required one to acquire a very high degree of subtlety. Only then would they know that he was vast as the ocean and his spritual stature was taller than Everest. Shantananda was recognised as a great master in his time itself. Hence, the title, *Maharishi*. Shantananda could be, but who knows? People recognised his stature but he never allowed people to build institutions or any paraphernalia around him.

Sometimes, he would be called upon to settle disputes. His mediation involved very little talk. If someone made a mistake, he would just say, "You shouldn't do that" or "Don't do this". Shantananda words would change something within the person and the person would not repeat the mistake. There would be no fanfare. If people didn't listen or understand, he would maintain silence and leave, understanding that the karmic push was too strong and his intervention would not help. His mild nature and simple responses sometimes made people wonder if he was truly the Master he was reputed to be. When one doesn't communicate, people get confused and start to speculate.

His responses to people in public were also generic and seldom understood well. Once a woman came and complained to Shantananda, "My husband is flirting too much. Can you please correct him?" Shantananda looked at her for a while and said, "All men are flirts." Saying thus, he walked away. She didn't understand anything. The Master said an important truth, "The male gender of a species is extroverted and flirtatious by nature so they can sow seeds for the propagation of the species." However, his response was not relevant for her since it solved nothing for her. She wondered with amazement and walked away feeling even more confused. He may have criticised something inside her. A realisation may have dawned. But that was not visible or tangible. People wanted more words, expressions and demonstrations.

Shantananda was not interested. He did his job silently and walked away which did not earn him a lot of popularity.

Gautama had been with Shantananda for a long time and was part of the *Maharishi* household. He mentioned that Shantananda used to instruct and train students explicitly, like a proper *acharya*. There were many batches of students who had learned under him. Gautama was one of those fortunate few. That was how Gautama had deep knowledge of Shantananda's teachings, methods, and timing of delivery of lessons. Over time, Shantananda grew more silent and delegated the teaching duties to other students including Gautama. By the time Vamadeva came, he hardly spoke, interacted or instructed and Gautama had taken over the teaching duties completely. In many ways, Shantananda progression reflected the future life of Vamadeva who after leaving the *gurukul*, wandered for many years delivering teachings and instructing followers and eventually grew quieter over time and became as silent as Shantananda in his later days.

GAUTAMA'S WORDS OF WISDOM

Here below, Gautama shares his thoughts on the stature of Master *Maharishi* Shantananda for the benefit of the junior students.

"Our Master is an *Avadhoota*. He is a great Yogi who came accomplished. Those who come fully accomplished can be considered as *Avataric* births. They chose their births consciously, while most of us chose our incarnations out of the need to fulfil the unfulfilled desires from our past incarnations. They have taken birth on *dharmic*[11] basis to preserve *dharmic* causes. They abide by

---

[11] based on dharma

dharma[12] and their life itself is their biggest teaching. Those who come accomplished have nothing to achieve in this incarnation. They only have to deliver over time. They reveal themselves accordingly, as per necessity and need. They do not display anything which is unnecessary. They will neither pretend or demand, nor will they expect anything from the world. They are totally detached from the *samsara* (mundane existence), yet will perform as per the demand of the incarnation and time.

Most teachers of the world are only *acharyas*. They have only acquired knowledge from the external world. Their knowledge has boundaries. Until one becomes the Source, the source of all knowledge, there are always boundaries. *Acharyas* can only teach from what they have learned. Most of the knowledge that we receive from outside consists of concepts and opinions of people, which are relative truths, often far from the absolute truth. When a man is fully settled in his inside world, he remains totally empty, while he is always full. Knowledge flows from within as per his external need.

The problem with acquired spiritual prowess is that the power achieved through the *mantras* and practices needs to be maintained through abstinence and rigorous practices, and is often difficult to maintain during fluctuating times. To retain this state, as well as to expound acquired knowledge, teachers need to dwell in sincere practices on a consistent basis while abstaining from many temptations of earth to keep what they earned or else they will soon lose them. Some observe strict celibacy, while others stay away from people, and yet others immerse themselves in severe practices. But the ones who come accomplished will walk and talk like ordinary men for they have nothing to do with name and fame, titles and

---

[12] *righteousness or one's righteous duty*

vain glories of the world. *Acharyas* with acquired knowledge cannot compare with such ascetics, who strictly follow the divine will, in divine order, and will never deviate from it, even if it costs their life. Their only interest is the establishment or re-establishment of *Sanatana Dharma*. They have neither excesses nor demands. They expect nothing from anyone and none can do them any favor. They accept alms and bless the giver with abundance of spiritual bliss. They neither beg nor demand, but accept what comes to them spontaneously. Even small acts of kindness are deeply appreciated and nurtured by them.

"Love is their food and offering. Fire is their ally. Silence is the bed on which they exist. Consciousness is their state. Their body is in alignment which AUM, the subtle vibration of Supreme Consciousness. There is nothing apart from them. So, friends, do not be confused between an accomplished Master (the Source) who has no interest to prove anything, and an acquired saint who is eager to display what he has learned through books or practices. People who do not understand the inherent silence will not connect with these established saints who often look like nothing conventional. Restless minds will leave them. The restless mind gravitates towards teachers of acquired knowledge who display their earned prowess efficiently. Such seekers easily get trapped in activities that maintain the inner noise for a lifetime and sometimes beyond. Even a spiritual enthusiast may take a long time to find his true path, and even if he does find it, it may take him a long time to recognise and embrace it totally.

An accomplished Master like our Master *Maharishi* Shantananda is total and complete. A pot filled with water never makes a sound. The noise happens only when the pot is half full. It shakes and spills. So, strive to be full pots by settling your faculties fully within yourselves and never ever compromise on this aspiration at any cost, because nothing in the external world is worth that subtlety and stability. There is nothing to prove to the external world. You have to stay rooted in your inner world, and for this you need to remain alert and attentive. Stay still, stay rooted in silence despite all the noise inside and outside. Sometimes, the noise within, the compelling noise of our thoughts that clamour for our attention, is usually louder than the fleeting noise of the world. We can avoid the external noise if we wish to, but the internal noise is extremely difficult to ignore. Inner silence is your highest treasure and greatest blessing. The association of an established Master will spontaneously and effortlessly remove the age-old karmic patterns and set us firmly in the direction of dissolution. So, never get confused between inherent and acquired *siddhis*[13]. The inherent always stays, whereas the acquired can vanish any time."

---

[13] *spiritual power(s)*

CHAPTER 5

THE GOLDEN PATH

The focus of Shantananda's method was dissolution of the mind – to gradually reduce the ripples created in the mind and eventually become empty. More activity means more accumulation. Hence, you reduce the activity to a level of inaction. Reducing activity does not mean laziness or avoiding action. On the contrary, it is necessary action or action only out of necessity. You are not involved in it but you have applied yourself fully. You don't own the activity. Hence, it is continuous repeated selfless action without ownership. When you're completely surrendered to the Master and are performing every action as a worship to the Master, purification happens.

When one is practising emptiness, one's words and expressions have to be used with extreme caution. Words become commands to nature when they come from an empty space. Even a single word. It can be detrimental as well as misleading. Either use words wisely or be silent rather than use words that create the wrong impact (read: create karma). Thus, everybody's doing everything in absolute silence and peace. It wasn't silence due to suppression of speech. You don't have to speak viz. necessary speech. You speak if you have to speak but that is also silence since it is born of necessity. This was reiterated by Gautama and believed to have been taught by Shantananda. This was an important direction and turning point for Vamadeva who was practising silence from childhood. He spoke only what was necessary and when it was necessary because he clearly understood the impact of a word when one is rooted in silence. He proved this many times later, such as when he stopped the rain during the floods.

There was a daily routine and a daily discipline. One gets up in the morning and attends to the various needs of the household. Someone cleaned the house, someone took the cows for grazing, someone got groceries, and so on. The show was going on. The routine was an education in itself when one applied the above principles of necessary action and necessary speech. Shantananda had no interest in teaching external knowledge because any input can create a ripple in the mind. Exposure to more information meant more impressions which required more cleansing to remove. They sat down mostly for practices such as meditation, *pranayama, havan* (fire ceremony), and so on. Gautama hardly sat down and gave lectures. Most of the talks given by Gautama in the *gurukul* were gentle guidances more than teaching. When they went for long walks while grazing the cows, he conveyed most of the teachings through appropriate stories. The students remembered the essence of the stories because otherwise it was silence. When more words are used, less is remembered. When one uses more silence and less words, those words become very important and stay etched in the student's memory. That was Gautama's method which he learnt from his Master, Shantananda.

Shantananda never looked at anyone as a student or a disciple where he had to teach or contribute to make someone complete. He saw everyone as complete. Shantananda never saw himself as a teacher but more as a sculptor. He worked to remove blockages that obstructed the progress or evolution of his students or introduce corrections or realignments to accelerate their progress.

With restrained discipline, concentration, meditative work, *pranayama*, outer silence, and subtle guidance, Shantananda moulded his disciples into empty clay pots ready for the Supreme Consciousness to completely fill them. Some of the practices were difficult because the mind faces boredom from repetition. The mind becomes tired of lack of dynamism. Repetitive work often leads to an aversion to it. This advanced method was not suitable for most seekers because their mind always demanded variety in activities and the corresponding experiences. Here, Shantananda's method of deliberate cleaning up of inner space, (the compulsive unlearning from past conditioning) often broke down acquired concepts, the systematic and progressive teaching activities that a student would usually expect. Purposeful action without ownership (surrender) leads to perfect inaction. This state leads to stable non-doership, annihilating karmic patterns, which leads to lesser desires, inner stillness and finally, a liberated existence.

Unhooking from desires and concepts leads to openness for the higher awareness, just like an empty bottle has the capacity to be filled completely, upto the brim. The Master fills that space with the fire (stable experience) of consciousness with a mere glance, touch or word. For liberated states, emptying takes more time than filling. The mind becomes uneasy, restless and confused when patterns are dissolved and that space is occupied by awareness and witness-hood. Restlessness increases when emptiness replaces thoughts, which are the pillars that support the very existence of the mind. When a thought pattern is annihilated through concentrated effort of conscious detachment, the substratum that consists of the mind, intellect, and ego immediately fills it in with another more compelling thought pattern, taking inspiration from something or anything external. The subtle method of perfect annihilation of the mind made Shantananda a difficult Master. His teachings were mostly intangible. His school made Masters, not disciples. And not everybody was eligible for that.

Those who weren't ready for Shantananda were unable to handle him. One who had no inclination for his teachings or wasn't ready to go all the way would be unable to connect to him or look into his eyes. This didn't happen during Vamadeva's time at the *gurukul*. Gautama mentioned that this happened very rarely because the Master would not admit anyone who wasn't ready. Shantananda never even connected to people who weren't steady. It had happened in the past where such people fell unconscious when they looked into the *Maharishi's* eyes. They had huge karma to clear and were not ready for realignment. The Master would gently ask them to return home and take care of their health.

Gautama mentioned a story that occurred a few years before Mukunda was born. The *gurukul* had a crazy group of students who had a background doing intense and extreme spiritual practices. They wanted something intense, dynamic and activity oriented which was the exact opposite of Shantananda's method which they couldn't cope with. They were getting restless in the *gurukul*. Around that time, there was a dispute on a land which belonged to Shantananda that was usurped by a local landlord. The matter was taken to court. Shantananda decided to fight the case himself. Everyone, including his students, was sure that Shantananda would win. After all, he was known as a great and powerful Master. He lost the case and consequently, the land. When he lost, the group of students were stumped. They discussed amongst themselves One asked, "How could he lose this court case?" Another asked, "Is his reputation real?" Yet another added, "He must surely be powerless." They mutually concluded, "Thus far, he has not taught anything of substance. His methods don't seem to lead anywhere. We may have made a mistake. He is not a real Master. We should look elsewhere." Thus, they left the *gurukul* immediately.

Gautama told the students, "Our path is the golden path. The path of fire. Those who are not eligible to walk our path won't stand the heat. Their feet will burn and they will leave. The path itself will ensure this, as happened in this incident via the court case." He continued, "People gravitate towards delivered knowledge or oral knowledge. They are not craving for experience. Only experience can give transformation. Words cannot give transformation. They can only carry information. Words are chaff. Words are unnecessary. The grain is hidden inside. Real Masters give experiences. People are afraid of them because they don't give these experiences easily. One has to crave for it and take the effort to extract it from the Master. Once you dig out, what you get is nectar, pure nectar. No beating around the bush. But people don't wait long enough for that."

To elucidate this, Gautama narrated a story of a young monk in the monk's own words when he was asked how he had acquired enlightenment at such an early age.

> "I served my Master in his house so I could observe him closely. Day and night, I kept looking at the Master. He never glanced at me as much. I sat on the ground and stared at the Master as he did his work. Initially, my mind was restless. And I saw the Master restless and often irritated too. I still kept doing the same practice. My Master asked me nothing and I asked my Master nothing. Slowly, I started feeling some emptiness inside me. Some things were leaving me. Perhaps I was merging with the Master's consciousness. What left

me was my restlessness. My mind started to settle down. When I looked at the Master, he seemed relaxed and settled too. There wasn't any restlessness manifested in him. I continued. My inner silence became deeper and deeper. An ecstasy started occupying the space. When I looked at the Master, I found him ecstatic and uncontrollably joyous.

When I asked a man sitting next to me why our Master was so happy, he asked me, 'Do you see happiness? I only see anger and restlessness.' I decided to follow my awareness which was the best thing to do. Truth was delivered to each according to his state of mind and capacity. Emptiness increases the capacity. We must be true to ourselves. We must trust our experience. Ever since then, I haven't asked anyone their opinions about my Master. My inner silence made me tranquil. I started sitting at the same place in deep silence with the absence of thoughts from morning till evening, and often through the night. Food or water were not in my thoughts. Often, they became a hindrance to my state of beingness. I understood that I had no other realms to conquer. I had attained the peak, the Everest of consciousness.

I waited for my Master's command. He never looked at me. He still played his role as always, and different people saw different facets of his personality and each one thought they knew him. The truth is that each one only saw him as they are, according to their own state. He played this illusion and existed for as long as it took. I felt complete, yet there was no "I" to feel that completeness. I asked nothing from my Master. I never even asked him if he was my Master. I just watched, watched, and watched. I realised that I was watching myself when I was watching him. My Master is my SELF. He is my soul manifested in another form. I understood the core of existence. I understood that I have no existence apart from the universe. "I" died. The Master called me one morning. He put his hand on my head and said, "I have emptied you. You have become Me. Now go into the world and be a beacon of light unto the darkness of ignorance. Be like a tree that gives shade to the woodcutter and fruits to a tiny bird as well as a nursing mother. You are not separate from me. We are essentially one. I gave you emptiness, which made you complete. Now I give you freedom. Be free."

The students were curious to know if this was his or Shantananda's story. Gautama smiled and clarified that it wasn't. He explained, "There are two clear messages in this story. The Master wasn't teaching. He was existing and doing his job. The monk was connecting to the Master. He initially connected to the Master's outer form and could only see the Master's outer form and his outward expressions (Master is angry, upset, sad and so on). Slowly, as he kept looking, he penetrated into the inner core of the Master and saw his still state – the state of absolute joy. Only the inner state can change one, not outward expressions. The moment he connected to the Master's inner state, he instantaneously became that state. Then it was ecstasy which is why he was happy. Then, the outer expressions had no value because he could only see the Master's inner state of ecstasy. The others saw the outward expression "Master is scolding", but he couldn't see that, because he couldn't see the outside anmore. The joyous state is all he could see because he had connected to the core of the Master. In recognition, the Master told him to go forth and spread that learning. There is no teaching. You are not asking anything. He kept watching and through watching, he became that. His consistency was the key."

Gautam indirectly explained how the Tradition worked. This was a prophetic story from Gautama because it was almost a reflection of the life of Vamadeva and his experience at the *gurukul*.

CHAPTER 6

PEARLS OF WISDOM

Gautama used to share stories with the fellow students when they went to graze cows. He would speak about the Master, how to handle different phases and situations in life, share different teachings and learnings of Shantananda, and so on. He used to share very deep insights on karma, especially about what one should avoid. Sometimes whlle walking, he would ask questions. There was no sitting down and teaching. When too many words are spoken, nothing is remembered. When one uses more silence and less words, those words are very important and remembered. That was Gautama's method which he had learnt from *Maharishi* Shantananda. Since they spent most of their time in silence, the students remembered the stories and their messages from the fewer occasions that Gautama taught. Since Gautama loved Lord Krishna, he usually quoted from or his talks usually ended up in stories of Lord Krishna.

The following are excerpts of some of the important teachings shared by Gautama with the other students.

On Bad Karma

In an incident at the *gurukul*, one student was given food to share with another. He lied to the other that he had no food and ate it alone. Gautama used the occasion to quote a similar story from Lord Krishna's life and explain the consequences of bad karma. Sudama was the Lord Krishna's childhood friend and classmate at his *gurukul*. Once as they were going to the forest to collect firewood, the Master's wife called Sudama and gave him some beaten rice for both of them to eat, in case they get hungry. Since it was not much, Sudama decided not to share it with Krishna. They spent a lot of time walking through the forest. As it was late, they were tired and hungry. Krishna asked Sudama if he had anything to eat. Sudama denied. Later, Krishna lay down on Sudama's lap and rested. Once Sudama was sure that Krishna was sleeping, he started eating the beaten rice. Of course, Krishna knew what was happening even though his eyes were closed. He asked Sudama, "Are you eating something?" Sudama said, "No. The cold is making my teeth chatter. That's all."

After he left the *gurukul*, Sudama had to suffer extreme poverty as a consequence of this minor betrayal. His wife requested him to seek assistance from his childhood friend, Krishna who had become a rich and powerful king. He was so poor that he had to borrow three handfuls of beaten rice from his neighbor as a gift for Krishna. When he came to see Krishna, he felt ashamed to offer the beaten rice to his friend Krishna, a king. The all-knowing Krishna however took the beaten rice from him and ate it with great relish. Unknown to Sudama, his family prospered instantly as soon as Lord Krishna ate the beaten rice. That was of course, the result of Lord Krisha's grace and compassion for his poor friend.

Gautama said, "When you betray, cheat or lie, you to pay many more times. Lord Krishna was very generous, He immediately compensated by cancelling the karma. But your karma may not get cancelled, because not everybody's Krishna. They may not have his compassion or his power. My job is to clearly make you understand the repercussions of your actions and tell you to avoid wrong action. If you still persist in committing wrong action, there is nothing for me to do. The karma of your wrong actions will, through suffering, teach you the right lessons at the right time in this life or in future lives."

He related another incident where a village youth had abandoned his wife and children to elope with the wife of a neighbour. The villagers came to Shantananda for guidance. *Maharishi* Shantananda prohibited the villagers from chasing the couple and asked them to have patience. He was against violence of any kind. He asked the village elders to allow them to have their chosen experiences even though it amounted to betrayal, and hence against *dharma*. He said that once they were content, they would return. Shantananda instructed the villagers to accept them like before, upon their return, because every incident has its karmic provocation and repercussion. All causes and effects are accounted for. Those who sow must reap. Our inherent goodness should transform others. Revenge is an ugly emotion; it is a sign of insecurity. Allow karma to play out completely and reap its fruits as well. No external interference was appropriate.

GAUTAMA'S WORDS OF WISDOM

"The one who betrays, cheats, steals, victimises, assassinates someone's character or acts in a way that creates pain in others will, in the end, fare worse. Hence, these acts should be avoided at all times. Betrayal is bad karma, very bad karma for the one who performs it and also for the ones who support it. It will haunt the one who betrays beyond lifetimes. Similar experiences will come back to him and disturb him time and again. Those who betray others will be betrayed manifold. Be aware. Never engage or support any of that. Lead your life as cordially as you can. Always tell the truth, speak your mind without prejudices and live a clean life. Extreme guilt will haunt those who betray and cheat. You may taste some initial success, but you will lose your conscience – the clothing of your consciousness. What is the use of winning the world by losing your soul? Eternal damnation will befall those who cheat, steal, betray and malign others."

"Every cause has its effect and every effect has its cause; this is unavoidable. The only thing we humans can do is to avoid insensitivity and acts of cruelty. Avoid bad company. Always walk with elevated friends or at least those who are compassionate and benevolent by nature. Never be lured by spiritual powers, its demonstrations or traps, or resort to practices of a dark, binding nature to acquire them. This will affect you through lifetimes. Always stay with the light path of our Master and the Tradition. Remember, help ever and hurt never. Never harm any living being, and never harm any saintly people through thoughts, words or actions. You will suffer its implication for hundreds of lifetimes. Bad causes will only produce bad effects. The major cause of all the sorrows of the world today is insensitive actions, resulting in undesirable results."

On Passivity

Gautama once recounted the following story from the Mahabharata – a famous epic from the Hindu scriptural treasures. The crux of the Mahabharata is the righteous war fought between two sets of cousins' of the Kuru dynasty – the five Pandavas and the hundred Kauravas. It was a war of epic proportions like a world war. This story occurs during the middle of this fierce battle. The regent, commander in chief of the Kauravas and the patriarch of the Kuru dynasty, Bheeshma has been incapacitated by the innumerable arrows that have pierced him in battle. He is literally lying in excruciating pain on this bed of arrows and awaits death. Since he has the boon to choose his time of death, he is waiting to leave his body during the favourable time of *Uttarayana*[14] which is best suited for transition to the higher realms. Exposed to the elements, he has to experience the cold winter, the harsh sun and the fury of nature during this long wait.

At the end of the day when the battle has paused, Lord Krishna and the Pandavas come to pay their respects to Bheeshma. Bheeshma asked Krishna, "What did I do to deserve this unbearable suffering? I have the power to see through my last hundred lifetimes. I have not committed any sins in any of them. Then why am I suffering like this?" Krishna replied, "To understand the cause of your current misery, you have to look at your lives beyond the hundred. In one of those lives, you were out on a hunt with a spear in your hand. A snake crossed your path. You flicked the snake with your spear. The snake flew in the air and landed on a cluster of cactus plants. He could not move anywhere due to the numerous pointed thorns piercing its body. It formed a bed of thorns for the poor creature. Exposed to the stark sun and unable to get any food, it lay there in unbearable pain and died of dehydration and hunger. The curse of that helpless creature has come to you."

---

[14] *The day after the winter solstice when the sun starts on its course towards the northern hemisphere*

Bheeshma enquired, "If that be so, how come this curse did not find fulfilment in these intervening lives? Why now?" Krishna replied, "Your karma was always waiting for the right time for fulfilment. However, since that life until this one, you only performed good deeds and never committed a sin. Hence, it could not touch you. The purity of your life protected you from this curse." Bheeshma got very curious and asked, "Then why this life? I have always followed my *dharma* in this life." Krishna said, "You did *adharma* (unrighteousness). You supported your wicked nephews, the Kauravas in their sinful acts. They cheated their cousins, the Pandavas, in the presence of the entire royal court (that included you) through a doctored game of dice. If not for my intervention, the Kauravas had almost disrobed the wife of the Pandavas in the royal court while all of you watched mutely." Bheeshma protested, "But I never participated in those heinous acts. I had nothing to do with them. I never supported them. I always looked the other way." Krishna said, " Not only the person who commits the sinful acts but also the one who mutely watches the weak and helpless suffer, performs *adharma*. Where the helpless are not supported, decline and decay befall. If you don't raise your voice against *adharma*, you are as guilty as the one committing it and will face the same consequences. Your passivity in the face of *adharma* has caused the waiting karma to befall you now. Hence, you are lying on a bed of arrows under the stark sun in the midst of harsh nature, awaiting death."

Gautama continued, "The scriptures say, '*dharmo rakshati rakshitaha*' (*dharma* protects those who protect it). When you protect *dharma*, *dharma* protects you. Do you know why our dear Master Shantananda who prefers silence and isolation and never interferes in anybody's life, gets involved in the local village issues when requested? Because once he has been informed about the issue, it is his duty to take a stand for *dharma*, and guide. He cannot keep quiet anymore, excuse himself or say it is not his concern, even if it is a minor issue. He performs his duty as mandated by *dharma*."

GAUTAMA'S WORDS OF WISDOM

One of the reasons why negativity thrives is the passivity of people who do not speak out against untruth. They know the falsehoods but do not challenge it preferring to maintain a safe distance. There will be times when our faith will be tested to see if we are speaking at the right time when it is most required. We may be called upon to speak to or against people whom we love the most. At those times, when we are supposed to speak, we should not remain silent. We may not have another opportunity to speak or even if we speak later, it may not matter since the damage may already have been done. We are held responsible for the damage done due to our passivity. We take on the same karma as the person performing *adharma*. Passivity is *adharma*. Passivity is equal to treason. An enemy is preferable to a passive friend. At least, we know where the enemy stands. Darkness may have a field day for a while but eventually the truth will come out.

On Possessiveness

An eagle was flying with a piece of meat clasped in its beak. He was in a hurry to take it to a safe location and eat it peacefully. The meat was larger than what he could've easily swallowed on its flight.

Suddenly a flock of crows started chasing the eagle. They flew with him and began to attack him. The eagle was helpless. He could not retaliate by pecking at them because he had this piece of meat held tight in his sharp beak. The eagle did not realise for a long time, why the crows were attacking him. He experienced intense suffering from the attack of the crows. Finally, he understood that the crows were after the meat, and not him. For a while, he was reluctant to let go of his hard-earned food. Finally, wisdom prevailed and he opened his beak. The piece of meat fell away and the crows immediately left him and followed the meat.

We are all like this eagle. We never drop the cause of our suffering, preferring to suffer eternally, often unconsciously and unknowingly. We work hard and earn our possessions suitable for our body, ego, mind, or intellect. When we have those possessions, irrespective of whether they are material possessions or siddhis of spiritual nature, the crows of society start chasing and hunting us. They come to take away our hard-earned possessions from us. We hang on to them because we believe that they are legitimately ours. Neither we nor the crows understand the fact that what we own is temporary, and can never truly be ours or theirs. Everything passes hands sooner or later. But we do our best to defend what we have. In the bargain, we may get hurt. Finally, when we become helpless, we will reluctantly let it go. Otherwise, death will detach us completely from our worldly assets. The more we possess, the more we will face attacks by the world. The lesser our belongings, freer is our life. Man holds on to his chattels and attracts many such crows. When he lets go of them at the physical, mental, and intellect level, the world of crows stops bothering him. *Avadhootas* are walking examples of this level of lack of possessions, possessiveness, and ownerships.

On Cows

On another day, while attending to the cows of the *gurukul*, Gautama told the younger students, "Our Master has said that cows are sacred. The Vedic wisdom rooted in *ahimsa* (non-violence) and respect of all beings, gave great importance to cows and considered them celestial beings. Do you know why?"

The other disciples listened to Gautama with rapt attention as he explained as follows.

The great sage Vashishta, one of the *Sapta Rishis* (the seven illustrious sages) requested the creator Brahma on behalf of all the sages on earth, "We need a completely *sattvic* being to help us lead a *sattvic* life on earth by providing us *sattvic* food, *sattvic* offerings for the fire rituals and ceremonies, as well as *sattvic* materials for purification of our homes, rituals, ceremonies and so on." Brahma replied, "The cow is such a being. You can take the cow to earth. Its milk will nourish you along with the products made from the milk such as butter, buttermilk, *ghee* (clarified butter) and so on. If the cow eats nutritious food, its dung will have no odor. All its products including its dung and urine will be sacred and *sattvic* and will have medicinal value. You can use *ghee* to purify your material and offerings for the rituals and ceremonies. Its dung and urine will be antiseptic and *sattvic* and can be used to clean and purify your homes, places of worship, rituals, ceremonies and so on. You can even use the solidified dung as fuel for your fire ceremonies. The dung and urine can also be used on the farms for organic cultivation of crops."

Brahma added, "Being *sattvic*, the cow cannot protect itself. Hence in return for its service on earth, the human species has to promise to protect the cow. Do you promise?" Sage Vasishta on behalf of the sages made a promise that the human species will protect the cow on earth.

Gautama continued, "Hence, cows are protected by the Hindu tradition in keeping with the promise made by the ancient sages to the creator. It is a grand collaboration facilitated to help the human species in their spiritual elevation. By protecting cows. Lord Krishna was actually showing the world that cows need to be protected and reminding us of our contract that Sage Vashishta promised to Brahma."

GAUTAMA'S WORDS OF WISDOM

Cows are peaceful, subtle beings and never engage in conflicts and fights. They absorb, store and release only pure products. This is why a cow can be compared to a tree. A tree takes in used and polluted air and gives out pure air that is good for our lungs. This is also why we always sit under the trees during spiritual discourses. The pure air refreshes and rejuvenates us. It makes our minds sharp and receptive. This helps us absorb more wisdom. Those who respect cows are spontaneously *sattvic* in nature.

Our scriptures say that the body of the cow is the abode of many deities. Each deity has a functional purpose. This purpose is fulfilled through the cow. It includes purification from gross to the ultimate subtle. Further, *sattvic* beings are very sensitive and absorb many toxins and negativities in a subtle form from its surroundings. Thus, the world is purified. The cow stores these negativities and toxins in her body and destroys it at death. Hence, a cow's meat should not be eaten, because at the subtle level, it contains all the toxins of the world which it absorbs every moment from society. People who slaughter cows and eat their meat incur extremely bad karma and also contaminate themselves severely. In the times to come, mankind will breach the contract even more. They will slaughter cows, even calves and pregnant ones, and steal milk from the calves. They will suffer immensely from the resulting consequences.

On Purity

Purity is a subtle state. Purity in thought is not just good thoughts. It also includes what you respond to. Your opinions, your criticism of others, and even getting involved in other people's affairs without their consent can all affect inner purity. We must help unconditionally and without expectations, especially if we see someone in need of assistance. Helping another is a pure act. But, if we decide to help someone unasked and unwanted, it can cause a karma transfer. This is a subtle matter. We should help, if the other does not have the capacity to ask or request. This is our *dharma*. But, if we try to intervene in someone else's matter because we think we can do something better, it will amount to karmic intervention. Preventing a person from falling is our duty. But if we hold the hand unasked, thinking that he might fall anytime, is karmic intervention and an impure action. Purity is an-every-\moment matter. Pure intention, combined with non-intervention, is important to preserve it.

On Violence

Our predecessors, saints, and sages constantly asked us to stay away from *himsa* (violence) of any kind. They kept reminding us: *Ahimsa*

Paramo Dharmah (Non-violence is the ultimate religion). Violence disturbs the vibratory level, both inside and outside of us. Violence in thoughts, words, and actions binds us to emotions and emotions lead us to further karmas. Karma has its root in unfulfilled desires combined with emotions which reinforces an operating character and constitution. So, a true *sadhaka* (seeker or practitioner) should be aware of such traps on the path of liberation and stay clear at all times. We should not harm any beings of any species. Always be compassionate and kind. Never be selfish and upset anyone's life. Life is the bed where you experience your karma on time. Always keep your bed tidy and clean.

On Fear

Fear destroys like fire. Fear is one of the most formidable enemies in the path of liberation. Sometimes, religions, sects, cults and possessive teachers use fear to control their followers because they have nothing else to give. This eventually affects the teacher, the follower, and their path adversely. In our path, we don't need to control people. We are trying to liberate people. In liberation, there is no room for fear. You need fearlessness. In the path of liberation, we should conquer all our fears before we set out on the conquest of our mind. Fear is ignorance. When you have fear, you are entertaining ignorance. What is the worst that can happen? Death! You will die anyway.

If you are really in the path of spirituality, there can be no fear. You will be protected. Trust in yourself, trust in nature, trust in existence, trust in our Master, trust in God. Our Master is the epitome of fearlessness, he is our leading light. We dissolve our fears in the consciousness of our Master and lead a life of total emptiness and lightness. Have no fear. Opposite of fear is faith. Have faith.

We have no reason to fear when we have unshakable faith in our Master. Our Master takes care of us at every step. Faith eliminates fear, like water extinguishes fire. Faith is the most reliable method to stub out the flames of our fears.

Awareness is the permanent way to tackle our fears. In other words, the best way to conquer one's fears is to face them and burn them in the fire of awareness. To an ignorant mind, a rope feels like a snake in the darkness and arouses fear, but in the light that provides clarity and awareness, that fear disappears. Likewise, most fears are related to inherent insecurities such as darkness, death, personal loss, or the fear of the unknown. They have no value in the daylight of awareness. Unfortunately, fear is the trap that the world uses to bind people for selfish gains. This is wrong. When we delve deeper and deeper into our inner silence, all the stored fears will begin to surface. Watch and let go... Watch and let go... They have to escape through the conscious mind. Do not panic or meddle with them; they are to be released gracefully. Our Master is protecting us, watching over us. All fears are illusions. Let go of your illusions and you will be established in the Absolute Truth.

On Fire

Be aware that we are all essentially the fire. The fire of creation that rested in the 'stomach' of the Sun became the Galaxy. The fire of will in the consciousness of *Parabrahma* (the supreme unmanifested consciousness) manifested as the universe. The fire of your mother's womb created you. The fire in your stomach sustains you. All existence is connected to fire. Fire is the only element that burns everything, and never gets contaminated. It just leaves behind ash, which is beyond any flavor and design.

The flames of fire only go up, never down. Hence, it is considered as the chosen carrier of offerings to all deities. It is always pure and sacred. This is why our tradition keeps fire as our closest ally and best friend. We offer all our impressions and afflictions to the sacred fire. All our intentions and all our impressions are offered to the fire every day.

Fire takes them on and releases us from their effects each day, yet it itself never gets contaminated by anything. We worship the Sun as the source of this platform called the galaxy, where life could thrive. We worship the Sun as the source of energy, and it creates, sustains, and dissolves life on earth. We worship the Earth because she gave us the platform for our existence, gratifications, and survival. We keep our bodies sacred and lust-free because our only plan and aim in life is liberation. When we burn all our identifications and identities, along with the stored impressions, in all our layers especially our causal layer, we dissolve into the supreme *Parabrahma*. When we stop existing, only the supreme, unsullied consciousness exists. Thus, we systematically nullify ourselves into the fire, using the fire of awareness.

On Exercising Choice

Gautama once asked a question, "Why do people say, 'Don't be like an animal?'". Some said, "Because animals are bad." Gautama said, "No." Several others tried but none could answer properly. Gautama said, "All creations of God are good and considered equal. There is no bad. All creations are made of a varying degree of three flavors – *sattva* (goodness, constructive, harmonious), *rajas* (passion, active, confused), and *tamas* (darkness, destructive, chaotic). Animals are programmed with one prominent flavor and they stick to that predominant flavor. A tiger is *rajasic* by nature and it stays *rajasic* till death. It will not be a *sattvic* or *tamasic* tiger. A monkey will always be like a monkey. It will not be a better monkey. They do not have the choice of raising themselves to the level of *sattva*. Human beings do. A human being through his choice of thoughts, words and actions can be a sinner or a saint. If one just follows their predominant flavor as animals do, say for example *rajas* – chasing money, material pleasures, and so on, then they are not even exercising that choice of *sattva*. If you don't use your choice as a human being, then you are almost like an animal. Hence, it means don't live unconsciously.

On Suicide and the Aftermath

One of the disciples asked Gautama, "What causes someone to commit suicide?"

Gautama replied, "There could be various causes such as disappointment, depression, expectations, unfulfilled desires, and so on. But these are all expressions or external causes. The root cause is a pattern of resistance or escapism where the solution for an inability to face a situation or fear, is suicide. This resistance could manifest externally as fear, self-doubt, lack of self-confidence or self-esteem, fears, prejudices, inability to face reality, and so on. Even introversion and shyness can be a pattern. People may be boiling inside but pretend to be shy because they can't handle a situation.

One's predominant emotion at the time of death becomes one's predominant pattern in the next life. This is why the scriptures encourage people always to keep their mind focused on their Master and God. If one is absorbed in intense devotion at the time of death, they return as a devout soul. Similarly, when the person exhibits a pattern of resistance for a long time, they exit in a confused state (regrets, guilt and so on). Thus, these patterns of escapism stay and get repeated over subsequent lifetimes. A person who commits suicide in one life will tend to do the same in the next life. It is an extension of self-destructive tendencies similar to people who drink or smoke uncontrollably and destroy themselves. The person will have some reason to commit suicide.

The same is the case with accidental, unnatural deaths or premature deaths that are manifested by trapped emotions or fears of an abrupt ending, such as a fear of accidents. Fear of theft can usually lead to a robbery in the house. Similarly, a fear of attacks from unknown people can manifest. In all these cases, the cause is a trapped fear. One's lineage can also push that kind of karma, especially in regions that have faced many natural disasters, wars, displacements, betrayals and so on. These unfortunate events affect many families from that region."

The disciple enquired further, "In the above cases, what happens to the soul after death?"

Gautama replied, "In these cases, the soul exits or leaves in a hurry, unlike natural death. The soul can exit through the nine holes of our body: top of the head, eyes, ears, nose, mouth, genitals, and so on. The soul transit at the time of death is significant. The lower the exit, the lesser are the choices available for evolution. At their chosen time of death, saints and elevated souls consciously exit through the top of the head. Likewise, karmic beings typically exit through the mouth during a natural death. Hence, a dead person's mouth is usually open. For the above cases, the soul typically exits through the genitals. This kind of exit indicates a return in the next life with more torturous, bizarre situations and increased agony.

Imagine a person was supposed to live to an age of eighty years. The person decides to end his life at the age of sixty. There are twenty years of potential life pending on the earthly plane. The person has exited the body, but it is not yet time for the person to exit earth. If they were deeply connected to a Master or God while living, either the Master helps them transcend the earthly plane, or they can try to reach various Masters in physical and non-physical form, to ask for help.

In most cases, there is no faith and no connection to a Master or God. Then, they are doomed to remain and wander on the earthly plane. The vessel is gone, but the soul is stuck on the earthly plane, not knowing where to go or what to do. Everything minus the physical body remains for the next twenty years – the mind-matter (mind, intellect and ego, the processors of our system), all other sheaths (energy, mind, knowledge, bliss) with their pending desires, attachments, inclinations, tendencies, and so on. They carry all these as a burden, yet they cannot have any fulfilment or experience during their remaining time on earth, because they don't have a body. They have all other emotions and feelings, except the body. They want to do something, but they can't. They are neither here nor there that results in deep helplessness. We may not see them, but many beings in various levels of subtlety exist on our earthly plane. Animals can see some of them.

Some deeply crave redemption in this disembodied state and may attract the grace of a Master who helps them overcome and change the pattern with awareness in their next life. These souls can also transcend during eclipses and times of upheavals in nature. Hence, Masters work during these periods to release these helpless souls craving for release. Some start bothering other beings, out of helplessness and jealousy. They still have emotions and desires but cannot express or do what one can do with a body. Hence, they connect to people with similar emotions and desires who are insecure or weak, enter them and use them. Sometimes, there's a conflict between the original soul and the intruding soul, which we term as possessed. Once they intrude, they accent the emotions and desires of their victim that are of interest to them, inducing the victim to indulge in those emotions and desires and thus experience fulfilment. In some cases, they influence their victim's thoughts through intense concentration without entering them. A third of the souls wander until the end of their original life period and then exit the earthly plane.

The two-thirds majority is not so fortunate. Helpless and vulnerable, they are trapped, captured and bound by predatorial beings who control them and use them as slaves. The hunters can be embodied (people engaged in dark practices) or disembodied (non-physical beings but using similar techniques). Once bound, there is no guarantee on their release. They are used to disturb people and for other harmful purposes. They have no choice. Since they are doing the dirty work in the front, the karmic impact of their actions first comes to them. Thus, they accrue bad karma which further delays their spiritual evolution on release. This is the biggest tragedy for these unfortunate souls who were regular karmic beings on the path of evolution.

Hence, the scriptures prescribe the fourteen to sixteen-day rituals after one's death to protect and help elevate the soul during the transition period. In other religions, there is only heaven and hell – no rebirth. They do not address the transit of the soul, which leaves the soul vulnerable. Nothing can touch one who is deeply connected to a Master or God. People who are depressed or have self-destructive tendencies must understand the subtleties and seriousness of suicide and the dire consequences. Rather than escaping from a situation, it is better to face it and solve it in this life, stay in the body and have a natural death. Likewise, emotions and fears can become diseases or even death. For women, the uterus stores trapped emotions or fears. For men, it is below the ribcage. Those focal points impact every other dimension. Even though it takes a lot of effort, one should remove and destroy these trapped fears and emotions and become free. One should elevate one's awareness to the level where these fears and emotions drop off, and one becomes clean and serene."

CHAPTER 7

A TALE OF TWO FRIENDS

Govinda was a classmate of Vamadeva. Unlike the others, Govinda was from the neighborhood. His father provided supplies to the *gurukul* and was connected to the *Maharishi's* family. Govinda probably owed his presence at the *gurukul* to his family's personal connection with the *Maharishi*. His house and father's shop were close to the *gurukul* and Govinda often visited his house while at the *gurukul*. Unlike the others who were silent and reserved, Govinda was more flamboyant and hence easier for Vamadeva to approach and connect. In the beginning, one needs support to adjust in a new place. Govinda provided that support for Vamadeva when he first came to the *gurukul*. He was the same age as Vamadeva, just a few months older. They were also the same build, with Govinda being slightly taller. In the beginning, they became very close, bathing in the river together and sleeping next to each other. In their early years, their resemblance was striking and some people believed they were twins. Govinda behaved like an older brother, which Vamadeva accepted and allowed.

As they grew into their teenage years, their interests diverged. Govinda developed a fascination for women whereas Vamadeva fell in love with isolation and silence and became introverted. Neither could Govinda understand the sudden change in his friend, nor did Vamadeva explain anything. His sudden lack of interest for almost all worldly things puzzled Govinda. He tried his best to bring him to his own ways, even introducing him to some of the prettiest girls in the neighborhood for sensual pleasures, but nothing made any impact on Vamadeva. He remained aloof. Later, Vamadeva was closer to Mukunda. They hardly spoke but he had a personal rapport with the smiling, ever peaceful Mukunda who got along well with everybody. However, his companionship towards Govinda continued, and he accompanied his friend everywhere. Vamadeva was more like an enigmatic shadow for Govinda – inevitable, disinterested, and non-interfering.

There was a shop not so far from the *gurukul* that provided groceries and rations to the *gurukul*. Every couple of days, the students took turns to get the groceries in bulk from the shop. On one such visit, Govinda saw the beautiful daughter of the shopkeeper and fell in love with her. Their love affair started soon after. Since then, Govinda volunteered to pick up groceries everytime. None objected or questioned. Later, he started picking up the groceries once or twice a day rather than in bulk. No on asked why. There were no hard and fast rules at the *gurukul*. There was complete freedom on what someone wanted to do and the way they wanted to do it. As long as the groceries and rations were available on time, nobody cared at the *gurukul*. He sometimes took Vamadeva along to avoid arousing suspicion on his frequent trips to the shop. His secret, of course, was very safe with Vamadeva.

This new interest of Govinda allowed Vamadeva to segregate from him. While Govinda would be busy chatting with his girlfriend, Vamadeva would, at every opportunity, withdraw his mind from the outside world and plunge into the inner pool of consciousness. However, Govinda could only confide in Vamadeva. When Govinda spoke, Vamadeva was a sympathetic listener. He saw Govinda's emotional involvement as a drama with different flavors. He neither participated nor objected. He didn't judge either. He just listened. That was all that Govinda wanted. On several occasions, Govinda tried to pull Vamadeva to his path of pleasures, but in vain. Vamadeva had no interest.

The key to Govinda's charm was his ability to predict the future. It was partly skill and partly intuition. Govinda impressed everyone, beginning with his girlfriend who later became his wife, to the old toothless woman who wanted to know if there was marriage in her cards. All were enchanted by his skill. It was Gautama who initiated Govinda into astrology on *Maharishi* Shantananda's instructions. Given the show that Govinda displayed in his practices, Gautama also guided Govinda in the path of devotion. The Master's assessment was accurate, as always. He had known that Govinda would lead a terrestrial existence immersed in his personal glories and accolades. What he gave to Govinda was exactly what the boy had come to him for. Every disciple always got exactly what they deserved. Govinda had his place in the *gurukul*. He was accepted as he was. Neither Shantananda or Gautama questioned his instincts or behavior. They allowed the show to happen. Gautama told Govinda, "You need gratification since it is too strong for you. Neither can you control it, nor can you come to terms with it. Don't pretend. Don't suppress. By suppression, you cannot evolve since the weight will be on you which will eventually pull you down. Experience and let it go. Have no guilt." As with all disciples of Shantananda, Govinda also became a master in his own right, albeit in different fields – romance and astrology.

Govinda's journey was colourful and rough until his marriage. His father-in-law to be, the shopkeeper, never really liked him. His flirty, talkative nature and smug manner while making predictions did not go so well with the older man who believed that Govinda was an upstart and would eventually abandon his daughter for other women. In those days, two or three wives were a status symbol. He understood that Govinda may walk that path to show off, because he thrived on praise, accolade, and applause. In fact, he trusted and respected Vamadeva more and would have been very happy, had Vamadeva married her.

At one point in time, Govinda had no choice but to elope with his girlfriend and get married to her in a temple in the next village. Vamadeva was his companion in that adventure as well. Although he was silent and preferred to stay in isolation, Vamadeva was a loyal friend, unafraid of social repercussions. He was unaffected by the display of romance by Govinda either, it never created any ripple of desire in the absolutely still consciousness of Vamadeva. Upon their return back home, the helpless father-in-law was forced to accept his flamboyant son-in-law. That was the beginning of Govinda's setting himself up in the city of Varanasi as an established soothsayer, visited by the rich and the famous, as well as the poor and the needy. He was a good man with a kind heart, always ready to help. Eventually, he became rich and popular and lived happily with his wife and children.

After Vamadeva left the *gurukul*, Govinda was always concerned about his friend. Although Vamadeva preferred solitude and silence, Govinda would have preferred Vamadeva to be a householder like their Master Shantananda. Whenever he could, he would bring Vamadeva home and make him give lectures on philosophy to an audience he would gather effortlessly. Vamadeva was quick to spot the hidden agenda, he knew Govinda was trying to fix him up with a potential bride. He knew his friend meant well, but Vamadeva would quickly escape. Often, Govinda invited

Vamadeva to his house on the pretext that his wife had been enquiring about him, or that Govinda's children were waiting to meet their uncle Vamadeva. Since Vamadeva loved the children, he could not refuse such invitations. When he arrived there, he would see a lot of people waiting to meet him, especially potential brides and their family. He would then try and escape, but his friend's grip on his arm was firm, and he couldn't get away.

Once, a rich and powerful local landlord asked Govinda to check the horoscope of his daughter. Govinda was a very talented astrologer. Using his personal calculations, he found out that Vamadeva had a great future no matter what path he chose – terrestrial, spiritual, and so on. To strengthen his relationship with the landlord, he suggested, "Vamadeva is the perfect match for your daughter. This man has the stature of an emperor. Their marriage will bring immense prosperity and blessings to your household and lineage. I will personally convince Vamadeva. He will not decline me." When Govinda approached Vamadeva, he politely but firmly told Govinda, "I have committed to a path of renunciation. Marriage or family life is not for me." Govinda was in a very sticky situation. Not only did he lose his favour but also incurred his wrath. This incident led to a parting of their ways. Govinda stopped seeking out Vamadeva and ceased his attempts to get him married. He understood that there was no point in chasing Vamadeva since he had already chosen his track. In his heart, he also suspected that Vamadeva may not have a long life and may choose to leave at a young age. He had already attained the silence early enough and, barring his purpose, did not have a reason to stay on earth for too long. A fter this, he stopped tracing Vamadeva and never brought Vamadeva back. A few years later, Vamadeva wandered away from Varanasi. The two friends met only once before Vamadeva left his body at the age of forty-nine.

CHAPTER 8

THE FAREWELL

Vamadeva had been in the presence and guidance of *Maharishi* Shantananda for fourteen years. Govinda had left the school before he got married and and was now well settled with his family in Varanasi. Vamadeva had stayed on, bathing in the pool of silence of his Master and the tradition. His dispassion reached a point where he decided to live the life of an ascetic. He discussed with Gautama to get ordained as a monk by taking the vows of renunciation. Gautama conveyed Shantananda's earlier words on renunciation to Vamadeva, "Renunciation is not an external clothing. Inner renunciation makes one a monk. Your connection with me is your greatest wealth. As a monk, that is the only wealth you need – your deep connection with me." Gautama knew that Vamadeva, in his mind, was already a monk and was living these words of his Master.

Since one is ordained by one's Master, Gautama discussed with Shantananda to get his approval and directions. The initiation ceremony is very elaborate which takes around a month or two, requiring many dips every day in the river Ganga in between the ceremonies. Through Gautama, Shantananda arranged to have the ceremony done through another saint who had an ashram close to the river by the ghats. This Master had immense respect for Shantananda and gladly agreed to perform it. Vamadeva took a month and a half to complete all the ceremonies and formalities including performing his own funeral rites as well as those of his parents to signify the end of his past life along with its commitments and responsibilities. The person ordained as a monk is given a new name signifying their rebirth. However, the saint only gave him a temporary name for the sake of the ceremonies because he felt that it was Shantananda's prerogative to give Vamadeva his monastic name. When done, the saint requested Vamadeva to return to his Master.

Gautama used to frequently travel to attend to Shantananda's matters. More students had joined the *gurukul*. In the absence of Gautama, Vamadeva took the new disciples under his wing. Unlike Gautama, he was a man of silence, so the students preferred Gautama's classes to Vamadeva's. Vamadeva was almost like his Master, *Maharishi* Shantananda; he too was always immersed in unshakable silence. He went about the daily activities, doing all that was needed immersed and saturated in that silence. He had progressed rapidly in those fourteen years. Like a piece of dry wood that gets a spark, blows smoke initially and then suddenly catches fire. Each student's progress was different and not all progressed equally. It was fine since each one was allowed to progress at their speed. Vamadeva used the time fully to empty himself completely.

It reached a stage where Vamadeva lost interest in all activities. He lost interest in food and he was in an extreme state of penance. He was continuously fasting. Gautama and the other disciples didn't interfere. It reached a stage where he would be experiencing ecstatic states in a trance for a long time. Gautama understood. He told the others, "Don't disturb. Let it be." Since he was not doing anything, his chores were getting affected. Others automatically took over. That was the *gurukul* way. No job was left unattended. Somebody would do it. This went on for more than a week. He was lost in the serenity of inner calm, making his mind float on it like a log of wood over still water, unattached to anything. Slowly but steadily, as his dependency on the outside world reduced, his mind was getting dissolved into the pool of silence. His mind matter started diminishing day by day and finally, it totally merged into the pool. It was as if Shantananda was preparing him silently for the final transfer.

The technique of floating in the inner pool of silence was finally delivered by his Master, *Maharishi* Shantananda, in silence, without any verbal guidance. One day, *Maharishi* Shantananda signalled to Vamadeva to come to his room. When Vamadeva entered, the Master was sitting on the floor on a rug in the lotus posture with his eyes closed. He stood there in silence until the *Maharishi* opened his eyes. It took a good half an hour. He motioned to Vamadeva to sit facing him. When Vamadeva settled down in the lotus posture, *Maharishi* Shantananda looked into his eyes. He was probably measuring the depth of the pool of silence and his vision penetrated through the disciple's eyes into the inner ocean that was waiting to be explored and awakened. Vamadeva sat with his eyes open, totally mesmerised. Persistent waves of inexplicable bliss rose higher than the tallest mountain and roared within Vamadeva at the steady gaze of his Master. Oceans of energies clashed together and merged inside him and huge blasts of powerful forces rose into his inner sky. The Master was activating something powerful inside Vamadeva. He was changing, delivering, as well as collecting and removing the residue of the streams of karmic sounds from him.

Vamadeva felt as though he was floating, and at the same time whirling uncontrollably. He felt he was dissolving. He had no awareness of his body or of what was happening. He felt total stillness and the unbound joy of stillness! No person, no personality, no world outside. Finally, the inner blasts stopped and everything dissolved into perfect silence which nothing can ever disturb. Only silence existed. The sound of the ocean was silence. When Vamadeva finally came back to terrestrial awareness, it was well past midnight. His Master had left the room. He sat there much longer, until daybreak just being in silence without the burden of thoughts – in total and complete bliss. He knew that he had arrived. His Master had given him the greatest gift – he had arrived! The permanent, unshakeable, unfathomable experience called consciousness that he had been searching for within, was finally here! Gratitude welled as joyful tears in his eyes. It started streaming down his cheeks. When he heard his Master and his fellow disciples leave for the bathing ghat, he also got up to accompany them.

When they returned from the ghats, *Maharishi* Shantananda indicated to Vamadeva that it was time for him to leave the *gurukul*. It was to be his final day at the *gurukul*. The final day of departure. Vamadeva felt no emotions. The world that he was deeply involved in was within him. There was nothing outside that he connected with or considered as his own. When an old lady asked him for a piece of cloth, he gave away his only shawl to her. Why did he have to worry? The heat was inside and he was always basking in the inner warmth. How could the cold outside bother him? *Maharishi* Shantananda had asked him to meet him one last time before he left the *gurukul*.

As instructed, Vamadeva came in the presence of *Maharishi* Shantananda. *Maharishi* Shantananda was a man of very few words, and whatever little he uttered was deep and meaningful. He said to Vamadeva, "Never give in to pretentious image. Stay true to your true image which is formless. Do not easily display yourself or your stature to people. If you do, it will only increase their expectations of you. Expectations will distract their inner silence. Reveal yourself to those who are ripe and ready to dissolve, they would need no display to know who you are. Walk the path inside. There is nothing outside to conquer. You have already earned your throne. This throne is eternal. You will always be watched and protected. You need to care for nothing. You need nothing, because you have become everything."

"You have nothing to do with the pretentious world. You have nothing to do with worldly possessions. You have to visit your parents one last time, serve them for a year, settle them well, before you start your journey, thus completing the *dharma* of a son. You will not stay in one place for more than three days, so as to avoid attachment to places and things. You will not develop attachment towards anything. You will have followers, not disciples. Even though you are a *raja yogi* who is established in silence, you will be known as a *jnana yogi*. In your next incarnation, you will be a complete *raja rishi*. But, do not worry about titles, name, or fame – all these are earthly lures and bindings. Always be aware of who you are, and stay true to your true image."

"From now on, you will be known as Atmananda Chaitanya and will be recognised as a perfect *Avadhoota*! Do not disclose your name unless absolutely necessary "

Maharishi Shantananda took his vessel that was filled with the sacred water of the Ganga, took some in his hand, and sprinkled it on Atmananda's head. He took two flowers, did some silent chant, and gave them to Atmananda. A profound and inexplicable transformation happened within Atmananda at this stage, it was almost like a metamorphosis – as if the past was completely dead and a new life had begun at that point. He then sought *gurudakshina*.[15] Atmananda took out a pomegranate from his cloth bag and placed it at the Master's feet. He prostrated full length at his lotus feet. The Master accepted the offering of his disciple. He placed his hands on his head and said:

"Be blessed. Be a blessing to many. Be useful, and live a life of purpose until you leave this body at the age of forty-nine. I will again meet you in *sookshma* (subtle) before you leave the earth. When you see me, you will know that it is time for you to leave. Prepare yourself and leave within two days. Go now, do not look back. You have nothing left here to take. Whatever you need further in your life, you already have. You are self-sufficient. You are free."

"Self sufficient… self sufficient… self is sufficient… accomplished… fully accomplished… fully settled within… free… free… freedom from everything outside…" These words kept ringing inside him for a long time, as he left his Master's abode with a grateful heart.

He sat for a while on the banks of the Mother Ganga. He looked at her for a long time. Slowly, he stepped into the water and took several dips. He gulped many mouthfuls of water. After wiping himself with his only towel, he wore the only clothes he had and started walking in the direction of his home and his parents.

---

[15] *the tradition of repaying one's teacher or guru after a period of study or the completion of formal education, or an acknowledgment to a spiritual guide*

CHAPTER 9

THE HOMECOMING

It was fourteen long years since Vamadeva left for Varanasi in order to be with his Master. Vamadeva was one of the very few boys who had left the village for education. He was one of a kind, and the community appreciated the courage and conviction of his parents in sending him to a city so far away, without knowing what it entailed. It hadn't been easy for his parents to deal with the absence of their only son especially as they had no idea when he would return or whether he would return at all. Vishnu Sharman had had no discussion with *Maharishi* Shantananda when Vamadeva was accepted as his apprentice. He was ashamed that he had nothing to tell his wife. Everything was vague and uncertain. When would Vamadeva complete his education? When would he return home? Would he return at all? There was no clarity.

Being part of a village community, where the presiding deity was considered the Head of the village, life was almost always in balance. Vamadeva's parents did not pitch themselves into the sorrows of ownership because they lived in a loving, uncontaminated society that was untouched by selfishness or grades of supremacy. Lord Shiva was the village deity and was respected and revered by all. Every house in the village contributed in kind to the temple. The rich contributed a substantial share of their wealth to the temple. The farmers contributed a good share of their crop for the grace that got them the harvest, the right weather, and protection from disaster. Members of each home took turns and served the Lord as priests and attendants. There was perfect harmony, balance, and togetherness in the village.

Whatever contribution came to the temple went back to the community in the form of education, healthcare, food, and clothing. Nobody in the village ever slept hungry. Everybody helped each other as children of the presiding deity and considered one another as equals. Almost all the families lived together – uncles, cousins, brothers, sisters, parents – in one extended house as a joint family and worked in the fields sowing, reaping, and harvesting together. Also, most families of the village were interrelated either by marriage or because family members separated in order to better manage crops or business. Everybody had equal worth and respect in the family and the society. The elders and the experienced people were always respected and consulted for all major decisions of the family as well as society. Thus, there was harmony everywhere.

One day, tragedy struck a household of the quiet village community when a fever took the lives of almost all the members of one particular family. The villagers took care of the ailing family members with immense care. However, the village doctors failed to diagnose or cure the illness, which had occurred for the first time in the village. Almost all the afflicted family members succumbed to it. The villagers blamed it on bad karma, suspecting the head of the family, who was also the chief caretaker of the Shiva temple, of engaging in malpractices. The only survivors were three little children. Fortunately, the illness did not spread beyond that family. The elders unanimously decided to place the children in the care of other households so that they stayed safe. One of the children, a young girl, was adopted by Vamadeva's parents who were also related to the family.

This beautiful little girl was full of life and enthusiasm and brought a lot of happiness and fulfilment to Vishnu Sharman and Savithri Devi's lives. With Vamadeva absent, the couple was delighted to have a child in the home once again. The child grew up to be a beautiful lady full of kindness and charm. The time had come for the young lady to be married and the old couple were looking for prospective grooms. It was at this time that Vamadeva completed his apprenticeship with Shantananda and returned home.

Every practising Hindu believes that leaving the body at Varanasi is the most auspicious way to attain liberation from existence. Vishnu Sharman and his wife were no exception. Over the years, they had contemplated visiting Vamadeva many times and have the *darshan*[16] of Lord Kashi Viswanath of Varanasi, the aspiration of every devotee of Lord Shiva. They considered spending the rest of their lives in Varanasi if their son chose to live there after his apprenticeship. However, they became responsible for the upbringing of this young girl-child whom they had adopted, which they considered an order from Lord Shiva, the presiding deity of the village: "Remain in the village and serve the Lord there, for He is the same Shiva who is present everywhere." So, they stayed.

Not a day passed when the couple did not think about their son or talk about him. However, they were wise parents with no feelings of possessiveness, but complete understanding of the karmic flow of existence. They regularly attended the discourses on scriptures that were held in the temple so that their mind was also calm, with wisdom and awareness. Before the little girl became a part of their

---

[16] divine sighting of a saint or a deity

lives, one reason that held them back from going to Varanasi was that they were unsure if Shantananda would welcome any intrusion in the training of their child. Even while accepting Vamadeva as an apprentice, he had not discussed anything with his father including the duration of the tutorship. He just accepted the child and walked away with him. Vishnu Sharman had not even seen the conditions and facilities of Shantananda's *gurukul*. When his wife asked for details, he was ashamed that he knew nothing.

This whole thing was a bit strange for the parents and they naturally felt uncomfortable to approach Shantananda fearing that it might affect their son's education in some way. They were aware that some Masters did not approve of relatives visiting their students while in apprenticeship. Not only did they wish to maintain discipline, but they also wanted to avoid different emotions and sensitivities entering their sacred space. In the *gurukul*, disciples experienced perfect togetherness of a traditional family with the Master and his family, even though they were far away from home. This experience also helped them gain independence and freedom while learning selfless servitude. Shantananda sent homesick children back to their parents as he never forced anyone to stay in the *gurukul* against their wishes. Similarly, if the parents asked too many questions, he would ask them to take their child back. He did not want any student whose focus was anything other than education and learning.

Vishnu Sharman and his wife were confident that their son was in safe hands and they did not wish to disrupt his education. They waited patiently for Vamadeva to return home. In the meantime, Vamadeva had completed his education with Shantananda and was now called Atmananda Chaitanya. He left the *gurukul* and, as per his Master's instructions, decided to visit his parents and serve them, as any son would, for a year before embarking on the journey of a monk. It took him a few weeks to reach his village from Varanasi.

Atmananda was now a handsome, lean and tall *brahmachari (celibate)* with long matted hair that had formed dreadlocks, and a natural beard, his face unmistakably expressing the calmness and peace of a perfectly settled mind. His eyes were very distinct – commanding, very powerful and transformative. Anyone looking into his eyes could see the ocean of stillness. When he looked at people, it seemed that he was looking inside them. He mostly walked and sometimes travelled in animal-drawn carts in order to reach his village. It was noon when Atmananda arrived at his parents' home. Seeing his mother through the open door, the young monk called out, *"Bhavathi bhikshamdehi."*[17] Savithri Devi came out and respectfully invited the monk into the house, as was the custom in the land of *Bharat* (ancient India) – no wandering monk was ever sent away without food and water. Those who could afford would offer clothes and grains to carry. Even if they had only a little food and would starve without it, they would give all the food to the wandering monk. They followed the maxim in the scriptures, *"Atithi devo bhava"*[18]

She gave him water to wash his feet, hands, and face before ushering him in. Then she respectfully offered him a traditional wooden seat and on a banana leaf, served him a delicious meal, freshly prepared, with great love and devotion. The monk ate silently and with perfect mindfulness. Savithri Devi took a handheld fan and fanned him gently, murmuring under her breath, "My son would have been this age. I wonder where he is now." Hearing

[17] *"Mother, some food for a wandering ascetic, please"*
[18] Literally *"The guest is God"* or *"Rever guests like God"*

those softly spoken words, Atmananda, who had finished eating, looked into the eyes of his loving mother and said, "Dear mother, I am your son, Vamadeva."

For a few moments, there was complete silence. Savithri Devi took a while for the monk's words to sink in properly. A multitude of emotions rose within her, and for a while, she alternated between laughter and tears. She knew that her son would return one day, but his sudden miraculous appearance and dramatic revelation brought up so many sentiments and memories. Meanwhile, Atmananda quietly stood up and took the banana leaf he had eaten from outside the house and threw it into the garbage. He then washed his hands and re-entered the house, giving his mother time to compose herself.

By then Savithri Devi was ecstatic. She immediately sent a young boy to fetch her husband from the temple. When Vishnu Sharman returned, he saw his wife beside herself, unable to contain her joy. "Vamadeva, Vamadeva," was all she could say. It struck Vishnu Sharman that the tall and handsome monk sitting in their house was their son who had returned from the *gurukul* after so many years. His thoughts went back to the day when he had last seen him as an eight-year-old boy. The usually non-demonstrative Vishnu Sharman hugged his son tightly and was unable to stop the flow of tears that kept rolling down his cheeks. For the next few months, the happy couple spent several hours a day telling their son every detail of their life so far – all the events in the village, their aspirations, and so on.

The naturally reticent Atmananda, on the other hand, had not much to say except how loving his Master was, and that he had experienced the best time of his life in his abode under his tutelage.

His parents were overjoyed to learn that their son had become an accomplished Master in his own right. They were also pleased to see how the village respected their son and treated him like a great sage. Atmananda earned their respect in no time. The priests washed his feet when he came to the temple to give discourses on subtle aspects of spirituality in the temple amphitheatre. None of the villagers ever missed these talks. They especially appreciated his simplicity, humility, and unassuming way of handling great truths – explaining in simple words the truths that he had seen and experienced.

Atmananda served his parents and conducted discourses in the temple. He did not waste a single moment. His parents watched him all the time, filling their eyes, ears, and minds with his sight, sound, and touch. A new life and purpose had dawned into them. They recognised the great brightness and glow in their son, and the clarity of purpose clearly visible on his face and in his actions. They understood and respected that their son's preference for silence. His love and acceptance of the whole world was overwhelming. While he cared for his parents in great measure, he also cared for all parents – human and non-human. He cared for all life. His love had no boundaries. All this gave tremendous joy to his parents. Atmananda didn't want his parents to get hurt by a sudden departure. Hence, he had informed about his ordainment as a monk on several occasions as well as hinted several times that he may have to leave the village. Despite that, his parents still hoped that their son would marry and settle down in the village.

Two years after his arrival, Savithri Devi brought up the topic of his marriage into their conversation. Their adopted daughter was a very pious girl and they were keen to find a match for her. They broached the topic with Atmananda on the possibility of his marriage with the adopted daughter. Atmananda gently denied the proposal before it went too far, saying, "Mother, I look at her as my sister. She is beautiful. She deserves a learned husband with whom she can experience a complete and proper life, not a life of uncertainty. I have chosen the path of a renunciate, a wandering monk. History will know me as an *Avadhoota*. I will not be able to do justice to marriage and a family life. I will soon have to leave." His parents initialy found it very hard to accept his words, especially his decision to eventually leave them and the village.

Before his re-entry into their life, they had prepared themselves for the possibility that they may not see their son again. But now that he had come back, they expected him tob e around the village neighborhood, stay there and practice. They didn't expect him to leave the village for good. They had brought in the topic of marriage to explore the possibility to get their son to stay back. Over the next several days, the parents had many discussions between themselves as they debated on how to request their son to change his mind. Morning and evening, the husband and wife deliberated over this dilemma. When they were unable to decide, Savithri Devi asked Vishnu Sharman to consult with Trivikrama, who was now the seniormost priest of the temple. Priests were very deeply respected in the village because of the balance and poise they had achieved through years of diligent spiritual practice coupled with consistent daily rituals.

Trivikrama understood and lauded their son's decision. He told Vishnu Sharman, „It is a matter of grace and great fortune that Vamadeva was born in your family. But he is a saint now. A saint cannot be owned by a person, family or a village. He belongs to this whole land and will bring immense grace to his family, his clan and the whole vllage. It is futile for you to try to possess him or pin him down with marriage. Please realise that such an ocean of mercy cannot be contained in a small house or village. Accept the fact that one day, he wil have to leave so his love can reach the whole world." Vishnu Sharman understood the clear perspective given by Trivikrama and made Savithri Devi understand as well.

The parents then approached Atmananda. Vishnu Sharman said, "We perfectly understand, my son. Right from childhood, you have chosen to be alone. You had clarity and purpose. I have never seen you confused about your life. I have never seen you accuse or criticise anybody. I have never seen you upset with any situation, even now. We understand you, son. You have great work and glory ahead of you. The world needs you. We are grateful that you chose to take birth in our home. We are grateful to our Lord Shiva for this great opportunity. We understand that we do not own you nor will we ever make the mistake of imagining that you belong to us. You truly belong to the world. We are grateful that you started your journey from our home. We are honoured. We are thankful. You have our blessings, if we are eligible to bless you at all."

These beautiful words of Vishnu Sharman pierced Atmananda's heart, filling it with joy. He got up and hugged his father, and then prostrated at his feet. Vishnu Sharman's eyes filled with tears as he blessed his beloved son with a mixture of fatherly love and gratitude, with full awareness of his son's stature. He helped his son back on his feet and hugged him again.

Atmananda then moved towards his mother, and after reverently prostrating at her feet, said, "Mother, you have served me unconditionally during my most helpless times when I was a newborn, a toddler, and a child. I am eternally indebted to you. Tell me, beloved mother, what can I do for you?" Savithri Devi could not control her tears. She blessed him whole-heartedly.

"My son, you are the dream of every mother. You are *amritasya putraha* (A son as precious as *amrit*, the celestial nectar). My womb and life are blessed to have carried you for nine months. I am beyond happy. There is nothing that I want from even the Gods, as I already have everything a woman can aspire for and a mother can dream of. You are truly a blessed soul whose divinity has elevated this household. Just like the touch of a hand that converts an ordinary fruit juice to *amrit*, you will elevate many children of many mothers. You will not only have our blessings with you but also the blessings of numerous incarnations of this generation and beyond. We do not ask for anything, we only offer tears of gratitude to our Lord, Lord Shiva, the presiding deity of this village and the universe to have sent you to us, and allowed this humble woman to mother you. We are blessed, my son. You are free. You are freedom incarnate. You are an incarnation of the unbound and the unfathomable. Just accept our gratefulness. Gratitude!"

So saying, she hugged him again. It was a great event in the life of Atmananda – a clear understanding and completion. This was also a moment of realisation for the parents that their son will walk into the world to complete and fulfil his life purpose that, in turn, would bring glory to the entire village.

In the next few weeks, Atmananda spoke to all the villagers about his intention to leave the village shortly, making no promise of his return. He asked that his parents and adopted sister, be completely taken care of, which everyone in the village wholeheartedly agreed to. He also ensured that his parents and sister were well cared for, planning even their funerals in the future, and his sister's marriage to a suitable groom. Before leaving, he manifested a string bag containing money that he handed to his mother, saying, "Dearest Mother, this bag must be handled only by you. Do not open this bag fully. Put your hand inside and the exact amount that you need will be in your palm. Spend it, but do not count the money inside the pouch, or look into it. This will take care of all your needs. You will have no dearth of money ever."

Then he told his father, "My dear Father, I am deeply grateful to you for allowing me to be myself. You never interfered in my decisions and will. You are epitome of purity, innocence and goodness. There is not even a speck of negativity in your mind. You have spoken ill about anybody. You have never suspected anybody. Even if people abused you, you have never reacted. I assure you, with all humility, that you will attain your favourite Lord Shiva in this life, just because of your innocence and goodness."

Vishnu Sharman's eyes filled with tears of joy and gratitude. He was a very pure and innocent man. His mind was spotless with not even a tiniest spot of evil. He never spoke bad about anybody. He never suspected anybody. Even if people abused him, it never bothered him. He was an epitome of purity and innocence. He had been waiting to hear this all his life – the assurance of liberation. Atmananda then called his sister to his side and told her, "My dearest sister, you belong to this house much more than I do. You are taking care of our parents with so much devotion and with total dedication. How can I express my appreciation in words? When I leave, my parents and this house I leave in your hands. I owned nothing, anyway. I will own nothing in the future too. The pouch that I gave to my mother must be floated in the river, in the early morning hours, before sunrise, upon the demise of both parents. If you keep the pouch with you, it will affect your life adversely. But I assure you, you will also have no shortage of wealth to live a noble and good life. I bless you and I shall always be with you."

Thus, Atmananda ensured every aspect of his *dharma* was completely attended to. He spent another week with his family and then, early one morning, just as the temple door opened, he embarked upon his journey after prostrating at the feet of his parents and blessing his sister who prostrated at his feet with utmost reverence. He walked towards the temple door. He chatted briefly with the priest and told him his intention to leave the village, which the priest already knew. He blessed Atmananda with a pure heart. Atmananda waited until the priest entered the temple and lit the lamps. Atmananda then prostrated in front of the Shiva *linga* while the priest offered him sacred ash and water. Receiving that with utmost reverence, he walked into the darkness towards the dawn of another life.

SECTION 2

Atmananda's Memoirs

"Every communion is important, every meeting has meaning."

CHAPTER 1

CAUSES AND EFFECTS

After leaving his parental home, Atmananda started his wandering life as a *parivrajaka* which would continue for the rest of his life. The only habit that he consistently had, throughout this life was his early morning bath by taking full dips in the river, ensuring that his body was fully submerged underwater. Hence, he preferred to stay close to a river. His usual practice would be to find a resting spot close to a river or pond, during the night. In the morning, he would start his day by taking dips. Rarely did he make an exception to this habit, irrespective of his health or the weather. He was also very fond of temples, even though he never worshipped in them. He ate only one meal a day and avoided food otherwise. These habits were very similar to those of his Master Shantananda. As much as possible, he would eat consecrated offering from the temple, that the priests generously shared. While wandering, he ate fruits from the trees or plants. Very rarely, he would accept alms from people. He also never ate food after sunset. Atmananda seldom used any water except flowing water or water from a well.

His mode of operation was simple and revolved around the pattern of rivers and temples. Temples meant the temple deities and rivers meant nature. He was always around rivers and travelled through river basins and alongside the banks of the holy rivers like Narmada, Kaveri and so on. He constantly walked and never stopped walking till the end. Sometimes he would take long walks alone covering a few villages or a few places until the next river. During his travels, Atmananda used to mostly sleep in open spaces under trees or highway inns. He preferred to rest in places slightly outside the city that had minimal traffic and not many people around. Wherever he went, people from the villages along the way requested him, a wandering monk, to stay in their homes. However, he usually avoided people's homes and rarely stayed there, perhaps a few times a year. He had few dependencies and avoided anything to do with people. If people approached him, he spoke to them and delivered as per their requirement.

Atmananda decided to return to Varanasi. He was walking alone without any companions, a rarity in his life of forty-nine years. He travelled through the day and searched for a place to rest around nightfall. Along the way, he was walking and decided to halt somewhere and rest for the night. He saw a faint light in a hut and walked towards it. He knocked on the door and asked, "I'm wandering and on my way to Varanasi. Can I rest here for the night?" A feeble voice answered, "You are welcome. Please come in. The door is open." He opened the door and saw an old woman lying on the bed. He realised that she was unwell and asked her, "I don't wish to trouble you. I will seek accommodation elsewhere. May I help you with anything? Do you need anything?" She said, "I am fine, *Swamiji*[19]. Please pardon that I cannot assist you at the moment since I am unwell. It would give me great pleasure to have you stay in my house. Please consider this your home. Whatever little I have in this hut is yours. Please make yourself comfortable." He thanked her, took a spot in the hut and rested the night.

---

[19] *a respectable address for an ordained monk*

He woke up early in the morning, took dips in the river close by and returned to the hut. He sat outside the hut wondering what to do next. If not for the saintly old woman, he would have continued on his journey. From their brief conversation in the night, Atmananda understood that the old lady lived alone and was now almost unable to move. She had injured her calf while collecting firewood from the forest. When Atmananda had approached her in the night, he had observed that the wound was deep and the bluish red patch around it indicated that the wound had aggravated and the poison may have spread around. The hut was located on the outskirts of the village and the surrounding area was almost like a forest. Barring an odd woodcutter or a bullock cart, he hadn't seen anyone in the neighbourhood. There was a pathway to the next village, with a village junction a couple of kilometers away that had a few shops. Though she never asked for it, the old woman was clearly in dire need of help. He also realised that there would be no one available to help her. Since he couldn't abandon her in her current state, he decided to take care of her until she recovered fully from the injury.

He proceeded further into the forest area to find a medicine to treat her wound. His knowledge about herbs and medicines was minimal. Yet, he connected to his Master and proceeded with full faith. He used his divine will to be guided to the right plant and plucked its leaves. He made a paste of the leaves, applied it on and around the wound and held it in place with a soft cloth. When she was resting, Atmananda went into the forest to look for fruits and also into the nearby villages to beg for alms. He shared the food that he received in alms with the lady. He also helped her around the house, when needed. He took care of her as one does for one's mother or a dearly loved one.

It took her two weeks to fully recover. Once he was sure that she had recovered and could comfortably manage by herself, he requested her permission to leave. With tears of deep gratitude in her eyes, the saintly old lady hugged him tight and said to him, "In these last two weeks, you have been more than a son to me. You took care of me in every possible way. I have no words to express my heartfelt gratitude. I have nothing to offer you. I bless you that there will be no dearth in your life. When you are hungry, there wil be food for you. After a while, you will have no need for food. You will not even feel hungry. These words shall always come true. Remember this always." The old lady's blessings held true in Atmananda's later life. He was always taken care of and food would come to him in some way. He eventually reached a state where food was no longer a necessity.

Moving back, his trip to Varanasi had a few such detours. During the journey, he rested for a short while in a village temple. The temple's annual festival was to take place in a week. The villagers had planned a big feast for *brahmins* (Hindu priestly class). They approached him, requesting him to stay until the end of the festival since there were fewer people than expected. The temple was taking care of everything – food, accommodation and so on. He agreed and stayed there until the end of the festival. In the evenings, people would gather around and there would be some discussions where he shared his knowledge. He would say a few things and people would listen to him. These were to be the first of his public appearances.

He eventually reached Varanasi after a few months of long, tiring travel. One day in the early hours of the morning, he went to a ghat in Varanasi, finished his bath and sat for meditation. A group of people brought a dead body for cremation at the ghat.

A few relatives were crying while the corpse was bathed before the cremation, and some looked relieved. By 7 a.m., six dead bodies had been prepared for cremation. Atmananda was in deep meditation and was not aware of anything around him. At around 8 a.m., when he opened his eyes, a group of men and women had huddled around to take his blessings.

Atmananda was generally averse to attention from anyone. Perhaps being in his early twenties at that time, he was not yet ready to wear the burden or the responsibilities of 'Master-hood'. He tried to stand up and get away from the mushrooming crowd, but they had circled him and were prostrating before him. His escape routes were closed. So, he sat down and started blessing them one by one. They kept a respectful distance, and took extra care not to touch Atmananda because they had reached him after a cremation. As per the Hindu system, relatives of the dead usually stay away from sacred spaces, they do not visit Masters or temples for about fourteen days after the death of a family member, because of the belief that one becomes impure after attending a cremation.

An elderly, bald man requested Atmananda to answer the queries of some of the people who had assembled there. Atmananda, who had been practicing various levels of silence with his Master in the *gurukul* and had continued that practice while wandering as well, agreed but only half-heartedly. The questions covered various topics like death, karma, suffering, and attachment.

"Death is inevitable. We know that all that is born will die. Then why do we suffer so much?"

Atmananda replied, "Ownerships, attachments of relationships, and familiarity. We become used to the presence of bodies around us, start owning them and develop emotions around them. You are sad because of your attachment and ownership.

Rewards of life are the fruits of your attitude, expressions, and actions. Your mind is both your enemy and friend. Whatever you experience is your creation, born out of your disposition. Every experience has its invisible root stretching into the past."

The next question was from the relative of an elderly gentleman whose last rites had just been performed.

"My uncle who we just cremated, suffered a lot before his death. In fact, we are relieved that he is free from suffering. What action or karma causes that kind of suffering?"

Atmananda elucidated, "Actions of an impure nature cause that kind of suffering. These actions could be from this life or other lives. When one goes against another person, displays hatred, anger, jealousy, and so on, towards them, they accumulate heavy karma, and then suffering is inevitable. Whatever we do against another comes back to us, sooner or later – in this life or another. There is no escape or reduction possible in karma. Whatever you do in life – good or bad – affects not just you, but leaves an inherited impact on all the people born in your lineage. Every person in every lineage must know this and be responsible."

"What then is the solution, respected Master?"

Atmananda answered, "Good merits that we earn through good thoughts, words, and actions. Do not envy another's possessions that karma has distributed as per their karmic merits. Be aware that your actions have brought your experiences of life. Nothing can be changed. However, the future can be changed if you lead a conscious and contented life today."

He paused and thought for a while before continuing.

"I would advise you to avoid a situation, place or person that disturbs your mind or your mental stability. Avoid being influenced by other minds. If you cannot totally avoid, at least ignore them, and do not absorb the effects of their presence. Instead, focus within and chant the name of your chosen God or Master. Stay away from things that make your mind restless, rather, give preference to inner peace and tranquility. When everything we do is in surrender to God or to the Master, we come close to the Supreme Consciousness. Embrace external things that do not affect your inner tranquility. Avoid the rest. Live a simple, benevolent life."

A young man asked: "Will our actions affect our children and their children?"

Atmananda answered, "Yes! Whatever you earn, your children and their children will inherit. Lineage always carries the burden of individuals that it has given birth to. Lineage holds the collective *karma* of family members. This is inherited in various degrees by all their offspring. When family members perform significant acts and good deeds, the effects reach every person in the family, just as a family feast reaches every stomach."

Atmananda's simple language and his unassuming, gentle nature was reassuring to everyone in the crowd. Soon the others asked him questions too.

"What can be the worst situation for any lineage?"

Atmananda responded: "Passive, selfish, and indifferent people, as well as insensitive generations born into it. Just like the air in a room becomes stale when the windows and doors are closed for a long time, selfish and passive people of a generation stagnate the lineage. Selfishness and self-centeredness are bad karma. Giving and sharing from the heart brings fresh air into the room. We can call it grace, created out of positive action.

"What can we do from today?"

"Be responsible," said Atmananda. "Know that you are not just an individual, you are a lineage. Respect your position and the power to make the lineage a better place for those before you and those that are yet to come. Love is the best medicine for karma. Do not discriminate. Just love. Love is the best medicine for karma. Be good and do good. That is the secret. Share and grow. Life should be totally selfless and free. Give more than you take. Be kind always. Be generous. Respect saints and spiritual people. Respect farmers as they are working hard in the rain and sun so that you do not sleep hungry. Respect lawmakers and law protectors. Because of them, you are safe and protected. Respect children, because they learn from you to respect their contemporaries.

Maintain purity and maintain peace. Never compromise inner peace for anything external. It is not worth it. Avoid all situations of praise and applause. Even if destiny brings you accolades and applause, understand that everything is temporary; remain humble. Never fall prey to ego or get addicted to your possessions or relations. Consider everything you have as a gift from God, and handle it with respect. Always be aware that whatever comes will also leave. Never cry over what is lost and disrespect what you have. Life is moment to moment. What this moment has given you is your gift. The next moment may take it away and replace that space with another reality. Keep flowing through these realities without attachments or expectations.

"We can own nothing here. Nothing belongs to us here. All experiences have eligibility behind it. We earned those experiences – good or bad. Be grateful, whether the world respects or disrespects you. Both are just experiences, as well as lessons. Learn to detach from everything using awareness as the thread. The key awareness is the basic nature of our existence – impermanence. Your conscience is your personal guide. Be a friend to your conscience and never do anything that will affect it. Rest in your conscience which is your personal protection from all negative karma. Adulation is an addiction. It is indeed a trap. The result is spiritual stagnation. The mind rules instead of giving way for the consciousness to shine forth."

"What can we really call ours?"

Atmananda replied, "Memories of experiences, desires, and the merits and demerits of our expressions and actions. The merits and demerits of our past lives determine the flavor of this life and the lives beyond. If a person has done spiritual practices with concentration and dedication through lifetimes, he will be born in the company, family or lineage of saints and holy men, and will have the opportunity to continue their practice until dissolution, based on the quality and quantity of their karmic baggage."

"Swami, what is the cause of human greed?"

Atmananda replied, "Identifications."

"What causes identifications?"

"Ignorance caused by *Maya*[20]."

"What is ignorance?"

Atmananda said, "There are various layers of it. Ignorance that we (as individual incarnations) will always be here on earth (illusion of permanence), that we will always be healthy, that all that we consider as ours (materials, positions, possessions) will remain with us, and so on."

"But isn't all this our reality?"

Atmananda explained, "It is our relative reality, as all these are temporary. In fact, our body, mind, intellect, ego, positions, possessions, likes, dislikes, and all aspects of human existence change, evolve, and dissolve each moment. There is nothing permanent in our life except the One who enlivens us and helps us experience this drama called life."

"Is all that we experience is a waste of time?"

"Not at all," said Atmananda. "All experiences are important. Every moment experience is what we call life. Every moment experience is our life purpose. Life happens each moment. When we knit together various temporary states, we finally arrive at the permanent state. Every experience is born and does die each moment."

---

[20] *the grand illusion*

"What is the problem, then?"

Atmananda replied, "There is no problem at all. It is our wrong understanding and identification that cause pain. Me and Mine cause pain. We cannot own anything. We cannot own even this life. Everything that comes also goes. Your own childhood died before you became a young girl. No state stays forever. Everything that is born will die too. When we are occupied with relative truth, that itself is the primary ignorance factor.

"Then what is truth?"

"Whatever that is unchangeable is truth. Only the pure energy is truth. Our soul is part of it."

"That means the cause of all the agonies of this world is our ignorance?"

"Indeed," said Atmananda. "Me and Mine are the causes of all the agonies of the world. In other words, ownership. We feel that we own our life, including decisions, possessions, positions, relations, and so many other things. When we realise that we cannot control any aspect of our life, disappointments take place. We fail to accept the very truth – the impermanence of life. This resistance causes all the pain."

"People work hard to earn a living and own a lot of things, for the sake of their children. So, is this all a wasted exercise?"

"Not at all. They are all aspects of existence. Working as per the orientation of the individual, earning wealth against the time we trade, having relations, responsibilities, accountabilities, likes, dislikes as per individual character traits as well as orientations, all kinds of gratifications, and so on are all natural, and part of the experience called human life. The only problem here is the ownership – the 'Me and Mine'. If we know all the time that 'we came to this earth empty-handed and will leave the earth the same way we came', life comes to a matured level. We also realise that all that we seemingly own has no value in our life, if it is not usable by us. Imagine a rich man has much land in his name. Yet, he can only sleep in one bed, in one room, the rest of his possessions have no real value except in the eyes of the world of egos and ownerships. In real terms, all that you use and experience is your only reality, the rest are all just paper documents. What we cannot experience is not ours. What we can experience is ours and that is our real possession. If we understand, appreciate, and perform that, life will be totally complete and meaningful each moment. Nothing will be wasted, and everything will be appreciated. Everything on earth belongs to earth, including this body that we took to experience various things on earth. Apart from that experience factor, nothing has any value."

"What is the core of human existence?"

"*Purushartha* is the essence or tapestry of human existence. It consists of *dharma, artha* (materials), *kama* (desires), *and moksha* (dissolution).

Dharma is the basis of existence of everything. *Dharma* is righteousness. The right method of existence provides guidance even to the mind-oriented people. Being natural. Being with nature. Truthful. Rightful. Righteous. Righteous living means living in tune with nature, the nature within and outside, without disturbing and destroying anything in and around us. The universe operates on *dharma*. Birth is *dharma*. Life is *dharma*. Death is also *dharma*. Every breath is *dharma*. Earth, wind, water, fire, space, and ether's function is based on *dharma*. *Dharma* is inevitable. *Dharma* operates the whole universe. When we are in tune with *dharma*, without resistance, we have a complete, unfluctuating life. The scriptures say, '*dharmo rakshati rakshitaha*' (*dharma* protects those who protect it).

Artha is material. Regular karmic existence needs material assistance. Materials include food, clothing, and shelter. *Artha* is important for existence. *Artha* also demands maturity. Immature handling, possession, and control of *Artha* leads to imbalance and eventual destruction of oneself and one's wealth. *Artha* belongs to nature. Nature alone can own nature. No being within nature can own it forever.

Kama is desire. Desire for food, shelter, clothing and every aspect of human existence, created by destiny, is *kama*. *Kama* is the fire that keeps life going. Even desire for liberation is *kama* in a sense. Inclinations and tendencies are also *kama*. *Moksha* is dissolution which is beyond enlightenment. *Moksha* is total liberation.

Dharma, *artha*, and *kama* exist in all parts of this world, amongst human and non-human beings. *Moksha* – the desire and sincere conviction for liberation from the karmic cycle of birth and death exists only in this land of *Bharat*. This is precisely what makes this land very sacred.

Do not take for granted this land that you are walking on. Great sages walked here. Masters like Agastya, Vishwamitra, Dattatreya, Vyasa, Valmiki, *Sapta rishis*, *Navnaths* (the nine *Nath* saints), Lord Rama, Hanuman, Krishna, Parashurama, Adi Shankaracharya, Buddha, Patanjali, Varahamihira, Bharata, Charaka, Narada, and so many others. Respect this soil. No other soil in the whole world has nurtured so many great Masters, traditions, and religions."

"What is the wise way of handling these aspects of existence?"

Atmananda offered a simple comparison. "Think of a garland. Let *moksha* be the thread. Make *moksha* the thread and make the other aspects the beads of the garland. When liberation is the thread, all other aspects will remain pure and righteous. When the key theme of life is liberation, life will be pure and truthful."

"Why are these young men sitting here near the burning human bodies?"

"Some are sitting here just to avoid the cold winter as they have no money and nowhere else to go. Some are sitting here to conquer their fears of death. Some, who are more advanced, are witnessing the state of the dead who used to walk the earth with pride and ego, over their possessions, positions, and achievements. The ash they wear on their bodies is a reminder to themselves and others that we are essentially just ash. Ash is also the sign of total detachment from all possessions of life.

Fire is a sign of the truth that has no discrimination. Death is the inevitable truth. The mind fears truth. It fears death. Fear is ignorance. When the mind continually watches bodies burning to ashes, it overcomes its fears and establishes itself in inevitable truth. Fear is against liberation. Having no fear is a sign of the liberated state. Those who are sitting here with abundance are avoiding the fearful society ridden by emotions, and they are not interested in material possessions, including name and fame. Everything can become detrimental and delay the liberation process and induce more births and deaths. So, one must be steadfast in one's determination for liberation. Nothing else matters."

"Karma follows man beyond his grave. How can we prevent karma?"

"Good and bad actions maintain the duality of existence. Actions that make us lighter, expand our hearts and earn us merits are good actions. Bad actions arise from hatred, revenge, enmity, and anger which make us heavier and bind us to the web of relationships by earning us demerits. Both good and bad actions keep us in the web of karma and keep bringing us back through many wombs. Dependency on the external world keeps us in the karmic web. Ownership of actions and manipulations of the mind maintain us here, birth after birth. Turning inward and steadily getting out of all dependencies of earth, and establishing oneself into oneself is the only way to break the karmic web.

Reduced dependency on anything and anybody, as well as no expectations from anything, will help us maintain detachment. Awareness that this body is decaying every moment, and we are all walking towards our inevitable end, is essential. All that is born will die. Hence, the state of not being born must be explored and established. This is essential for liberation. At some point in life, this question will come to everyone's mind, just as did yours: What is this drama for? The answer is: Divinity is experiencing itself in multiple frequencies, using duality as the medium. This is the awareness that is needed to stay afloat without drowning into the pool of karma."

"Do we have a choice?"

"Yes. We always have a choice. Staying as a witness, detached from emotions and expectations is our choice. Always being aware that this whole life is an unfolding drama and looking inward to our stable soul that is unaffected by anything inside or outside is our choice. Avoiding ego and identification to this incarnation is our choice. Detachment from our outside and inside world is our choice. Avoiding ownership of people and possessions is our choice, which helps us stay liberated. To share, care, and love ourselves and all things around us is our choice."

"Master and grace are synonymous. Is it not the Master's grace that helps liberation?"

Atmananda responded by saying, "Remembrance is important. When the mind marries negativity and pessimism, we forget the grace aspect of life. That leads to disillusionment and depression. Therefore, we have stories of Masters and the *Avatars* in literature that we label as 'good history' or 'good stories'. If we forget the good things a Master has given us and only remember the imaginary, bad things that our pessimistic minds churn out from illusions, usually based on concepts and prejudices, the negative aspect of it spreads like poison through our 'bloodstream' (system) and will waste many lifetimes. Grace flows when surrender happens. When grace stops, negative feelings envelop the mind. Like a person looking through a piece of yellow glass sees everything as yellow, a man with a negative mind sees only negative things around him. The mind will convert everything positive into negative. The Master and grace leave such minds."

"Can you be our *Master?"*

"No. Your Master is already within you. People like me are only guides," said Atmananda.

A short while later, he added: "I am a wanderer. I carry nothing with me. If you walk with me, I will not object, because the path belongs to everyone who chooses to walk. But walking is your choice and responsibility, just as staying or leaving is your prerogative. I will have nothing to do with it."

Saying thus, Atmananda got up. Everyone got up too. Bowing down to his audience with full reverence, he walked away without looking back.

CHAPTER 2

A SIDDHA OF THE HIMALAYAS

Many years ago, during one of Atmananda's journeys to the Kumaon region of the Himalayas, he happened to meet an interesting saint whom the villagers called *Mooli Baba*. White radish is called *mooli* in Hindi. When Atmananda met him, *Mooli Baba* seemed to be sixty years old. He was curious and asked one of the villagers why the saint was named after a root vegetable.

The villager replied, "We do not know where *Mooli Baba* came from or what his name is. He suddenly appeared in the village and wandered up and down, sleeping in various odd places and ignoring rain and sun. At first, we thought he was just a mad beggar, but then we realised that he was not begging at all. Instead, all he did was buy only one particular vegetable, *mooli*, with money that he fished out from his rough shoulder sack. We did wonder how he came to have money, but no one dared to ask him. Soon, he settled down close to the jungle trail, building a rough shelter for himself with bamboo, sticks, and pieces of cloth. It was not sufficient protection against the incessant rain, but he seemed to be satisfied. Soon, people started recognising his stature and began to visit him.

Since we saw him eating only *mooli*, everyone brought him *mooli* as an offering. As a remedy or cure, he always gave everyone a *mooli* in some form. Once, for a patient with throat cancer, he made him open his mouth and pushed a *mooli* inside and pulled it out thrice. The man screamed in pain, but was instantly cured. *Mooli Baba*'s methods were strange, but effective. A woman drank the juice of the *mooli* that he gave her, and it cured her stomach ulcer. His *mooli* cured all illnesses spontaneously.

On certain days, *Mooli Baba* would neither come out of his tent nor meet anyone. On those days, if anyone came near, he would throw a *mooli* at them and drive them away. If it hit them, it healed them instantly. *Baba* was that powerful. The strangest thing I ever heard was that Mooli *Baba* once pushed a *mooli* up the anus of an old man suffering from haemorrhoids and it healed him! They say that the old man bled so much that people were afraid he might die. He cried in fear and confusion but soon the bleeding stopped, and he experienced relief. He left, fully healed!

Mooli Baba only articulates one word – AUM – which sounds like 'Hmm' from his mouth. He never asks anyone for anything, and when he needs something, the money seems to appear in his hands."

Atmananda had to meet *Mooli Baba*. The pull was so strong that he could not imagine continuing his journey without meeting the saint. He spent seven days and seven nights in this remote village, and visited *Mooli Baba*'s makeshift abode many times. There was always a small crowd in front of the saint's tent. He always waited because he wanted the saint's patients to have preference. Each day, after the last patient left, *Mooli Baba* would always go inside his tent and draw the curtain, as if to test Atmananda's patience. Atmananda realised that even though he was accomplished, *Mooli Baba* did not give him any preference and was testing him. He understood that a saint or a sinner are the same in the eyes of a true

Master. There is no difference.

Seven days later, he threw a *mooli* at Atmananda. Atmananda took it and walked to his accommodation. That evening, he ate only that *mooli*. Something shifted in him. He went into a deep trance that lasted a few days. He did not leave his room, eat, sleep, or use the toilet. He did not even consume water. When he returned to the waking state, he realised what a powerful *Avadhoota Mooli Baba* was. He decided not to waste another minute and immediately went back to see the saint.

Rain was pouring from the dark cloud-laden skies. Thunder and rain. There was no one on the village path. Atmananda did not have an umbrella. He was determined to see *Mooli Baba* or at least be in the saint's presence. The flowing water was knee deep at several places along the village path and it was difficult for Atmananda to walk, but he cared for nothing else. Nothing could stop him from going to *Mooli Baba*. He waded through the water and reached the clearing near *Mooli Baba*'s tent.

The thin sheet of fabric that served as a curtain was drenched, and it flapped in thes strong wind. It was cold. Atmananda was shivering. When he came closer, he saw a hole in the curtain through which he peered inside. *Mooli Baba* was sitting there, with his eyes raised to the heavens, totally still and motionless, while the rain beat down upon him through the gaps in the sacking above. He seemed totally unaffected by the weather. Atmananda stood looking at him for some time. He could not move either. He stood outside the saint's tent in the rain, while *Mooli Baba* sat inside his tent in the rain. The same rain precipitated upon both of them. Atmananda felt as if both of them were under the same umbrella of rain.

Mooli Baba suddenly looked in his direction. He threw a *mooli* at the curtain, causing it to fall to the ground. With his eyes, the saint motioned him to enter. Atmananda entered. "Hmm," the saint said. "Aum," Atmananda replied. He then looked into Atmananda's eyes. Atmananda bowed down at the saint's feet, making sure he did not touch them, touching them only in his mind. He again murmured, "Hmm," as if acknowledging Atmananda's intention. Suddenly, he hit the back of Atmananda's head with a *mooli* and Atmananda went into a trance. When he came around, Atmananda found himself on his knees with his head touching the ground. He couldn't remember how many days and nights he had stayed like this.

When Atmananda came back to terrestrial consciousness, *Mooli Baba* was not there. Atmananda was alone. Neither the villagers nor Atmananda ever saw *Mooli Baba* again. All Atmananda saw when he looked around was a small pile of *moolis* near the entrance of the tent. He distributed the *moolis* among the villagers. Those who chose to keep those *moolis* claimed that they always remained fresh, for many years. Those who consumed the *moolis* were cured of many diseases too.

Both the times that Atmananda went into a trance, he had different experiences. The first time, he had left his body and was roaming in a plane of existence where there were only white bubbles all around him. Naked men and women floated around him like fairies in the bubbles. He could see himself looking at himself from the outside. He could see himself through the others as well. Everything was transparent. Then he realised that white conglomerates all colours – all colours came together to create white. So, in fact, this world is multi-coloured! There was no pain or fear here. There was no ego or loss. There was no duality or oneness. There was nothing. It was indescribable, it was more like a hallucination. When he returned from this plane, his vision had changed. He could see through things around him.

The second time he went into a trance was when *Mooli Baba* hit him on the head with the *mooli*. He became a splash of light. Everything gross dissolved. He became light. Just light. He saw many like him, but they were all essentially him. He could not understand if they were within him or outside. The light was blinding, yet soothing. The body was well beyond the earth and stars. He was light and there was nothing else apart from him. He was the creator, maintainer and destroyer. He was the witness too. He was everything and he was nothing! There was nothing neither created or destroyed. There was a thin veil between his earlier identity and the present one, which was now so fully torn to extinction that nothing existed anymore.

When he came back to his body, he realised that he cannot be this body. As a reminder of his shift, or as a witness to it, only a few *moolis* lay on the floor, nothing else. And *Mooli Baba* had disappeared forever. Did the saint really exist? Did the saint exist only for him? Had the saint visited this village just for him? Questions that need no answer. Questions that do not matter. The current state is the only reality.

He stayed in the same village, in the same tent curing people for three years, as his humble offering to the great saint, *Mooli Baba*. He fulfilled the saint's tasks as best as he could, in his humble way. The people to whom he gave *moolis* got relieved of their nagging afflictions. When the divine call came for him to leave that place, he took his bag and left. As soon as he walked out of the tent, it collapsed completely and merged with the earth, leaving no sign of its existence! It had miraculously stayed on all these years until he decided to leave the village. He faintly realised, "*Mooli Baba* and I were in fact one, and 'I' did not exist."

CHAPTER 3

THE FARMER'S SON

Once while he was wandering further north from Kumaon, he stopped for a meal at a little wayside hut owned by a farmer. He had a tiny farmland where he grew seasonal crops and took care of his wife and son. He also served refreshments, at a reasonable price, to the occasional travellers who passed through the village. There were no restaurants anywhere near. That afternoon, Atmananda was his guest.

The farmer was a selfless man and he always served freshly cooked meals. Atmananda told the farmer, "I am hungry. May I have something to eat?" The farmer asked Atmananda to sit on the cot outside and went inside his hut. Atmananda heard the farmer tell his wife, "The new customer is a monk. He must not be asked to pay for his meal." His wife asked if the monk could be given the remnants of their lunch, since it was charity, Atmananda heard the farmer admonish her, saying monks and saints must never be offered leftovers. The obedient wife silently went to the well to fetch water for cooking. Atmananda sat on the cot looking at the last rays of the setting sun as they cast a golden halo over the forest.

While the farmer and his wife were busy cooking a meal for Atmananda, their teenage son came from outside and entered the house. He looked at Atmananda and bowed slightly, more as a matter of ritual, without any reverence, and then went inside. He asked his parents what they were doing, whether they were cooking their evening meal. They replied that they were preparing some food for the monk. Atmananda heard the boy object. "He is a wandering monk with no money. He will not pay. Just give him the leftovers of our lunch and a banana and some water, and send him off before sunset. Otherwise, he will stay on for dinner, too." In continuation, he told his mother, "Ma, Father does not have any thought for our tomorrow. At least you should guide him not to be so generous."

Quickly, his father intervened with a whisper. "Hush! Silence, my son. Not so loud. Do you want the sadness of a hungry saint to affect our family? Keep quiet. It is our *dharma* to feed the hungry monks. Their blessings will keep us free from illness and poverty." As his wife cooked, he led his son behind the hut, perhaps to take him away out of Atmananda's earshot. Atmananda could still hear their conversation; it was quite audible to him. The farmer said, "Son, have you heard the story of Adi Shankara? While wandering, one day he reached a house and called out for alms. The householder was away looking for work for their daily sustenance, and his wife opened the door and saw a young monk calling out for alms."

"She told him with deep humility, 'Pardon me, Maharaj, there is not even one grain in this house. How can I serve you?' Adi Shankara looked at her and said, 'Kind Mother, I am very hungry. There will be something in your kitchen. Please check all the vessels and bottles.' The lady of the house went inside and searched. She found a single gooseberry pickling in brine in a bottle at the back of a shelf. She gave that to Shankaracharya, and he consumed it as though it was a delicious, full meal. He was happy. He blessed her with an outpouring of a song of devotion for to the Goddess of abundance, and golden gooseberries started falling from the skies and rolled on the ground. The family became wealthy and lived happily ever after."

He continued, "My son, never ridicule saints and monks. God can appear in their form. Lord Shiva has appeared to many, as a monk, saint, and beggar! He appeared to Adi Shankara as a cobbler, and to Sage Narada as a boatman. So, never count the money that you spend on their food. God will reward you with much more. If you displease a saint, as the scriptures say, you will face eternal damnation for yourself and your succeeding generations. Never bring wrath on yourself and your family, my son. God has given us sufficient food, water, clothes, this modest shelter, as well as good health. Why not share a bit of our food with a noble, wandering saint?"

There was silence. The farmer's son thought for a while and asked his father, "As you said, it is a deep sin to antagonise or offend saints. But what if they are not saints, and they are just lazy people pretending to be saints in order to enjoy free meals wherever they go, from people like us who work hard day and night in the fields?" The farmer replied, "Everyone will enjoy the fruits of their actions, my son. You will get what you deserve, and they will get what they deserve. Pretensions often become costly bargains, and pretenders suffer terrible damnation. Nobody can fool the world forever. This should not be our concern, let us leave it to the justice of the Almighty."

"My dear son," he continued, "according to the scriptures, all the sixty-eight places of pilgrimage are to be found at the holy feet of the saints. And the one who abuses a holy man will be cursed with spiritual blindness, or be spiritually crippled without any progress over lifetimes, and also will be in the hell of suffering – life after life. We may neither understand the stature of holy men nor their methods and actions. We accept and respect them. They will shower grace upon us. What is the worth of material richness, if the price we pay for it is deep suffering?"

"If one abuses saints, liberation is taken away from him and his kin. And the cursed ones will roam in the eighty-five million types of wombs available on earth including worms and insects, and suffer agonies in each existence. When a bit of kindness can ensure our liberation, why should we be rude, and let unkind words tilt the equilibrium of our whole family and the generations to come? Let us honour saints and let us be rich within – that is the true richness."

Soon, they brought Atmananda a hot meal, and both the farmer and the son served him respectfully. After eating, Atmananda prepared to leave. They requested him to stay the night and leave the next morning, for there was nowhere a person could rest for the night. Atmananda could not accept their hospitality as he had to reach further north and decided to be on his way. Before he left, he gave them three *moolis*, saying, "Plant these *moolis* in your yard before *brahma muhurta* tomorrow. You will have no dearth of wealth."

The whole family came and prostrated at his feet. He left them and walked away into the moonlit village path, heading north.

CHAPTER 4

ATMANANDA AND THE THIEF

At one point, Atmananda's only worldly possession was a begging bowl. One day, the queen of the kingdom heard about him and invited him to the palace. He was treated with great love and respect and offered food in gold plates. Atmananda said that he would rather eat from his begging bowl, so he received everything in that. After receiving the queen's hospitality, he prepared to leave. He asked the queen if she wanted anything from him, adding, "But what can a poor wandering monk give to a queen?" to which the queen immediately replied, "I would like to have your begging bowl." That was his only possession. Without hesitation, he gave it to her. The queen received it and said, "This is the most precious thing in this palace. I shall worship this in our shrine." Then she brought him another bowl to replace the one he had given her. It was made of gold and studded with diamonds and precious stones. She gifted it to Atmananda.

He received it gracefully. The queen's courtiers started murmuring amongst themselves, "Look, here is a renunciate, a wandering monk. See his greed. He is supposed to stay away from these temptations, but he happily accepts the golden bowl from the queen. What sort of a renunciate is he?" Hearing these comments on his way out, Atmananda responded by saying, "A bowl is a bowl, whether it is made of clay or gold. To you, what it is made up of is very important. To me, the utility of the bowl is more important than its material. I see a bowl, a receptacle. You see gold, a precious metal. You will only see as what you are. Do not judge another and collect those sins if you cannot see the truth." The courtiers felt ashamed at their audacity to judge a great *Avadhoota* who was an honoured guest of the queen. After speaking these words, Atmananda left the palace and went his way.

Later, whenever he went asking for alms, he would bring out the gold bowl to receive the offerings. People were surprised to see the diamond-studded golden bowl, which was too valuable for a wandering monk to carry. They felt it was inappropriate. A thief was attracted to this bowl, and he made plans to steal it at any cost. He started following Atmananda, waiting for the right opportunity to make off with it. In the evening, Atmananda found a rundown place to sleep that wandering monks and beggars used. The thief had been stealthily following Atmananda. He hid behind a wall and waited for Atmananda to fall asleep. Since Atmananda had no other possessions with him, it would be easy for the thief to find the bowl. Atmananda knew that the thief was waiting to steal the bowl. He took it and tossed it at the spot where he knew that thief was hiding.

The thief was astonished. He came to Atmananda and asked, 'Why, dear Master? Did you know that I was stalking you?" Atmananda said, "Yes, I knew. Why should you wait? Why should I prevent myself from falling asleep? Once you have the bowl, you will go, and I can sleep." The thief had never met anyone like this wandering saint. He could not believe what had just happened. He said, "It is such a valuable bowl. How can you throw it away without a second thought?" Atmananda laughed. "It may be valuable for you because you are obsessed with its material. To me, it is a container for holding food." The thief said, "O Great soul, I have never met anyone like you. Allow me to touch your feet and also tender my gratitude. I now feel I am wasting my life chasing possessions, while you seem always to be free."

Atmananda said, "I threw the bowl at you so that you could come inside the room and not leave. If I had kept the bowl, you would have come into the room to steal it, and you would leave before getting caught. Now, you do not have to worry. You can sit here as long as you wish. After giving you what you were seeking, I am free, and you are free. I can sleep peacefully, and you can leave peacefully." The thief was overwhelmed. He could not believe all that was happening. He effortlessly obtained the item that he chased. Additionally, he built a rapport with its earlier owner on equal terms, without guilt or obligation. He felt a change in his heart already as he could not believe that such amazing people existed on this earth. The incident humbled and transformed him.

He came to Atmananda and touched his feet reverentially. For the first time, he felt the fragrance of divinity and purity. He said to Atmananda, "I am the worst person in the world, a thief. You are the purest, a saint. How do you allow me to touch your feet? How many lifetimes will I have to take before I become as pure as you?" Atmananda said, "It can happen today, just now." The thief could not believe it. He asked, "How is that possible for someone like me?" Atmananda said, "I know who you are and why you are what you are. An old house that has been closed for centuries is filled with darkness, which can be dispelled by lighting just one lamp. The transformation from darkness to light takes no time. All you need is the will, the willingness. Darkness cannot resist light. Even the pitch dark ceases to be dark if there is one small source of light."

The thief understood the point. All he needed was the willingness to transform. His old habits ought not to come in his way. He asked Atmananda, "I am a thief by profession. I do not know any other work. Will I have to leave this profession?" Atmananda said, "I cannot tell you what you should and what you should not. It is up to you. But I can teach you how to light the candle of transformation." The thief said, "This is strange. Are you not angry or upset with me because of my profession?" Atmananda said, "That is not my concern; it is yours. Who you are is your burden, not mine." The thief joked, "No teacher will accept me as a student because of my profession." Atmananda said, "I need not accept you or reject you to guide you. Those who place demands cannot be teachers."

The thief's interest was aroused. He said, "Please teach me." Atmananda said, "Listen carefully. Just be aware of your breath all the time that you are awake. Just watch your breath, your inhalations and your exhalations, and the short gap between these two. Just remember this one thing always – watch your breath. That is all you need to do to start the light!" The thief asked, "Is that all? Is it as simple as that?" Atmananda replied, "Yes, but you need to remember this always, whatever you do." The thief was incredulous. He said, "You are not talking about morality? No do's or don'ts? No conditions?" Atmananda said, "All that is not my business. It is up to you. They are your thoughts, needs, and your burden, not mine." The thief sighed and agreed to do what the saint advised. He left with his newly-acquired bowl, clutching it tightly.

Two weeks later, he came back to Atmananda. He said, "Master, you trapped me very badly. I could not steal a thing in the last fifteen days, because activity and breath awareness were not happening together. Whenever I was observing the breath, I couldn't do a thing. This became a big handicap for me at work. I became aware, alert, and was living in the moment. In a matter of two weeks, precious metals seem to have lost their lustre for me. I am becoming more and more silent and disinterested in life around me. What should I do?" Atmananda said, "Go away. It is up to you. If you want this silence, you have found the path. If you want possessions, you are free to return to your old habits. Do whatever you wish. Go away. How can I tell you what to choose?"

The ex-thief said, "I don't want to choose my old habits and rekindle the insatiable greed for possessions. I want to go deeper into the path of silence and liberate myself from my madness and greed. Please accept me. Please consider me as your disciple. Please initiate me." Atmananda said, "I have initiated you already." The ex-thief pulled out the golden begging bowl from his bag and placed it at Atmananda's feet. Atmananda said, "I have given this to you. It is yours now. Go in peace."

CHAPTER 5

AT HOME WITH A TIGER AND A SNAKE

In the early days, Atmananda used to wander deep into the Himalayas in seeming purposelessness. Yet, he would be at the right place at the right time delivering what had to be delivered to earnest seekers. Always in the course of his journeys. Never as a detour. He used to have a particular pattern and was very clear in these movements. He would sometimes meditate in the forest for many weeks at a stretch. At these times, he would abstain from food and even water. Once he traveled deep in the remote stretches of the Himalayas where there were no villages or inhabitation for miles around. The place had five or six giant peaks of sand and mud that could be seen from even miles away. Atmananda could see through his inner vision that these weren't natural hills but in reality, structures formed over the bodies of saints sitting immobile and meditating for centuries. In the subtle plane, one could see the saints as transparent crystal bodies of light in deep meditation, sitting immobile in the center of the hills.

After completing their life purpose, these saints have to withdraw from the world. However, they may still have a future purpose and a need to interact with the world at a later point in time, maybe after several centuries. Instead of exiting and having to go through a womb again, they choose to become inanimate, park themselves in a certain place, go into hibernation and become dead for the world.

Given their high stature, they can exist in this inanimate state for as long as is required. Their nails continue to grow and enter the ground. Their hair also continues to grow. These are the only signs of their life otherwise they are completely immobile. They almost become fossilised. Eternal hibernation. Zero movement. They stay fully themselves, fully absorbed and fully aligned. If someone comes their way, they may feel inclined to deliver to that person. They may momentarily activate themselves anytime but only for a definite purpose.

Nature and almost everyone else, leaves them alone, undisturbed in that inanimate state. Similar to plants, trees and rocks that exist in the yard but hardly anyone pays them any attention. They choose places that are reserved, isolated and difficult for people to enter, and also allow wild animals, birds, snakes, etc to keep people away. The animals consider them a part of their clan and protect them as part of their territory. On rare occasions, elevated Masters and celestial beings may visit these saints to appreciate and experience their state and to be in the saints' presence which helps their alignment. When the time for action comes and their purpose begins, the saints revive themselves, come out of this inanimate state, shed their old bodies and appear afresh in the world.

Atmananda decided to spend some time in isolation at this location. Since it was a very remote location, there was rarely any human intrusion. He chose a cave on a mountain about nine hundred feet above the forest. This forest had many wild animals – tigers, snakes, elephants, and so on. He sat down to meditate at the mouth of the cave. After a while, a tigress came to the entrance of the cave. Atmananda was deep in meditation and unaware of the animal. The tigress wanted to enter the cave, but Atmananda was blocking her. In anger, the tigress let out a spine-chilling roar right in front of Atmananda's face. He opened his eyes and saw the tigress. He looked straight into her eyes and they understood each other. He moved away, and the tigress entered the cave.

In this story, the message from Atmananda is that fearlessness is important in the path of liberation. When the tiger roared in his face, Atmananda looked straight back at her with absolute peace and calm. The tiger understood that this man is harmless and fearless. Animals attack us only if we are afraid, else they won't touch us. So it is with life. Things seem dangerous only when we are afraid of them. Fear attracts and manifests the object or result that we fear. We have to be fearless. If we look fear in the eye, nothing can touch us. Nothing can dare touch us.

In the cave, there already was a huge and fierce serpent residing. People would have shivered if they saw it and wouldn't have dared enter the cave. However, neither was the serpent bothered by Atmananda's presence, nor was Atmananda bothered by its presence. Now that the tigress also occupied the cave, the chance for a conflict was inevitable. They didn't trust each other. But they trusted Atmananda. Hence, the two beings existed harmoniously in the cave, perhaps due to Atmananda's presence. In a short while, the tigress delivered four cubs and the family in the cave started growing. While Atmananda meditated, the cubs would climb over him and play in his lap. The tigress would go out in search of food. There were trees around laden with fruit. Sometimes, the fruits would fall and roll right near him either on their own or due to monkeys. Atmananda would sometimes eat but mostly he kept them on the side. Sometimes, the fruits would pile up into a small heap. Given the cold weather, the fruits would stay fresh for a long time. Atmananda seldom had a need for food and rarely ate. He was almost always fasting.

He was deeply connected with the elements of his body. Thus, he was deeply connected with the elements outside in nature as well. The physical body is made up of the five elements, viz. earth, water, air, fire, and space (ether). He was deeply connected in every aspect. He controlled all the elements within his body. He restricted the secretion of digestive juices, thus keeping the element of fire that controls digestion, in balance – insufficient to cook food but sufficient to sustain life. He kept the element of water in equilibrium to stabilise the body which is full of water. He controlled the element of air by either reducing the intake of air to an absolute minimum or sometimes, stopping it completely. He aligned and adjusted to the space around him to stabilise the element of earth. Finally, he existed in a near thoughtless state. Absence of thoughts ensured that there were no effects of the thoughts either, thus regulating the element of ether. He used to meditate in this state of total stillness and calm. Even, the outside temperature did not affect him. If it was too cold, he could increase his body temperature and vice versa.

The serpent did not eat either. It was alive but not moving, not even for food. It may have been an elevated being meditating as a serpent. It is believed that when an elevated being in the form of a serpent does not use the venom and meditates on the venom for a long period of time, the heat of the meditation saturates the venom and transforms it into a gem called *nagamani* that is more priceless than a diamond. It is the same for human beings. When we meditate within, without any distraction for a long period of time, we receive the precious gem of enlightenment. For human beings, it's also priceless but it is a state and not a physical thing. The snake existed in the cave before Atmananda and continued to exist in the cave even after Atmananda left.

Atmananda stayed with this strange family for around three years, coexisting in the most natural manner, and then proceeded with his wanderings. This episode gives a clear picture about the unity of consciousness in all beings that Atmananda always stressed upon. All beings are one in consciousness and there is no separation. All other species know it except humans. Atmananda always respected all beings on earth ensuring his life-flow never interrupted or disturbed others.

In those days, for travellers and wandering monks, free shelters were provided by the local rulers, usually outside the temple. They also served two hot meals a day. Typically, it was a stone platform for people to rest, that was covered by a roof to protect from the elements such as sun and rain. People typically spread their clothes on the ground to sleep, using their bag as a pillow. During his travels, Atmananda preferred to stay in these shelter inns. When sleeping in such places, he tried to occupy the same space as much possible. However, if there was a dog, cow or another being sleeping in his chosen space, he would never disturb them and find another suitable space. He believed that space belonged to everybody and all beings were eligible to have their space. He never discriminated another being's right to use a space, just because it was a man-made space. Atmananda always said, **"Respect space. Without space, there is no creation. Respect creation. Respect all spaces occupied by creation. Respect the space of each creation."**

He respected every space, considering every space as sacred. Not just temples but every space, including a toilet since it was doing ist job and maintained some creation – visible or invisible – that occupied that space. He said, "Do not discriminate any space. A junkyard may seem like a dirty space but it fulfils its purpose. How can you say it's dirty? If it were not there, that garbage would be in our houses. Maybe a rat lives in the junkyard and hence, the junkyard is important for a rat. Similarly, the waste bin outside is playing ist role. Thus, they are all important and sacred. We can't disturb any space or any creation. Mankind started discriminating spaces and messing with nature, which is creating problems that will grow into calamities. We decided that the forests belong to us, air belongs to us, the rivers and sea belong to us, and so on. We entered into those spaces, disturbed and destroyed the space as well as disturbed, fought and either ate or killed the beings in that space. Instead, we should encourage preservation by respecting space and creation."

If Atmananda consumed fruits, he made sure the seeds were planted four inches deep in the ground, near a water source. If he received food and a dog came by wagging ist tail, indicating that it was hungry, Atmananda would give the food to a dog. He would not eat since he felt that his hunger and the dog's hunger were the same – none more important than the other. Atmananda always loved to serve others before self. He also said, "Eating is for survival, to fulfil a necessity or need, not for pleasure. One must only eat as much as one needs at a time. You must eat the food that is available to you, without disturbing any other beings – people, animals, birds and so on." Once when he was offered a tender coconut to quench his thirst, Atmananda said, "The water inside is for the tender coconut to nourish itself. The seed needs it to strengthen itself to become a tree. I have no right over its food. Instead, let me have a bowl of water from the well."

He later clarified, "Every birth has its struggle. Every transformation has its process. We should neither block it nor abuse it. A worm weaves a cocoon to hibernate and meditate. It meditates and transforms itself inside the pupa that it created. It expands and develops its wings. Then it must experience its newly found state. It makes a hole in the cocoon and wriggles out into a whole new reality as a butterfly, while the cocoon tries to prevent it. It is a real struggle to break free from terrestrial bindings, comfort zones that we are bound to for a long time. Finally, it breaks free and the world has a butterfly. What the pupa calls the end of the world, the Master calls a butterfly. People of wisdom should watch it as an example of their own life. Every seed and sprout is awaiting metamorphosis. Some will make it and some won't. That is the principle of nature. We should not abuse it or stop it."

Thus, Atmananda lived with nature as nature. When one rests in that elevation, one cannot see difference between beings and species, let alone man made boundaries. One sees unity everywhere.

CHAPTER 6

A DAY IN THE LIFE OF ATMANANDA

On one of his journeys, Atmananda Chaitanya reached a city close to a great river revered by many. He and his entourage stayed near a big Shiva temple. Many people knew of Atmananda because of his travels and presence in many places. So, naturally, many people came to see him to take his blessings.

That day, the local magistrate and his wife were visiting the temple for worship. They saw an unusually large crowd in front of the temple. The magistrate sent his attendant to find out more details. The man came back and said, "There is a famous saint sitting by the pillar. People have assembled to take his darshan and blessings." The magistrate and his wife also decided to take the blessings of the saint. They came to where Atmananda was sitting and they prostrated at his feet.

Atmananda blessed the official and said, "You have prostrated at my feet today. At the same time next year, you will come to this temple with a baby boy." The magistrate and his wife were surprised that the saint knew they were childless, despite being married for more than twelve years. The magistrate was overwhelmed by this spontaneous prediction. He went and explained the day's events to the Collector of the city, an Englishman by the name of Sir Stephen

Howard. Stephen was a good, kind man, who was well-educated and full of respect for his foster country and its culture. As soon as he heard the story, he decided to meet the saint.

When the Collector reached the temple premises, the crowd had swelled. Due to his position, he was given preference and thus arrived in front of the saint within minutes. Atmananda looked at Stephen and said, "Your colour belies your inherent nature – an Indian born in England!" Stephen did not understand. Atmananda then explained about Stephen's past birth in India, his lineage from the family he was born to in his last life, and the current generation of that family.

Incidentally, after he had come down to India, Stephen had met the people that Atmananda referred to, and had surprisingly felt a strange familiarity and affection towards them – almost as if he knew them from before. He had helped some of them get jobs in government departments and thus ensured their proximity to him. Now, everything made sense to him. He was indeed an Indian! His heart was full of love for India. This was his home. He was so fascinated with the British and their ways in his past life, that he took birth in England in this life, but came back to India with the heart of an Indian. He felt at home in India.

Atmananda asked, with a knowing smile, *"Who are you?"*
Stephen replied with extreme humility, "My name is Stephen Howard."

Atmananda: *"That is your name. My question is who are you?"*
Stephen answered, "I am the Collector of the city. I hold the highest position in the governance of this city."

Said Atmananda, *"That is your job. My question is who are you?"*
Stephen was confused. "Well, as you know, I am from England and on deputation to this city, on Her Majesty's orders."

Atmananda smiled and said, *"You still do not know who you are!"* Stephen looked even more confused. "Well, I am a lawyer by profession. I am the second son of my parents who live in England. I have two brothers and a sister."

Atmananda laughed. *"My friend, you still have not told me who you are."*
Stephen surrendered. He then bowed down and requested Atmananda to save him from this embarrassment, and give him the answer to the question.

Atmananda then said, "You are neither your name, nor your position and qualifications. Neither are you the relationships that you mentioned just now. All these just add up to define your existence in this life. You are beyond all these. Most of the things that you mentioned are transitory and temporary. They are all relative terms. You are trying to understand your existence in relative terms. But your existence is not that. You are beyond nationality, colour, qualification, and position. You are an eternal soul, that is what you are! You are eternally flowing through many bodies that you have assumed over lifetimes."

"You are what you are, during your waking state, dream state, and deep sleep state. All that you assume is in relation to something. While in the waking state, you are a husband in relation to your wife, a son in relation to your father, a brother in relation to your sister... All these identifications dissolve completely when you enter your deep sleep state. You are everything and you are nothing.

Your whole existence is in relation to something. You have come to me for this clarity and understanding. I bless you. Go in peace."

Stephen stood there, spellbound. He felt something explode in his spine, an awakening, something that he had been waiting for since birth! Deep gratitude arose in him. Tears flowed down his face.

Stephen asked Atmananda, **"What is the purpose of my life?"** Atmananda replied, **"To do justice at every moment to what is given to you, with full application and without impartiality."**

Atmananda then turned towards a group of farmers who had come to see him, and completely ignored Stephen. Atmananda was not swayed by power and position. He had nothing to do with terrestrial hierarchies. He now addressed the farmers.

"Ignorance is not a virtue. Learn the ways of the earth. Apply that knowledge for the benefit of all. Respect nature and her subtle expressions. Do not exploit nature but never timidly surrender to it. Never surrender to silly emotions. Surrender to the will of God expressed through Mother Nature. Accept the will of God with extreme humility. Share selflessly with others and survive during tough times. Sow, when the climate is favourable; reap, when the fruits are ripe and ready. Follow the seasons."

"Never cut a tree that has not fully completed its life and willingly ready for the axe. Worship trees as they are great saints. Never destroy them insensitively. They are benevolent to the whole world. Leave the forests alone and do not farm in the forests. Forests are for the birds and animals which inhabit them. Stay away from forests and do not disturb the wildlife. Coexist in peace and harmony with all the birds and animals. Build your house with matured stones.

They can weather storms. Live in peace and harmony and never ever disturb nature."

Many people had placed offerings of fruit before Atmananda, and he distributed some of them among the poor farmers who left with a deep feeling of fulfilment. Stephen watched this with amazement. He sat down by the side of the road facing Atmananda. Atmananda did not bother to offer him a chair or treat him any differently. The police officer who had accompanied Stephen was concerned and asked Stephen if he should get him a chair Stephen waved him off and asked him not to disturb the proceedings. This caught the attention of Atmananda who turned to see the police officer.

He addressed the police officer, "Thieves and robbers are to be punished, so society does not move on the path of anarchy and lawlessness. Neither must we entertain violence. No contamination must be allowed or accepted. Destruction of public property should never be allowed. Nobody has the right to destroy anything. If the law is enforced without inflicting violence on people, this country will prosper. Any ruler or country that exploits the helplessness of its people will undoubtedly perish. Exploiting helplessness is a serious crime. Society will crumble. Children will rebel. Prevention of crime and the preservation of law are serious matters, both of which require sensitivity and care. It takes a heart of compassion to enforce the law. It takes humility and conviction. I bless you with that." The officer bowed down in extreme humility.

To a prostitute who was in the crowd, Atmananda said, "Divine woman, you are serving the society. Because of you, your sisters in this city are enjoying peace and security. Because of women like you, other women can walk freely, without fear, even at midnight. You are like a candle. You are burning yourself for the society's well-being. Because of you, lonely men are satisfied. Society trapped you and pushed you into this. You have been sold by your kin. You are burning inside, and you crave the normal life of a woman, which you cannot lead. No woman wants to be in a position of such helplessness. Your heart is pure. You mean no harm to anyone. You have neither hatred nor feeling of revenge against anyone. Your heart brims with kindness and love. I bless you. I bow to you, Divine woman."

Many could not contain their surprise at these words. Stephen, who was listening, thought to himself, "How true! The age-old profession contributes to the balance of society! The mental balance of people will certainly reflect in the balance of society, because society consists of people. This saint is calling a prostitute 'divine'! It is time that I change my perspective. Everything in society is divine!"

A businessman came up and prostrated at Atmananda's feet. When he saw Stephen, he naturally gravitated towards him. He tried to bow down to Stephen, who avoided him in embarrassment. Stephen thought, "Even in the presence of the holy man, this fool has a commercial mind, he is trying to establish contact with me, not caring about the saint or his blessings." In this congregation, the saint was the main person Stephen was a mere visitor. It was inappropriate for the businessman to ignore the saint and his messages, and instead focus on the visitor. Atmananda, as if reading Stephen's mind, addressed the rich businessman, "My beloved watchman, I believe you have reached the wrong destination. Are you sure you are in the right place?"

Suddenly the rich man withdrew his attention from Stephen, looked at the smiling saint, and prostrated at his feet again. "Dear watchman, these feet have no commercial value. I believe you are wasting your time." The businessman felt embarrassed. He thought that Atmananda had mistaken him for a mere watchman. He said to Atmananda, "*Swamiji*, I am not a watchman. I own the largest jewellery, restaurant, and garment shops and I also feed the poor in the temple." Atmananda laughed loudly. He laughed and laughed. The businessman's face turned pale. He felt he was sinking into the ground. The crowd watched with amusement.

Laughter is contagious, it spreads like wildfire. Everyone present started laughing. Even Stephen could not hold back his amusement. When the laughter subsided, Atmananda asked the businessman to sit down. "My friend, you have come here because your servants told you that Stephen has come to see me. You have not come out of faith. You have come to get closer to Stephen, just for the sake of some special favours that may increase your business prospects. Then, why are you pretending? You think you can fool me? I can see through you."

"You are a watchman of your wealth. You have no freedom. You are too possessive. You do not give any freedom to your workers either. You treat everyone as slaves, including your own family. Even though you have a lot of wealth, you never pay your staff on time, deducting money from their salaries, falsely blaming them. You do not enjoy your life. You have no peace, and your heart is filled with anxiety and fear as you are always worried about thieves. You don't sleep. Money has given you sleeplessness. Even the chickens in your house sleep better than you, despite the threat that you may kill them any day."

"You greedy man! Your children are also suffering because of you. Your whole family suffers because of you. Do you think that by bribing God, by conducting elaborate rituals every year, you can relieve yourself from all the sins that you commit every day? Certainly not! God has nothing to do with your lifestyle. You have alienated yourself from God. You are making your life miserable, and your family is also in chains. You are causing them to suffer further."

"You can get nothing from me. You are a filled cup. First empty yourself of your ego and attitude and then come to me. I will fill you with wisdom and understanding. As soon as you empty yourself, your life will immediately begin. You will stop being the watchman, only guarding your wealth. Remember, all that you consider as yours will be with you only until your death. You will depart alone. Death forcefully detaches you from everything. The fire will burn your body into ashes. Then, you will be just a handful of ash. A life of greed will ensure an end in grief. Greed, envy, jealousy, ego, and all such terrestrial emotions will lead to sorrows and diseases. Beware."

After a short pause, while all the others remained speechless, Atmananda continued, "Oh, foolish man. Do you believe that everyone respects you because they love and admire you? Nonsense! People pretend to be respectful to you out of fear, because through money, you have gained connections in high places. Nobody loves you, not even your own family members. They fear you. They feign their love. The truth is that they are suffering. Even your children will rejoice when you die. They will squander the wealth that you have accumulated through your selfishness, as liberation will create corresponding expressions, which are most likely to be wild expressions of freedom from tyranny! Sometimes, people who are chained do not know how to enjoy their freedom when they get it."

"This will be the case with your family members. Your children will cause you to suffer more and more. Your eldest son is already squandering your hard-earned money on prostitutes, and your daughter has many lovers. You will see that happening more and more. What impact are you creating in the world around you? You are not creating anything good. Wake up now. See the reality. See who you are. See what you are doing. If you wake up, it is good for you. Shed your ego and attitude, and for your own sake, shift to benevolence, and to sincere, unconditional love. Move away. I have nothing to give you. Even if I give you anything, you will not be able to hold it, let alone carry it. What I could possibly give you is more precious than all your wealth put together. You cannot buy it."

And pointing to the prostitute, he continued, "This poor woman here is wealthier than you. She has a rich heart, filled with compassion. She just took home a newborn baby girl found abandoned in the garbage, discarded by her unknown 'glorious' parents. Even though she is poor, she is taking care of this new soul with great compassion and love as her own child. Have you ever bought a meal for a poor man? Have you ever even considered such acts of kindness? Haven't you abused beggars, poured hot water on them, and driven them away? Haven't you let your fearsome dogs on poor rag pickers? All your money cannot buy what I can offer. Do not waste my time, Go away. Get lost now."

There was pin-drop silence. Nobody dared to move. The businessman sat transfixed as though he had just seen a fearsome ghost. He felt he was stripped naked in front of the crowd. He felt insulted. When a selfish person comes to a Master, they feel insulted when the Master tells the truth because they have their ego in front. In contrast, a selfless person or a person who really wants to transform, takes the Master's words as a stepping stone, knowing fully well that the Master's words are intended to remove, unburden and release their baggage. The businessman had come to Atmananda with the ego of his amassed wealth and seemingly great achievements. His ego was annihilated unceremoniously. He fell at the feet of the saint and wept uncontrollably.

Stephen pondered on Atmananda's words, "This person has no elevation. He has not come here for the saint's blessings or advice which are priceless. He has a lot of wealth and he sits safeguarding his wealth. But in reality, his stature is no better than that of a watchman. A watchman's job is to watch and guard the wealth but he can't use it. This is exactly what this person is doing. He is protecting his wealth all the time. Neither does he enjoy, nor does he allow others to enjoy. He will do this until his death. Since he does not part with his wealth, the people around him including his family and children are forced to steal it. His son is squandering his money through prostitutes. He must probably be under tremendous stress all the time."

Atmananda stood up. It was time for his bath, worship and meditation. It was already late afternoon and close to sunset. It was time to move on. Atmananda distributed all that he received to everyone assembled, and walked to the nearby river for his bath. He usually bathed once a day in the early mornings and sometimes in the evening. He would not take a bath at other times of the day unless he conducted a spiritual discourse or interacted with a lot of people. He would use the bath to wash away the low frequency energies absorbed during these interactions. Many followed him to the river. He quietly took a bath and went into the temple for worship.

This was a typical day in Atmananda's life.

CHAPTER 7

DIFFERENT STROKES

Though Atmananda was a wandering monk with many followers, he never referred to anyone as his disciple. People came to him and some followed him. Some stayed for some time, others came and soon went away. With time, the number of people increased. He never took responsibility for any of them. He would just be – people connected to his consciousness and thus became flexible. The more flexible one is, the more spiritual one becomes – this was Atmananda's message to the world. He let each person travel in their own path based on their constitution. He simply facilitated them to follow their individual orientation – devotion, knowledge, selfless service, and so on. He had no special affinity towards any place or person. He walked wearing only a loin cloth even in the harshest of winter. He didn't carry any blanket or spare clothes.

Whatever food there was, he shared with his followers. He related everything to what was available. Like Christ who shared his meal with his followers, and also went hungry when there was nothing to eat. To those that came, he delivered as per the required capacity and eligibility. As time went on, Atmananda seldom sat down to give discourses. There was no need to talk. He would deliver with a single touch and say, "Alright, son". One touch! That's all. A perfect *Avadhoota*.

Since he left home, he was known by the name Atmananda for only a few years while he was preaching and giving lectures. From then onwards, he never mentioned his name. Thereafter, the people who came, did not know his name. Some people call him *Babaji*, some called him Rasta *Baba*, some called him *Swamiji*. He accepted whatever name people gave him. His name Atmananda was only known through the earlier half of his life.

We conclude this section with a few more anecdotes that give glimpses of Atmananda's state and stature.

Silence Speaks

This incident occurred when he was still giving lectures. A theft had happened in the village where he was hosted in one of the houses. The thief silently entered Atmananda's room while he was meditating and left the stolen goods there. He then quietly merged with the crowd sitting at the village square. The village elders and others were seated on charpoys[21] as they smoked and talked. There was a commotion as soon as the theft was discovered. A silver anklet had been stolen. The village was small with only around twenty houses. The village elders decided to search every house in the village to recover the stolen anklet. Finally, they reached the house where Atmananda was staying. When he heard the commotion, he came out of his meditation and stepped outside the house. The village elders apologised for disturbing his practice and requested his kind permission to search the house. Atmananda relented. The anklet was found in his room.

The village elders were in a fix. Except for the loincloth he was

---

[21] *A light bedstead made of wood and coir rope*

wearing and the cloth on his shoulders, Atmananda had nothing else. They couldn't imagine that he would steal. They were also afraid to accuse a saint. They politely questioned him on how the anklet reached there. Atmananda shrugged his shoulders to indicate that he didn't know since he was meditating. Others started elbowing each other and hinting. Atmananda remained calm. He slowly turned and looked deeply into the eyes of the village chief. There was no discussion. No words were exchanged. The village chief suddenly exclaimed, "I know the culprit." Pointing to a person in the crowd, he said, "That's him." Atmananda responded to the village chief's question by transferring energy through his eyes to those of the village chief's. The village chief could see the flow of events through Atmananda's third eye and immediately identified the thief.

He straight away told the thief, "Come here." The thief shivered at this unexpected turn of events and tried to run away, but the others caught him. He was brought in front of the village chief who asked him, "Why did you steal the anklet?" and blurted out the truth. He was attracted to a girl who had shunned him. He had stolen her anklets to take revenge on her. The village elders profusely apologised to Atmananda and left him to continue his spiritual practice. The following morning, Atmananda left the village to resume on his onward journey. Atmananda, in many instances like these, expressed his Master Shantananda's calmness to resolve adverse situations.

Request to a Tree

Atmananda used to walk through places that were mostly by the side of the river. Most of these places would have no vilages and would be sparsely inhabitated. Some of these places had small hut like temples. Once while walking along the Narmada river, he reached one such temple of the Divine Mother which had an old priest. He was a bachelor in his seventies and he lived in the temple. The temple was tiny and one had to kneel to enter. The priest performed rituals thrice a day and made meagre offerings of whatever minimum was available.

Hardly anyone came there, mostly people who came to cut wood. They would offer something to the Lord. The priest would offer a flower or some fruit plucked from nearby trees or some fruit. He couldn't climb a tree so he had to make do with whatever came within arm's reach. Sometimes there would be nothing on the nearby trees and he had to go further away to bring fruits for the offering. Even though Atmananda had met the priest only a few times, he was very fond of the priest. He used to address him lovingly as grandfather.

One day the priest casually pointed to a tree in front of the temple and remarked to Atmananda, "This is the Mother's guava tree. It is barren. If it had borne fruit, I would have fruit everyday to offer to the Mother." Atmananda said, "Oh, okay." He then walked up to the tree, patted the tree and said, "You should offer fruit." Then onwards, the tree bore fruit and the priest never had any problems with making an offering. He would cut the fresh fruit and offer it tot he mother. Atmananda's workings were casual, without fanfare or demonstrations.

Shift the Deity

Once Atmananda was walking alone by the Narmada river when he stopped at a place to take a dip. After taking a bath, as he continued on his journey, he passed by a small hut where an old monk called

Vyasananda was sitting and meditating in front of an altar that had many small idols of the Divine Mother. Atmananda peered into the hut, addressed Vyasananda and said, "Change the deity. This is not yours." Vyasananda opened his eyes and looked at the stranger standing at the door of the hut. The stranger (Atmananda) was a young monk probably in his late twenties, wearing a loin cloth with his matted hair tied on top of his head. There was nothing distinguished about his appearance. In contrast at first glance, Vyasananda with his white hair and beard looked wiser in comparison. Vyasananda closed his eyes and did not pay the stranger any attention. Atmananda repeated his earlier statement. Without opening his eyes, he said, "Go away. Don't bother me." Atmananda in a commanding tone said, "No. Shift the deity now!" Vyasananda did not appreciate this intrusion. Even though he was upset with the stranger for disrupting his practice, he decided to ignore him.

Suddenly, Vyasananda realised that he couldn't remember the *mantra* that he was chanting. He had been initiated by his Master into the worship of the Divine Mother at a very young age and had diligently continued the worship for decades. Despite that, he had now forgotten all the *mantras* as well as the practices that he had been performing all these years. As hard as he tried, he drew a blank. Vyasananda realised that the stranger was no ordinary monk. The words he uttered became a command to Vyasananda and erased his memory completely. He immediately got up and prostrated at Atmananda's feet and said, "Revered Master, you are none other than Lord Shiva. Forgive my rude behaviour. Surely, the Mother has sent you to guide me. Please take pity on this ignorant child of yours. Kindly show me the way." Atmananda looked at him compassionately and said, "Connect to Lord Vishnu." Saying thus, he blessed Vyasananda and left the place immediately. Vyasananda took the young monk's words as a divine command and started worshipping Lord Krishna (an avatar of Lord Vishnu). His earlier practices were not in alignment with his constitution. Hence, he had not made any headway or attained much in his spiritual journey except the white hair and beard. Atmananda's unassuming but direct intervention and guidance allowed Vyasananda to attain a high spiritual stature later in life.

Anybody wants money?

Avadhootas are rarely bothered about money and wealth. They live in a perfect world of supreme consciousness and have no use for money, possessions or properties. Nothing to guard, protect or secure. Once Atmananda was travelling in Andhra Pradesh. He had finished his lunch and was sitting with a few people who had gathered around him. As mentioned earlier, Atmananda always preferred to stay near a water body. A short while later, a horse-driven carriage stopped, the driver untethered the horse and led it to the river to drink. In the meantime, a maidservant got down and helped her mistress (belonging to the local feudal nobility) alight. The lady walked around to stretch her legs while the horses ate gram.

The lady noticed that Atmananda was giving a discourse and approached the group. At that time, Atmananda was talking about the harmful effects of possessiveness and how illusions get strengthened when one is possessive. Ownership reinforces the illusion and maintains the mind. As soon as she heard this, it transformed her. She had recently lost a child and was in deep pain. Atmananda mentioned that most people are living in the past or dreaming about the future, while the present is wasting away. He added that the body is transient and people have a life of around

29,200 days. She realised the futility of holding on to the past, and her pain was released. She touched Atmananda's feet, and he blessed her, saying, *"Be happy."* She then placed a heavy silk bag in Atmananda's hands. He received it and held it for some time. He then kept it aside and continued with the discourse. She bowed to Atmananda, sat in the carriage and left.

Later that evening, as people came to the ghat for bathing, Atmananda noticed the bag and opened it to find silver coins. He donated three silver coins to the local temple in the neighbourhood. One silver coin was usually the amount earned by the temple in a whole month. Being completely detached from the world and not used to handling money, he had no idea what to do with the rest of the money given by the lady. He immediately got up and shouted, "Anybody wants money? Anybody wants money?" Many people came running. He proceeded to distribute the rest of the money amongst them and emptied the bag. In this way, he was done with it!

Walk till there is NO OTHER.

Atmananda was having lunch with his followers at the house of a businessman who had invited the wandering monks for a meal. While having lunch, the host's cousin came up to Atmananda, bowed in reverence and started a conversation. This incident happened when Atmananda used to give elaborate spiritual discourses and engage in discussions with seekers. As Atmananda was consuming food, he told the person, "I shall speak to you after the meal". Some people are absent-minded about the convenience of others before they engage in a discussion. They do not seek permission and automatically believe that people are always available for them.
After lunch, Atmananda sat outside the house, enjoying the gentle spring breeze. The same man came to him and started speaking

about his spiritual pursuits. He mentioned that he had a very powerful Master. Atmananda listened to the stories of his Master and the miracles that he continuously performed, which entertained his followers and also kept them hooked to him. The Master is also gently guiding his disciples into charity activities and thus purifying their inherent *samskaaras* (inclinations). Finally, when he had concluded, Atmananda asked just one question. "What did you gain from your association with your Master"? The man who was talking for an hour could not answer. He tried explaining the miracles and similar stories again. Atmananda cut him short abruptly. "I understood all that. My question remains. What did you gain from this association?" The man could not answer. He thought for a while, yet could not find an answer.

Atmananda said "You are certainly entertained and perhaps kept from the usual emotions of the society by the Master. But what did you gain? Did you lose from your system, your anger, hatred, jealousy, greed, possessiveness, fears, insecurities, pride, ego, comparisons, competition, enmities, ownerships, doer-ships and even compulsive thoughts and so on? If not, you have not connected to your Master beyond your mind. You do not have him. This is why your Master is your entertainer. Use him as your annihilator. Lose yourself in him. Become free. Completely free from your mind, ego and intellect. Be totally free. Destiny brought you a Master. Now it is up to you to use that grace and presence to empty yourself and nullify your inclinations completely. A Master is not an entertainer, or your servant paid to fulfil your inherent inclinations and unending tendencies. His job is to remove you from your limited selves and set you free from your mind."

"And as long as you witness differences around you, people, places and events around you, as long as you use your mind and memories constantly, as long as you keep your pride over "you and yours", you are a slave. Until you see no other around you and only you in many forms, you have not arrived. Keep walking until there is no other. Therefore, you should be with the Master brought to you by your eligibility, your destiny. The most precious gift in a human lifetime is the proximity of a man who has found himself. A true Master is one who has found himself and is fully settled within himself. One who has dissolved his ego, mind and intellect and existing only to serve humanity with his liberated body, mind and intellect. This is one of the gifts that money cannot buy. This is the gift of your destiny. Destiny brought you to a true Master. Let your mind not take you away from him. When you pin your various expectations to a Master, if unfulfilled, you will have disappointments. This may take you away from the Master. This would be your biggest loss of not only this lifetime but many lifetimes to come."

More than the feast that was served in that house with love and reverence that satisfied their stomachs, the feast of elevating words from Atmananda filled everybody's hearts.

Fair Weather Followers

Many liberated Masters have created situations that displaced their disciples from their comfort zones. The Masters often behaved in strange ways. Disciples who had expectations and set notions about their Master became disillusioned and quit. This is the aim of the Master as well – to shake the tree until the dry leaves fall off. Only those with firm faith need stay. Faith is the key. Faith takes them to the highest, with the guidance of the Master.

One day, Atmananda suddenly said to his companions, "There

will be heavy clouds and rain. There can be no shelter from the elements. We will be scattered." His companions were frightened and confused with the thoughts of rain and possible floods. Slowly, some of them detached from Atmananda and left for safer zones. Others tried to make a shelter or arrange for one in the vicinity, but Atmananda never stayed in one place for too long. Thus, all the plans that they made were of no use. Then, there were some who chose to be with him against all odds, confident that Atmananda would protect them.

Atmananda and his group reached a temple town in south India where they decided to rest. They stayed within the temple premises for three nights, as was their custom. On the last night, there was a theft in the temple. The police soon caught the thief and brought him to the temple to collect evidence. Everyone was asked to assemble outside and the offender was made to walk past them. The police were keenly observing the group to see if anyone showed signs of cognisance or familiarity, or if the thief looked at anyone in particular, any sign that he had an accomplice. They were disappointed as no one seemed to recognise him.

But when the thief came near Atmananda and looked up at him, Atmananda smiled and blessed him. The police immediately took Atmananda into custody, happy to have found the thief's accomplice. Atmananda's followers made themselves scarce. They did the same thing that Peter did to Jesus. They completely disowned their Master. All of them ran away, some even to other cities, to escape persecution. Atmananda was kept in the town prison for three nights, but it did not affect him in the least. Finally, the police realised he was innocent and released him. He blessed the policemen and the police station and resumed walking.

For many weeks, Atmananda continued his travels, wandering alone. It did not make any difference to him. Some followers understood Atmananda's prediction of clouds and rains. Some came back. Some went away forever. Human relationships are so conditional. There is no permanence. Today, we may feel inseparability and deep love, and tomorrow utter hatred. Relationships are so fragile and built on expectations. When our expectations crash, so do our relationships. Life after life, we have been living this terrestrial truth of impermanence. When can we truly understand our existential impermanence and genuinely embrace truth and permanence?

Complete and only then Come

One day Atmananda was walking down the street with a group of people. Suddenly he turned to one of the men and said, "Go to that alcohol shop and have your drink." The man panicked, "*Swamiji*, what are you saying? I don't need any alcohol." Atmananda said categorically, "No. You need alcohol. Unless you go, you cannot follow me." The man went to the shop while Atmananda and others continued to walk. Atmananda did not stop anywhere. One of the followers later asked Atmananda, "Why did you send him to the alcohol shop?" Atmananda replied, "He follows me, but thinks about alcohol all the time. He can get nothing from me. If he does not love to follow me or is not connected to my consciousness, it is an absolute waste of time. You must complete what you are supposed to complete and only then come, as by that time you will be okay."

Atmananda related a story of a person whom he sent to a brothel for similar reasons. When the person spent time in the brothel, he realised that he had many pending sexual desires. He had an active interest in women. After a string of bad relationships, he had chosen to follow Atmananda. He realised that his choice was motivated by escapism rather than an active interest in spirituality.

Atmananda continued, "Many people in the spiritual world are like that. They follow somebody on a whim, but their minds are elsewhere, on other things. Hence, they do not evolve. They just move from one Master or path to the other, but do not progress because there is no clear intention. Spirituality should never be a pastime. It must be a part of one's existence. Whenever people say, 'My Master, his Master!', I feel like laughing, because these are all various forms, it is all one Master, numerous expressions. Your attraction to one form makes you feel it is yours. This attraction is the illusion of ownership that you carry. In reality, I can own nothing. Nobody owns anything. Noboy can own anything – a Master or for that matter any relationship or object outside of you. You can only experience, that too only in your waking state not when you are sleeping. It is silly to express ownership because ownership is an illusion. Even more silly is to compare (my Master, your Master) and then compete. Another illusion. So many traps we go through. Respect every Master but connect to the one who has come to you and is talking to you, which is your reality. You connect to what you like and nobody can object to it. What you are actually connecting to is yourself through that mirror."

Respect for Prostitutes

Atmananda always used to respect prostitutes and always referred to them as mother. Survival instinct is a major human instinct of which sexual urges are a basic ingredient, primarily intended for propagation of the species. Denying, ignoring or suppressing this instinct results in internal calamity which will eventually show up in society by affecting social well being. The prostitutes provided a channel for men to satisfy these instinctive urges and thus maintained the balance in society. Like a candle, they burnt themselves to keep other women safe. Yet, no one respected them. Hence, he had an affinity towards these people and always blessed them.

During his travels, he would choose brothels for his resting place, if any were around, He seldom went inside and slept on the verandah outside the brothel. Some of them had latent desires which sprouted in this place and tested their resolve. Some got upset by Atmananda's association with a place of disrepute and left him considering him a fake. Atmananda would be unaffected but it was a test for the people who followed him. Thus, the brothel served to filter out the people who were still not ready to be with a Master of Atmananda's stature.

He would give them whatever he had with him. Especially, he always gave something to the prostitutes' children whenever he saw them outside the brothels. Since he rarely carried anything with him, It was probable that he was materialising the things that he gave these people. All these prostitutes were very fond of him. Due to him, other people also started respecting them. When they died, there usually was no one to take their body to the funeral. Most times, Atmananda would arrange somebody to do the needful and make sure that their bodies were properly cremated. Once Atmananda encountered an old and sick prostitute who was dying. There was no one to look after her last rites. Atmananda stayed in that place for a few days and waited until her demise. He paid the required money, arranged for her cremation and only then left.

All Lives Matter

When Atmananda was wandering, he would stop to rest under a tree or at the verandah of a temple or a highway inn. When a few people gathered, he would start giving a discourse. The crowd would gradually increase. If it went on for a while, the neighbouring people would bring food and give it to him. He would distribute it to the people who had assembled. Once he was giving a discourse in a temple in a remote village. Most of the people in the village were from the weaving community. One of the people in the audience was a cloth merchant from the city, who used to buy his material and also get his clothes stitched from weavers in that village. He had come there to pay the workers and cloth sellers in the village. He wanted to feed all the people who were attending the discourse. He requested Atmananda's permission for the same. Atmananda neither accepted nor declined. He said nothing. The cloth merchant assumed Atamananda's tacit acceptance and proceeded with his request.

He brought the food and placed it near Atmananda. Atmananda stopped talking, kept some food for himself and asked to distribute the rest of the food to everybody on leaf plates. Everybody started eating quietly. The unspoken command was "no talking while eating". Atmananda as usual offered the food to the deities and started eating. Suddenly, a monkey came down the tree and snatched the food from Atmananda's hands. Even though there was some food left in the utensils close to Atmananda, the monkey ignored it and instead grabbed the food from Atmananda's hands. There were a few more monkeys on the tree. Atmananda exclaimed, "Oh! I'm sorry." He offered the remaining food to the monkeys. Suddenly, the people started feeling guilty. The saint (Atmananda) had no food while they were eating. Since they had started eating, they couldn't offer him their food because that would mean giving leftovers to a saint.

An elderly woman from the crowd told him, "You are younger than my son. Maybe the age of my grandson. I can feed you from my plate. You can eat from me." Atmananda politely declined saying, "Mother, with due respect, please eat your meal. I am very grateful that you are offering this to me. Your possession belongs to you. I have the power to distribute my hunger to these people. I have no hunger because I have already dissipated it. When these people satiate their hunger, I also become contented. I have no need for food. I don't need to fill this stomach to satisfy my hunger. I can fill any stomach and satisfy myself. However, your stomach needs that food. I can't take it."

He continued, "I made a mistake. I didn't distribute the food properly. I only gave it to the beings in front of me, not to those behind me. I did not consider the monkeys and other beings on the tree. They penalised me, which I gratefully accept. Since I didn't give the food to them, they took my food away from me. But they also took my hunger." It is possible that Atmananda himself created this drama to convey a point to people that they should consider all beings not just human beings and also that hunger is the same for all beings.

Redemption of a Bull

Once Atmananda went with his followers to a Krishna temple where he received a lump of sandalwood along with the consecrated offerings that had been served to the Lord. Atmananda distributed all the offerings except the sandalwood, among the group of people who were with him. He then continued walking with the lump of sandalwood in his right hand. He didn't give any of it to the others. Some amongst the group wondered why the Master was walking with the sandalwood in his hand instead of keeping it somewhere or distributing it. Of course, Atmananda did not bother to explain anything. After walking about six kilometres, he stopped a hundred yards away from a butcher's shop. In the distance, they could see a calf was tied to a tree facing the butcher's shop.

The calf was a very handsome bull, fully white in colour with a golden brown patch on the head near its third eye. He was young, probably two or three years old. Atmananda went to the calf, applied the sandalwood to his third eye and then continued on his further journey. The group was bewildered by Atmananda's seemingly arbitrary action. Some questioned why the Master wasted the sandalwood on a calf that was doomed to die. Some thought that the butcher may let the calf live if he saw the sandalwood on the third eye. A very remote and wishful possibility. Some questioned why they did not receive any of the sandalwood. One of the followers who was deeply connected to Atmananda had a vision that explained Atmananda's action. Later that evening when they stopped to rest for the night, he related his vision to the group.

The calf was a butcher in his last human life. Since then, he had taken two hundred and eighty lives. In each of those lives, he had ended up in a slaughterhouse and was mercilessly killed for his meat. This life was no different. His mother in this life was his father in his life as a butcher. She was alive because she gave milk and was hence useful to the butcher. Soon after birth, he had been separated from his mother. Both of them went through the intense agony of separation. She knew that her child would be slaughtered and always lived in fear for his life (and her own). Rarely were they allowed to meet. On those occasions, she used to lick the child and express her love. When they started communicating, the mother told him that they would not be together for long. Every time they met, it was always with the fear of parting.

He was kept in a separate place with other calves and cows, and was fed well to make him plump for slaughter. Most of them were unfriendly because they knew that they were going to die. It was like a place for inmates on death row. When he was a butcher, he never spared a thought for the animals he killed – their feelings, their pain, and so on. He did not even think of them as living beings or care about their agony when they see their loved ones suffer and die. Many a time, the animals he was about to slaughter looked into his eyes with tears of pain and begged for mercy. He did not care. His focus was on delivering meat to his clients. The animals were just a source of meat.

Through each of his two hundred and eighty lives since then, he was doomed to suffer the same pain and agony that his animals suffered. He had various reflections from the other side of all that he chose not to see or feel in his life as a butcher. He could see his own people getting butchered and the complete lack of emotion on the face of the butcher. Each time he hoped and begged for mercy from the butcher. The butcher never showed any mercy. They just did their job with complete insensitivity and didn't even look. They had no feeling. They were only thinking about the meat. They did not even treat him like a living being. While he awaited his turn to be slaughtered, he helplessly watched his kind being killed, dismembered, chopped and their meat kept for display.

His saving grace was the selfless action that he had performed in his human life. He regularly gave the old leftover meat to poor families in the neighborhood. He also selflessly took care of a family of six children who got orphaned due to the untimely death of their parents. Atmananda's intervention was the result of these good acts coupled with an intense and overwhelming cry for redemption born out of the repeated unimaginable suffering over his two hundred and eighty lifetimes. He was destined to suffer this fate for a few thousand more lifetimes. Atmananda intervened to give him deliverance by compressing all those lifetimes and making this his last lifetime of suffering. In a way, this story tells us about the eligibility to earn the proximity of a Master of the tradition of liberation.

SECTION 3

Atmananda's Odyssey

"I shall talk to the world through the positive transformation and metamorphosis of my consistent companions."

CHAPTER 1

A STRANGE TRYST WITH A BEGGING BOWL

Manav sat on the steps leading to the Ganga and stared at the water flowing hurriedly. It was just like time. The moment you think of the present, it had already become the past. The moment you look elsewhere, gallons of water rush past. This is Life! What a mad rush! When will this restless rush end? Where will it end? Where is this water going? Where is time going? Time has no problem. It has always been like this. Only those who chose to watch it become tired. Time is never tired! Everything goes through time – people, seasons, events, everything. Life flows through time just like a big log moves down a river – helplessly, uncontrollably, and unconsciously. Just like the log, people vanish, new people come, and they too vanish. Thus, time and the river have many similarities. What are we holding back? What can we hold back?

Manav looked up at the sky in helplessness, as if seeking a divine communion. Where is the answer? Who can answer? And at that moment, he made a decision. He would leave everything and walk north. NORTH! The Himalayas lie to the North, and the Ganga flows from the Himalayas. So, technically, Manav was already there. But he stood up and walked further north. Somehow, in his mind, North meant some surety, a sort of refuge that he did not quite know yet. Anyway, what more can anyone lose than his life?

Manav considered himself quite brave, in terrestrial terms, and believed that he was not afraid of death and darkness. So, he walked further North into the darkness of uncertainty and embarked on his search for the unknown.

Tough terrains of existence. Tough times. Unknown paths. Unknown destination. Unknown people. Everything strange. All are strangers. Amongst the strangers, he found familiarities. Familiar strangers. One man asked him, "*Swami hai kya?*" (Are you a saint?) Manav replied, "*Nahin, Sadhaka hoon.*" (No, I am a seeker) The stranger then asked, "*Mila nahi ab tak?*" (Did you not find it so far?) Manav stared at his eyes without answering. How could he tell him that 'getting it' was not his primary search, but knowing what to search for was? He took his backpack and walked further. The stranger shouted, "*Atmananda ko zaroor milna. Milega tumko, jo tum dhoond rahe ho.*" (Definitely meet Atmananda. You will get what you are seeking.)

Manav did not look back but kept walking. Atmananda! He kept repeating the name. Did the stranger imply that if he looked for *ananda* (happiness) in the *atma* (soul), he would find what he was seeking? Or was Atmananda a person who could give him answers? Where would he find this Atmananda? Manav smiled to himself, thinking, "Do I move forward and face the uncertainties that lie ahead or stay back and experience eternal stagnation? I am caught between the devil and the deep blue sea. Death is sure in either case! The question is, do I walk on that path or not." Manav feared stagnation more than uncertainty. He decided to walk further. It was the best decision of his life.

On the third day, when he reached Rudraprayag, a local temple priest guided him to Atmananda who sat amidst a large group, cracking jokes and laughing. To Manav's great surprise, Atmananda resembled the stranger who had suggested that he meet Atmananda. He was perplexed – was it the same person who came to guide him a couple of days earlier? Nothing made sense. Even though Atmananda looked at him, he showed no recognition. He went on with his jokes. Everyone was laughing. What sort of a saint was he, Manav wondered, just cracking jokes and laughing. For a moment, he asked himself if he was searching for laughter? Maybe he was! Laughter is indeed an expression of happiness. Everyone searches for happiness, and they never find it, except for a fleeting moment or two.

After contemplating for a while, Manav approached Atmananda, who continued to ignore him. He seemed busy, applying sacred ash on his forehead and various parts of his body, after a dip in the river. He was reciting some *mantra*. Manav waited, and when Atmananda left with his followers, Manav followed them. It was only on the third day that he got to talk to Atmananda. The first thing that Atmananda said after looking at Manav was, *"Jad hai"* (This is dead) *"Jeevan kidhar hai?"* (Where is life?) Manav did not know the answer. Atmananda did not wait. He kept walking. Manav followed, mesmerised. Finally, the entourage reached a city. Manav hated cities. He preferred the relative isolation that the mountains provided. He wondered why Atmananda loved the city so much that they had walked all the way downhill, over days and weeks, to reach this place of filth and greed! As if reading his thoughts, Atmananda turned and said to no one in particular, "I exist in the mountains, yet my feet are on the ground. My body does not signify my 'size'. What I see is what you cannot see." Was this a statement or a warning, wondered Manav as he struggled to decipher the meaning in the message. Atmananda just continued walking.

Manav wanted to return to the mountains. The Himalayas! What peace! What tranquillity! He felt as though a part of himself was still in the mountains. Attachment! One part of his mind told him to leave Atmananda and go back, while the other kept convincing him that he had finally found his Master. However, Atmananda did not seem like a typical Master. He was just wandering all the time and wasn't teaching anything significant to anyone. His behaviour seemed so bizarre to Manav, but none else seemed to be bothered. None seemed to care about the uncertainty and hardships. Everyone seemed to enjoy Atmananda's company and aimlessly wander! Was this spirituality, pondered Manav who became even more confused than before.

Unexpectedly one day, Atmananda looked at Manav and asked, "Whom can you wake up?" Atmananda then answered his question, "Only those who are sleeping, not the ones pretending to be asleep. Whatever you do, those who pretend to sleep will not wake up. Many in the Himalayas are pretenders. I am collecting pearls in the marketplace!" This was a revelation for Manav who thought he understood the real purpose behind Atmananda's visit to the city but was never sure. It was tough to put Atmananda into any frame. Perhaps he is here to 'awaken' the ignorant sleepers to the ultimate realities or truths. This made some sense. This was probably Atmananda's mission. A noble mission indeed! But, in this drama, what was Manav's role? Once again, deep uncertainties started to plague Manav's mind.

Atmananda again read his thoughts. He looked intently into Manav's eyes and in a stern voice, he commanded, "Go begging. Do not return for one week. Bring whatever you can save after spending on your basic needs." This suggestion completely shook Manav. Many disturbing thoughts flocked into his mind. "Go begging? Why? Do Atmananda or his followers need the money or food that I, Manav, may gather through begging?" Atmananda did not look at him; neither did he show any inclination to answer the questions in Manav's mind, nor explain his command. He just repeated, "Go begging from tomorrow." Manav could not sleep that night. Many conflicting thoughts ran through his mind, "I have not witnessed Atmananda ask anyone in his entourage to beg. So why me? Does Atmananda want to teach me a lesson because he hates me?"

Manav hailed from a respectable, affluent family. He was now twenty-three years old and had not experienced any lack of food or facilities since childhood. During his travels, whenever he needed money, he did odd jobs. He was skilled in finance. He worked and earned a living, but he could not bring himself to beg from anyone. He also felt that people and other beggars might mock him since he did not look like a beggar. This would result in considerable embarrassment for Manav. He didn't want to have anything to do with it. He could not make up his mind until morning. Atmananda woke up at 3 a.m. and saw Manav sitting under a street lamp. He walked towards him and said, "You did not sleep? Good! When you look tired and unshaven, you can fetch more money!" And he burst out laughing. It sounded like a cruel joke to Manav, who became angry and upset.

By this time, Manav felt that Atmananda intended to make money by using him. He thought that Atmananda was not a saint but a businessman who knew his trade well. He thought that he should leave Atmananda immediately. Ignoring Manav's churning emotions, Atmananda handed him a broken bowl and said, "Okay, leave now! Come back after a week!" And without waiting for Manav's response, Atmananda turned and walked towards the river for his bath. Manav stood there, undecided and utterly confused. Finally, before daybreak, he made up his mind. He decided that he would go begging! At first light, the city came to life with the hustle and bustle of people going about their business. Manav started his journey with the begging bowl.

He had left his backpack with one of the followers of Atmananda, who accepted it rather matter-of-factly and expressed no compassion whatsoever at Manav's predicament. Manav took him to be as insensitive as Atmananda! Partially out of anger and resentment against Atmananda, and partly out of determination and ego, Manav took nothing with him except the broken begging bowl that Atmananda gave him. He extended his bowl towards the passersby with a lot of trepidation. Some people gave him a few coins, others shooed him away, and one man ridiculed him, "Look at you, such a healthy boy and begging!" Another admonished Manav, "Why can't you do some work and earn a living? You lazy bum! Is it easier to beg than work, eh?" And even though Manav begged till noon, he could not gather sufficient money for a meal. No one seemed to care, let alone show any compassion.

He felt a strong urge to throw the bowl away and do something meaningful, more dignified to earn some money and buy at least one meal. Atmananda would never know. He could return after eight days, with money that he received through work, too. After all, Atmananda only wanted money. But something stopped him – possibly an attitude of revenge towards Atmananda or a strange satisfaction in this self-inflicted pain? Atmananda must have had some reason to instruct him to beg, which he did not know. But, slowly, as the day grew, so did his hunger, and strangely, his determination. He had survived the whole day, only by drinking water from the street taps. By evening, he got sufficient money to afford some bread. He ate that bread and drank more water. At night, he slept under a banyan tree in front of a temple. It was cold and windy. He had not carried a blanket or any other protection against the cold. The strong wind made it difficult for him to sleep. He shivered. His teeth chattered.

He also started getting fearful. Every sound made him shake and shudder. All night, he mentally berated Atmananda with the choicest of abuses. He had believed that he was fearless and had no fears because he had travelled alone in the Himalayas. He had led himself to believe that he had always braved darkness and death. Both these fears surfaced now, and he had to face them. He thought that if he closed his eyes, an unknown creature or perhaps a ghost would attack and kill him, or enter and occupy his body. The darkness and shadows seemed alive, potent, and heavily threatening. He realised that the seeds of all possible fears existed deep within him, lying dormant, waiting to germinate in the right environment. He spent the second sleepless night in fear and confusion. His mental tirade against Atmananda continued through his waking moments in the night.

Atmananda had warned him to return only on the completion of eight days. Somehow, Manav decided to fight it out. He was more worried about Atmananda ridiculing him and making fun of him in front of the others. His ego did not permit him to stop begging or go back to Atmananda. Strange are the ways of ego, indeed, even at the toughest of times! At daybreak, he walked towards the nearby river, cleaned his teeth with a paste made from the tender mango leaves that he crushed using a stone. Then he took all his clothes off except for his loincloth and kept them on the river bank. He did not want to wet his only set of clothes. Even though the water was ice cold, the bath rejuvenated him tremendously. He took many dips in the river and felt more refreshed and cheerful. When he got back to the shore, he was shocked to find all his clothes stolen. There was nothing left except for his broken begging bowl! It was such a big embarrassment for Manav. How could he go anywhere like this? He only had his loincloth to cover himself. Even that was wet and cold since he had no change of clothes. "Oh, God! What will I do now? Why am I being tested like this?" he lamented. He held Atmananda responsible for all his troubles and resumed his mental assault on Atmananda.

Hunger crept in. He walked towards the main streets of the city, in his drenched loincloth holding the broken bowl. People looked at him with contempt, pity or compassion. Many thought that he was mad. Some gave him some money, even without his asking. Quite surprisingly, the new costume enabled him to collect sufficient change to buy himself a decent breakfast, without much effort. When he approached a restaurant, they would not allow him to enter. He asked for some bread and curry and paid them the exact amount of money they demanded. Every penny was precious to him. He started taking money seriously and started realising its worth. He even felt that he understood the reason why people worshipped money as the Goddess Lakshmi!

The waiter put the bread and curry into his broken bowl, as the staff refused to give their utensils to a 'mad beggar'! This was further humiliation for him. Quietly swallowing his pride, Manav sat under a nearby banyan tree and started to eat. Just as he was about to put the first morsel in his mouth, he noticed a little girl sleeping next to her mother under the tree. She peeped at him from under a blanket that was covering both her and her mother. She smiled at him. A cute little smile. She looked like she was hungry. Her mother was still sleeping. He smiled back and extended his hand to offer her the bread that he was about to eat. She crawled out from under the blanket and towards him, smiled and opened her mouth, expecting him to feed her. Not being very familiar with children, he showed her the bowl of curry, expecting her to join in his meal. She smiled again, innocently.

Manav realised that she was too young to eat by herself. He dipped a piece of bread in the curry and put it in her mouth. She only had a couple of teeth, but she properly chewed and then swallowed the food. He wound up feeding her most of his bread and curry. It seemed like she had not eaten all day because she ate with gusto! Manav observed that she did not cry or wake her sleeping mother, even though she had been starving. She was probably used to hunger. What a lesson, he thought, that too from a toddler! She smiled at him, as if in gratitude, and went back to her mother, who was still sleeping. Manav found himself left with only a tiny portion of his meal! But somehow, he felt deeply satisfied with this whole event. He looked again at the little girl. She was already cuddling to her mother under the blanket and was settling down to sleep.

Manav looked at mother and daughter and was lost in thought for a few minutes. The mother could be a single parent living on the streets. Maybe a prostitute? The child might never know her father. For a brief moment, Manav felt that he had fulfilled the role of a father to a hungry child! A deep satisfaction welled in his heart. He felt ecstatic with joy, despite his seemingly pathetic situation. He began to understand his mission. Slowly, Manav got up and walked towards another busy street. On the next road, he encountered many beggars who shouted and threatened him if he dared to enter into their territory. He got an experience of the struggle for survival and silently walked away to another street. This time, though, he did not feel any humiliation or bruising of ego. He had been walking from place to place in the hopes of getting enough money for food.

He started experiencing hunger pangs and had a dull headache due to hunger which reduced his momentum. He saw a small restaurant around the corner. Even though he did not have sufficient money, Manav approached the restaurant and asked for a banana from the display shelf, expecting a little compassion from the owner. His pride was steadily evaporating; he had decided that any food would do, even remnants from another customer's plate. The restaurant owner, however, yelled and chased him away with a stick, clear that they did not want a naked madman on the premises. He walked to another restaurant nearby, where he was treated even worse. When he approached a table where their customers were having food, the restaurant owner threw a jug of hot water at him and drove him away.

Thus, hungry, drenched, and slightly burnt, he sat under a tree, with his begging bowl kept in front of him. Suddenly sadness, isolation, and hunger overwhelmed him, and he wept bitterly. People who noticed the crying beggar dropped coins into his bowl. Slowly, the despair subsided, and Manav discovered he had sufficient money for a couple of meals. He bought lunch from a restaurant that had a yard in front of it. Again, the restaurant owner did not allow Manav to enter his establishment. He even forbade Manav from crossing the yard and asked him to stay at the other end. He packed the food, crossed the yard and gave the food to Manav. Manav sat by the wayside and had his meal. He found that he had over-eaten, so he decided to skip the evening meal.

That night while fears still gripped him, he managed to sleep for a few hours. He realised there was nothing to protect and guard as he had nothing except his loincloth and his begging bowl. He did not even have a blanket to cover himself. He spent the night hiding behind a wall, in front of a shop. This sheltered him from the cold, howling wind. At night, a realisation came over him. When he begged, nobody gave him anything. When he sat down and cried out of deep frustration, a lot of money came to him even though he wasn't begging. He realised that one might not find when one goes seeking the truth. Frustrated in their search, when one finally gives up, sits down and connects to their state, the truth reveals itself. A profound spiritual and philosophical truth!

Finally, he completed eight eventful days and decided to return to Atmananda. He had begged, managed to save some money after his expenses. He believed that Atmananda was only interested in money. When he reached the place where he had left Atmananda, he could not find Atmananda or any of his followers. They had already left the area. Nobody knew where they had gone. Because of Manav's condition, no one was willing to even talk to him, let alone guide him. He was naked and unpresentable with a thick stubble, unkempt matted hair, a shabby face and a dirty body. His intuition guided him that Atmananda would be close to the river. Thus, he walked further north following the river and found Atmananda a week later. It had been two weeks since he had left Atmananda to embark on his begging adventure.

He walked up to Atmananda and gave him the coins he had saved. As expected, Atmananda did not display any compassion, kindness, a smile or any sign of recognition. Atmananda took the money and without saying or asking anything, immediately distributed it among the people who were around him! Manav felt like crying. Every penny was so precious to him because it represented the enormous pain and humiliation he had endured.

Atmananda did not even say a word of consolation or respect his hard-earned money! Thoughts of suicide flooded Manav's mind. He felt utterly despondent.

"Look at you. You are so shabby. You stink. Take a bath!" said Atmananda. Some people around Atmananda laughed out loudly. This was the limit! He had spent two weeks working hard to collect money. These lazy bums were doing nothing, merely following Atmananda everywhere, and they had the nerve to laugh at him. A frustrated Manav immediately left, collected his baggage from the keeper and went to the river for a bath. He sat on the shore and wept in dejection. He felt utterly useless – a complete waste. He felt stupid and lost. After he had cried and had taken a long bath, he felt slightly better. Once he wore his clean clothes, Manav felt even better. After thinking about it for a while, he made up his mind to leave Atmananda and pursue spirituality on his own. He could not accept or approve of Atmananda's style of functioning. He considered it insensitive, sadistic, and cruel.

Manav walked back to inform Atmananda about his decision. Before he could say anything, the saint said, "You are now ready to be with me. Good. You have come to terms with all your fears and have conquered them – fears of being alone, being naked, having to beg for a living, asking strangers for help and so on. You have already conquered your ego to a great extent. Now, you are fit to be on my path – the path of being in the now, the path to the present, the path of pathlessness, the path of simplicity, the path of purity and lack of expectation. You are welcome to travel with me." Saying this, Atmananda started walking.

Manav suddenly realised that he no longer felt any anger or humiliation. In the past two weeks, the many harsh realities he faced as a beggar had smoothened the sharp edges of his character. He had many experiences which helped him to see life from a different angle. It helped him develop a sense of detachment to life. He started respecting everything, every being. He started seeing the value in everything. He started appreciating food and clothes. He started noticing the difference in the awareness of people. He started feeling the importance of kindness and compassion. He started feeling and understanding the relevance of love in existence.

So many changes in just two weeks! He was a completely new person. It was like his old self had been burnt to ashes and his new self had been reborn from those ashes. Manav now understood why so many people were Atmananda's followers. He felt ashamed at having mentally abused Atmananda all these days. He regretted considering Atmananda as his primary enemy over the last two weeks. In his mind, this was a great insult to the venerated Master. He did not mention this to Atmananda because he realised that it did not matter to Atmananda whether people praised him or cursed him. He delivered to each person as per their need, expecting nothing in return. Manav understood how he was imparting knowledge – by practical training and complete annihilation of the ego. He felt sincere and immense gratitude for the Master, his teaching and his methods. To compensate for his actions, he decided to resolutely follow Atmananda for his own purgation. Thus, Manav found his path of liberation. He knew that he would never be the same again.

CHAPTER 2

SWEETMEATS TO LIBERATION

Towards the latter part of his life, Atmananda had five followers who always moved with him – Srinath, Manu, Panduranga, Ramakrishna and Aruna. Many others came and joined the core group but left him after a while. Atmananda never bothered about who came or went. When people came, he shared food with them. That was his only sign of approval of anyone's company. No other approval or disapproval. He just flowed, and the rest flowed with him in absolute faith and surrender.

Once, Atmananda sat in a village park in front of a row of shops, one of which sold sweetmeats. Panduranga loved sweets, and his eyes constantly darted to the decorated stalls displaying colourful sweets. Despite sitting with his back to the shops, Atmananda said, "When the eyes have focused with the mind on an object, the man is lost to temptations." No one, including Panduranga, knew the depth or purpose of this statement nor did Atmananda explain it in detail. Atmananda spontaneously took some coins from his cloth sack and asked his follower Aruna to fetch some sweets from that shop. Aruna was surprised. In his experience, he had never seen his Master using money, especially for the sake of sensory pleasure. He also wondered how *Gurudeva* (revered Master) got the coins. Usually, *Gurudeva* gave away all that he got to the people around him or those that came to visit him. He never kept any money with him. However, he would never dream of questioning his *Gurudeva's* actions.

Aruna immediately got up and left for the shop while the others sat around the Master. On reaching the shop, Aruna asked the shopkeeper to pack some sweets that he thought *Gurudeva* would like. The elderly shopkeeper was a very pious *brahmin* called Rama Shastri. He guessed by Aruna's attire that he was a wandering monk. While packing the sweets, he asked him who he was. Aruna gave a brief explanation about himself and his dear Master, sufficient for the shopkeeper to get an idea. The shopkeeper handed over the sweets, much more than what Aruna had asked. When Aruna tried to pay, he refused, saying, "Please allow me this opportunity to surrender my humble offerings at the feet of a great soul, your *Gurudeva*."

He asked his granddaughter to manage the shop while he went with Aruna to meet Atmananda. As soon as the shopkeeper saw Atmananda, a strange feeling came over him, and he prostrated at Atmananda's feet in complete humility. He said, "Lord, my life is complete today. You are Lord Dattatreya Himself. I am ready to lay my life at your feet at this very moment." Atmananda blessed him and said, "Rama, two steps above and two steps below; one step in the centre. This is what you have. When you leave the five steps, you will become me. Nine steps above and eight steps below; one step in the middle. When you complete the steps, then you will become my father. My Father and I are one."

Atmananda's followers were surprised that he knew the name of the shopkeeper. Rama started crying like a baby because this was what he had been taught as a child by his own Master. Atmananda's followers did not fully understand the meaning but kept quiet.

Atmananda hugged the sobbing Rama. Aruna and others were surprised since they had never seen *Gurudeva* so involved with anyone. They were curious about their apparent past association but were afraid to ask Atmananda. The meeting ended abruptly. Rama Shastri left. Aruna handed over the packet of sweets and the remaining money to Atmananda who distributed the sweets to everyone except Panduranga.

Panduranga craved sweets the most, but he was the only one who got nothing! In his mind, he yearned to taste at least a crumb. Atmananda ignored him totally and did not even look at him. Atmananda and the other four emptied the entire box. When Aruna tried to give a piece to Panduranga, Atmananda turned and said, "Yours for yourself." It was a karmically perfect statement. Even more and more sweets were given to Kalikananda who never liked them. Only the one who wanted it the most, did not get any. None of the followers understood the strange ways of Atmananda. Yet, their devotion towards their *Gurudeva* was absolute, and they did not ask questions.

Panduranga had joined Atmananda's group when Atmananda and his group were visiting a temple in central India. At their first meeting, Atmananda had looked at him and called him by his name, saying, "Panduranga, I have eight years, and you have eight years. Come with me and go before me." Panduranga left what he was doing at the temple and, as if hypnotised by Atmananda, followed the Master without even a spare cloth in his hand. His faith took root, grew into a giant banyan tree within moments, and soon became unshakeable. As they walked out of the temple, a businessman came and prostrated at the feet of Atmananda. He offered him two lengths of cloth – one for below the waist and one for above, a few coins, and some fruit. Atmananda blessed the businessman, gave the clothes to Panduranga, kept the coins in his bag, and distributed the fruits among his followers.

They had travelled together for almost eight years up to now. They had travelled through many parts of India. While Atmananda taught them nothing specific, the followers picked up many jewels of wisdom, observing his way of life, which slowly transformed them. The simplicity and total unpredictability of the Master kept them alert and grounded. It also helped them to stay fluid and flexible. Three days was usually the maximum time Atmananda stayed at any place. At this place, near the river, Atmananda stayed for almost four days. Every morning, the elderly shopkeeper brought fresh sweets and some food to Atmananda, and Atmananda distributed the sweets to everyone except Panduranga. He shared the food equally with everyone. There was always sufficient to appease the hunger of all. They ate only once a day, as true yogis did.

This was not the first time that Atmananda was distributing sweets in this manner. In all the eight years that they had been together, Atmananda never gave even a tiny portion of sweets to Panduranga who craved them the most. They rarely received sweets, except in temples in which everyone, including Panduranga, was given some. But, Panduranga who craved the multicolored sweets from the sweet shop, was severely disappointed by the seeming discrimination of Atmananda.

On the third day, Atmananda sent Aruna to the shop again early in the afternoon with the same coins. Aruna hesitated to take the coins as he knew that Rama, the shopkeeper, would not accept them. Rama had been delivering food and sweets to Atmananda and the group at no cost. But his beloved *Gurudeva's* instructions could not be questioned. There was always a higher purpose behind

Gurudeva's every word and action. So Aruna walked towards the shop. The shop was open, but the elderly Rama Shastri was not at his usual place at the counter. Aruna called out to see if he was inside. His granddaughter came out saying that her grandfather and other relatives had gone to attend a wedding in the village. She also informed him that most of the sweets had been sold to fulfil an order from the bride's family. The shop had very few sweets left.

For a moment, Aruna admired the devotion of the elderly businessman. He had offered fresh sweetmeats to Atmananda that very morning despite his commitment to provide sweets for the wedding. Aruna asked the girl at the shop to pack whatever sweets remained, gave her the money and left. The girl had no problem with accepting money. For her, Aruna was just another customer. It was 5 p.m. and time for Atmananda and his followers to go for their bath and evening meditations. When Aruna brought the box of sweets and handed it to Atmananda, he immediately gave the box of sweets to Panduranga. He said, "It is all yours. No more unfulfilled desires."

Receiving this precious gift from his beloved *Gurudeva*, Panduranga cried like a baby. He fell at Atmananda's feet and begged pardon for having nurtured thoughts of hatred against his *Gurudeva*. He apologised over and over again for considering Atmananda as partial and cruel. Atmananda smiled and said, "Have the sweets, they are all yours." Panduranga began to eat them with great relish, and when he offered some to the others, they declined, saying, "You deserve them all." Panduranga was deeply satisfied. It was a feast for him. He could only eat half the quantity, saving the rest for later.

After the evening prayers, Atmananda called Panduranga and said,

"If you flow with time, time is your friend. If you do not, time is your foe. Have you kept time? Now release time. Time cannot be held by man. Only immortality can hold time. Remain blessed. Be immortal." He asked Panduranga to meditate facing the North and to remain awake that night. At the time of subtlety, the time of *brahma muhurta*, when the group woke up the next day, they saw Panduranga still meditating in the lotus posture. When they tried to wake him, he fell backwards. His body had frozen. His soul had left!

Rama Shastri arranged for a proper funeral on the fourth day. At the funeral, Atmananda said to Rama, "His only desire on earth was sweets. He had transcended all other desires. He would have left his abode (body) much earlier if this last desire had been fulfilled. He had to serve me for eight years, so I kept him in his abode. Now he has to leave ahead of me. With the fulfilment of his last wish, he has attained immortality." It was only then his followers understood the reason behind this dramatic sequence of events.

Exactly eight months after this, Atmananda also left his body and thus fulfilled his first words to Panduranga.

CHAPTER 3

AGHORA BABAJI AND RAMA SHASTRI

Aruna and Rama Shastri were obtaining the materials required for Panduranga's cremation. Aruna asked Rama Shastri what Atmananda had meant when he had said, "Two steps above and two steps below; one step in the centre. This is what you have. When you leave the five steps, you will become me. Nine steps above and eight steps below; one step in the middle. When you complete the eighteen steps, then you will become my father. My Father and I are one."

Rama replied, "I do not know if I have the eligibility to explain this code that the great Master who walks with you, told me. He is the Supreme Lord Dattatreya himself. He is verily the holy Trinity – Brahma, Vishnu, and Shiva. I shall explain according to my understanding. Pardon me if I fall short.

Beginning from our first until our last birth we take on earth, the total completion of various aspects of various lifetimes attains its ultimate completion when the soul merges with the supreme Consciousness. Eighteen signifies completion because nature has eighteen aspects – the five senses, our mind matter (mind, ego, intellect), the eight most powerful and extremely dangerous enemies of human existence (*kaama* –terrestrial ambition, *krodha*

– anger, *lobha* – greed, *moha* – attachment, *mada* – lust, *matsarya* – competition, *ahankara* – pride, *asooya* – jealousy), the three flavors (*sattva*, *rajas*, and *tamas*) and operating consciousness (waking, dream and deep sleep).

We have a tangible physical body; along with its senses to sense the world outside. Then, we have the mind matter which has the three processors – the mind, intellect and ego – that process everything that comes through the senses into us. Just as the organs of our body process the food that we consume, mind processes emotions, intellect processes information and ego processes aspects related to ownership. Further, each person has a different mindset. The three flavours create our character and constitution, and makes each of us distinct. Every being is a different combination of these three. All these combinations are important and add to the flavour of existence. The mind matter and the three flavors make up our subtle aspect. We must also tackle the eight enemies that bind us and prevent our liberation, as well as the patterns, prejudices, emotions, feelings, memories, impressions, etc that are stored inside. Finally, we have the consciousness aspect which operates in the three states (waking state, dream state and deep sleep state) and processes and supports our subtle aspects (mind, intellect and ego) twenty-four hours every day.

Collectively, each man has a unique nature. All of us base ourselves on this multiple nature as well as one nature. This is where we are progressing from, and into the path of pathlessness. We have to travel from our outside nature to our inherent nature, crossing over even the minutest of nature to attain the Ultimate. 18 is also 1+8 = 9. It signifies the nine avatars of Maha Vishnu – the maintenance aspect of existence. These nine avatars are Matsya (aquatic), Kurma (amphibian), Varaha (animal), Narsimha (part animal, part human), Vamana (dwarf), Parashurama (animal human), Rama (saint human), Krishna (God human). They signify the progression and refinement in the path of evolution. Then comes Kalki, the last avatar of Maha Vishnu. Unlike the nine avatars, Kalki is not a person but a situation which signifies dissolution. 10 = 1+0 which means one, unity, or back to the original form.

He reminded me that in our path of complete dissolution, I have to travel these nine steps. Our great Master also indicated that I may take nine more births. With his grace and blessings, I may need no more births and also transcend them in this life itself. I am not worried. As long as I have his grace, I am ready to take another million births too."

Aruna admired the wisdom and understanding of this elderly businessman. He had truly recognised Atmananda. Aruna noticed that from the moment he saw Atmananda, Rama Shastri did not waste any time, and connected to Atmananda immediately. Aruna, of course, knew that it was due to the grace of his *Gurudeva*. It was not easy because Atmananda had no paraphernalia. He walked around, wearing just a loincloth. So, people easily dismissed him. But this businessman recognised him instantaneously. He also never charged Atmananda any money for the sweets that were purchased by Atmananda's group.

Aruna and another follower, Kalikananda were genuinely interested in knowing about the shopkeeper Rama Shastri's Master. While preparing for the cremation of Panduranga, Rama Shastri narrated, "Our great Master knows him. It is Himself. Nobody knew his name. He was called Aghora *Baba* by the villagers because he was mostly naked, and sometimes he wore bizarre clothes. He used to carry a skull in his hand, and people were afraid of him. He had many spiritual powers.

He was not exactly my Master, as I was just a young boy of five or six years. I believe he left his physical body when I was thirteen or fourteen, some say he just disappeared along with his disciples. Nobody has seen them ever again. Physically, our great Master is much younger than me. So, there is no way that he would have seen Aghora Babaji.

Babaji was my grandfather's Master and also my father's. I was afraid of him and always avoided him whenever he was close. He lived in the burial ground. People say that he brewed and drank alcohol, smoked, and also slept with many women. There were about twenty-five people with him all the time, many of them women of various ages. No one knew from where these women came. His eyes were always bloodshot, and he looked as if he was under the spell of alcohol. I even heard that he performed many bizarre rituals and fire ceremonies at night in the funeral fire, stark naked. People said that they saw him dancing in the fire too.

Pointing to an area in the burial ground, he continued, "Right there, he had a small thatched hut where he slept. My mother's younger brother hated him. He would tell my mother, "That *Baba* is creating prostitutes here in our village. He sleeps with many women, and all men and women perform naked rituals at night with him. He drinks alcohol and uses other intoxicants too. The *Baba* is immoral and should not be worshipped. Do you want our young Rama to copy these bizarre habits? Talk to father and grandfather, make them understand that he is not a good Master to follow." All this made my mother very anxious.

When I started recognising Babaji, he looked to be in his sixties.

He had long matted hair that cascaded to his knees. Sometimes, he would circle and tie his matted hair around his head to form a big turban of hair. He had an unkempt beard which often had food particles stuck in it. He had fierce eyes, an athletic body, a powerful physical form and a deep scar on his chest like a knife wound, which possibly looked like a battle scar. There used to be many women with him, most of whom wore saffron. The men looked like they were intoxicated, high on drugs, and almost always wore only a shawl. They were a strange group.

I had no choice but to pass the burial ground on our way to the teacher's house every day. My friends and I used to quiver in fear whenever we heard any sounds from there. We saw Babaji in our dreams, coming and killing us and eating our flesh. Later, I realised that my mother also had such dreams! Once I overheard her telling my father about her dream, and he just laughed and said, "If Babaji commands that the sun shall not rise again, the sun will obey. If he commands the earth to rotate backwards, Mother Earth will obey. He is an *Avatar*. Do not fear him. Worship him. He is our protector. If he comes in your dream and eats your flesh, it is an excellent sign. It means he has accepted you. It is not just a dream. Your dream is symbolic and is actually a blessing. Your flesh consists of five elements. Eating and digesting your flesh is symbolic of reducing your lifetimes. What you had to experience through thousands of future lives has been taken away by Babaji in this lifetime itself. He has liberated you."

When I was perhaps ten or twelve years, my friends and I were walking past the burial ground and somehow came right in front of Babaji. He was alone, and his bloodshot eyes made us shiver. One of my friends even wet his *dhoti*[22]. We tried to sneak past him. 'Stop!' he commanded. We were trembling. He asked me to come

---

[22] *A garment consisting of a piece of cloth tied around the waist, and extends to cover the legs.*

to him. My knees were shaking as I went closer. He gently took my hand with a lot of love and kindness. Instead of the stench that I expected from his unkempt body, I caught the fragrance of divine flowers.

"He looked at me with compassion. I lost all my fear. He held my hand and spoke the same words you heard our great Master utter. Those exact words! 'Rama, two steps above and two steps below; one step in the centre. This is what you have. When you leave the five steps, you will become me. Nine steps above and eight steps below; one step in the middle. When you complete the eighteen steps, then you will become my father. My Father and I are one.' Even though I did not fully comprehend the meaning of those words, they remained firmly etched in my memory. He made that possible.

Now, I genuinely pity my uncle and others who criticised and despised him both privately and publicly. They missed the chance of many lifetimes, absorbed as they were in the superficial incompatibilities, pretentious moralities, and non-conformities based on their preconceived notions. They were trapped in the cages of their mind, self-created cages of conditioning. Babaji's aim was perhaps to shatter that conditioning. Total ignorance made them miss it in this lifetime. When would they get another chance? I clearly understood from my father that if we cannot develop the eyes to see beyond the superficial obvious, we miss the opportunity, especially with Lord Dattatreya, the supreme *Parabrahma*. However, not everyone is so fortunate. It is immense luck in human existence to have eyes to perceive truth.

Aghora *Baba* and our great Master are the same. He came back in this form to bless my family and me again, and I had the good fortune of serving food to him. Before his death, my grandfather had said, 'Babaji will never leave your hand. He will watch over you through time. You will meet him again before you leave your body.' I knew from the bottom of my heart that it is true. I experienced the same fragrance when our great Master touched me. It is all one. All are undoubtedly Datta. Babaji came to destroy our concepts and take us to higher awareness, and now our great Master is doing the same.

I understood that the bizarre lifestyle was to protect him as well as those who followed him. I even feel that the naked women and men who lived with him in the burial ground were not humans. They could be celestial beings. I believe this was Lord Datta and his followers enjoying a terrestrial existence, just like our great Master. The fragrance that emanated from his body was unmistakable and celestial. Praise be to the Lord Guru Datta!"

"I hope that I will someday have inner eyes to see the glory of my Lord, and all the petty doubts of my silly mind will vanish forever. It is never easy to understand a Datta Master unless they choose to reveal their true stature. In that way, I have not been lucky to see beyond the physical dimension. Unfortunately, our eyes can only see the superficial substance. But I am satisfied with this confirmation that Babaji has appeared again to touch me and love me. My life is fulfilled.

One more thing which you may not know is that there were no sweets in our shop yesterday. We had taken everything for the wedding. What you bought had appeared miraculously, and my granddaughter did not know about it. What she gave you happened there just because of the will of our dear Master. It was a miracle for sure. What Panduranga consumed before his death were no ordinary sweets. They were celestial sweets. Also, the sweets had to be bought as per *dharma*. It could not be a donation since someone was attaining *mahasamadhi*[23]. Hence, this happened in my absence else I would not have taken the money."

Rama Shastri's eyes welled up in tears as he said, "Such is the love of our tradition which provides for us to the minutest detail. We need to have a non-judgmental mind at all times. Glory be to Lord Datta and his many Avatars.

---

[23] *conscious exit of the soul from the physical body accomplished by yogis to merge with the supreme Consciousness when their time has come*

CHAPTER 4

THE *AKSHAYA PATRA* (INEXHAUSTIBLE VESSEL)

"I cannot believe I am so limited! I cannot feel I have a body. Master, what is this?" Manu asked Atmananda. Atmananda paid no attention to his words. Accustomed to many such exclamations from his followers, he knew their cause – the mind. He was never impressed with anything that minds ever produced. Why would he be? Minds were all that he saw around him. Walking, talking, sleeping and dreaming minds; heavy minds laden with concepts, prejudices, fears, memories, and desires; nothing else. Ever since he had started following Atmananda, he had connected his mind on the heart centre of the ever-meditating Atmananda sitting just a few feet away. With steady focus, he had brought Atmananda's heart centre from outside into his heart centre. At that moment, a melting, dissolving feeling enveloped his mind as his heart centre merged with that of Atmananda. He then felt and experienced Atmananda within his heart centre and consistently worshipped Atmananda within his own heart. Finally, on that day, he saw or rather felt in his inner eye, the fathomless, unlimited vast sky of Atmananda's heart centre. The whole universe seemed to be resting there. That glimpse pushed him into a blissful trance state, which lasted for a few hours.

Atmananda neither guided him into that state, nor did he pay any attention to it. He knew that one could only feed minds. Consciousness needs no food. His very presence was his highest teaching. To those eligible, he delivered the unasked merely by his presence. Eligibility was in inner emptiness, unshakeable faith, lack of doubts, total surrender, and clear purpose of liberation. On the tree of liberation, healthy leaves seeking the ultimate remained on the tree. In contrast, the leaves that were dry, confused, prejudiced, and decayed with heavy emotions, kept falling off periodically. Even a light breeze was enough for those leaves to fall off. Whenever this happened, and someone commented or asked about it, Atmananda would reply calmly, "It's not their time as yet. (They are not ready for liberation)" Many a time, the requirements of his followers would be terrestrial. To such people, he would say, "You are wasting your time with me. You should address your needs and be done with it."

The sun had set. Atmananda stood up and walked a few steps towards the river bank. He intended to take a dip and meditate in the nearby temple. The local temple priest had always offered food to this wandering monk and his followers whenever they went there, even though they never asked or expected anything from anybody, anytime. On the way, they met an old woman. She was limping and walking with the help of a stick. She was rheumatic and seemed to have a frozen leg. Atmananda would always ask, "Have you eaten?" to every old and sick person he met on his way. He asked the same question to this lady. She said, "No, it has been two days." This place was away from the city and sparsely populated, so it was unsuitable for wandering monks and helpless old people.

Atmananda turned to one of his followers called Ramakrishna and asked him, "I gave you three fruits in the afternoon. Do you still have them?" Those had been offered to Atmananda by a fruit vendor as *dakshina*[24]. "Yes, *Gurudeva*," Ramakrishna replied. "Give them to her," instructed Atmananda. Ramakrishna hesitated for a moment because that was the only food that this group had at that time. Without any emotions, Atmananda signalled to Ramakrishan with his eyes as if to say, "Give them to her now," and then started walking ahead. Ramakrishna rushed to hand over the fruits to the old woman and then caught up with the quick and agile Atmananda. All of them were quite hungry, and there was no assured source of food. While walking with Atmananda who never stayed at one place for more than three days, nothing was certain. This was a test for most of his followers. Atmananda never cared who dropped off and who stayed. He continued wandering. After bathing and performing the evening rituals, they walked into the village temple. Lord Krishna was the principal deity of the temple. The sweet scent of *tulsi* garlands that adorned the beautiful idol of Lord Krishna greeted them. The idol shone in the light of the *ghee* lamps.

ATMANANDA'S WORDS OF WISDOM

Atmananda always had a clear reason for taking his followers to temples – purification. It was never for his own sake. Purification has multiple aspects. First the senses, then the mind. Senses have no meaning or existence without the mind. Each deity in the *Sanatana Dharma* is a representation of different ideals or dimensions of human existence, such as action, will power, abundance, wealth, love, knowledge, peace, and so on. The eyes capture the bright, shining, decorated positive glory of the idol, which is nothing but the representation of an ideal that is represented by the deity. These ideals are also frequencies and all these frequencies are present in the human body. Each organ has a different frequency. Hence, when

---

[24] *donation or offering*

we worship and respect those frequencies, it silently and indirectly rejuvenates those aspects within our body as well.

The ears are awakened through *mantras*, bells, drums, conch and other sounds of the temple. The nose is awakened by the fragrance of basil leaves, flowers, incense sticks, camphor, and perfumes used on the idol that represent the purity of our state, the fragrance of pure consciousness. The skin is awakened by the application of sacred ash, turmeric paste, sandalwood or vermillion. The tongue is awakened by the sacred water, fruits, or other offerings. The sound of the conch, supposedly as powerful as a thousand OMs, is powerful enough to ward off all the negative elements and awaken the human *naadis* (meridians). Finally, the mind is awakened through all these senses as well as the vibrations of chants and songs, which detach it from the outside world and keep it steady in the present. Thus, the whole body is awakened. This helps inner and outer purification.

The *aarati* lamp has five wicks representing five elements, five *pranas*[25], five *koshas* (sheaths), etc. and essentially, the fire element in us. The wet cloth used to hold the lamp to prevent the heat from affecting the palm, represents the water element, vital for sustaining life on earth. The peacock feather fan represents the air element. The flower represents earth. The yak tail fan represents the subtle form of ether. Thus, the five elements that constitute earthly existence are offered to the Lord. Also, the offerings made by the devotees at the temple signify sacrifice, surrender and sharing what you have been blessed with. Thus, we are offering every aspect of our existence to the Lord Almighty and live our life in total surrender to His will.

Humility is the most important aspect of human existence that

---

[25] *life force*

brings forth grace in abundance. Humility has four aspects. The feeling of insignificance in a positive way, is one aspect. If one feels lower than the lowest, it's a clear sign of established humility. This is also why people prostrate in full length at the feet of an idol or a spiritual Master. It is an act of total surrender, making oneself insignificant, so that the ego is brought down to the lowest possible level. Man minus ego is equal to God. The second aspect of humility is being tolerant, nurturing high level of acceptance, without judgement of oneself and the world around. This acceptance keeps our mind steady and calm. On the other hand, resistance, judgement, prejudices, hatred and anger towards anything makes the mind turbulent. The third aspect is acceptance and respect of all beings – human and non-human. Respect them as you would like to be respected. The fourth is to have no expectation. Do not expect respect, acknowledgement or anything at all while giving forth your best. This is symbolised by giving a variety of offerings to the temple or idol of the deity. All these put together become the experience called humility. Humility ensures grace in life.

After the aarati, the priests extend the aarati plate to the devotees to purify themselves with the fire that has caught the essence of the deity/divine. The priests also offer sandal wood paste to the worshippers, to apply on their third eye, to cool the heat generated through intense prayers communicated through the third eye (with eyes closed) and flowers, which represented the earth, to stay grounded and grateful.

The day is started with the request to Mother Earth, to forgive us for stepping on her, or walking over her body. Earth is a gift to us from God, for the fulfilment of our desires or to exhaust our vasanas of earthly nature. The flowers remind us of this beautiful gift from God, with a warning to handle it delicately, with care, as we would handle a delicate, tender flower.

Rejuvenation, purification, and nurturing goodness were the reasons why Atmananda took people to the temples. For him, temples were meeting places for sharing, caring, nurturing and expressing our innate goodness and kindness. He never encouraged prayers of requests for material or spiritual benefits from the deities. He used to say, "Increase your inner space, you will carry more grace."

Whenever people asked Atmananda, "What can we do to get the state of God?" Atmananda always answered, "By doing, you only get more karma. Only through non-doing or detached existence from actions and the results of actions, while in action, can you realise God. You cannot "get" God. God can only be realised. God is always there. Godhood has to be earned through emptiness. In silence, you become aware of it. Actions and expressions often take that opportunity away."

There were hardly any devotees in the temple that day. It was a village temple that was away from the city crowd. An old woman and her teenage granddaughter circumambulated the temple chanting '*Aum Namo Bhagavate Vaasudevaaya*', the sacred *mantra* of Lord Vishnu. -When the priest saw Atmananda and his entourage, he came out of the temple and gave them some flowers, sandal paste, and two bananas.

The priest said, "Don't leave. Let me complete the rituals and close the temple. I would like to share a meal with you." He went into the temple to complete the evening rituals. Atmananda gave one banana to the old woman who came near him to touch his feet. He did not allow her to do so. Instead, he touched the ground near her feet. She exclaimed, "Oh no, *Swamiji*, I will be committing a sin if you touch my feet." Atmananda smiled and said, "If I am the cause of your sin, I shall take it away too. Bless this son, Mother. I am touching my mother's feet."

Atmananda and his group of nine sat outside the temple waiting for the priest to close the temple and join them. The priest lived about a hundred feet away from the temple. After the daily rituals, he usually took home the fruits and grains that devotees had offered to the Lord. This sustained his family of five. They did not complain of poverty or their circumstances.

He came to Atmananda, bringing with him a few plantain leaves that served as disposable plates, and spread them on a flat stone seat near a banyan tree. He started serving them rice. He gave them almost half of what he had received that day. He kept the rest for his family. Atmananda watched silently as the priest, using a folded leaf as a spoon, poured some *ghee* over the rice. He looked at Atmananda apologetically and said, "This is all I have. Please accept my humble offering and bless me."

Atmananda held the hand of the priest in gratitude and said, "O great embodiment of unconditional love, your generations will not know hunger." The priest's eyes filled with tears as Atmananda continued, "You have hungry children waiting for this food, yet you have given us half. They may sleep hungry tonight because the food you have is insufficient for five people. I will not allow that."

He took a plantain leaf and covered the vessel that the priest held in his hands, tapped the pot thrice and told the priest, "Do not remove this leaf until it is time to serve. There will be sufficient food for all." The priest was overwhelmed. He tried to prostrate at Atmananda's feet but Atmananda did not permit it. Instead, he held him and said, "You are taking good care of the beloved Lord Krishna without any demands and expectations. You are a pure and selfless man. You never care about yourself or your family while sharing food with any stranger who wanders this way. Your family is also good and pious. Only goodness and blessings will come to you. You may be materially poor, but you have a rich heart. You will never be short of anything from this moment. Your next seven generations will experience the goodness of your actions."

The priest felt that the selfless worship of Lord Krishna by his family for generations had borne fruit. He had been serving Lord Krishna unconditionally without any expectations, as his father had done before him, and their previous generations had done before his father. Whatever little he had, he offered to the Lord. Despite the meagre quantity and his large family, he always shared whatever he received with wandering monks. He only served and never asked or expected anything. Even the blessings of abundance that he received from Atmananda were given unasked. That was his power. The priest concluded that the moral of his story was that generations of pious activity brings forth abundance. In the priest's mind, Lord Krishna through Atmananda, appeared and spoke to him, and blessed him with abundance. The priest left with tears of gratitude in his eyes. Atmananda always used to reach such places to fulfil the Lord's wish to either elevate, bless or remove blockages and allow the person to reap the benefits or receive abundance. These incidents would happen in the course of his wandering and never as a detour.

Atmananda closed his eyes, chanted a *mantra* and then began to eat the food on the leaf. They all ate the rice flavoured with *ghee* to their heart's content. Nobody knew how that little quantity became sufficient for all. Everybody was amazed how Atmananda had performed such a miracle. Although they witnessed it, they did not realise the magnitude of the extraordinary action because of their extreme hunger. It struck them much later and they realised that they really did not know Atmananda or how he operated at any time. The same thing happened at the priest's house later that evening. Everybody ate to their heart's content, and there even was some food left back. The vessel that Atmananda had touched remained with the family for seven generations, and their home never had any shortage of food.

They left the temple premises the same evening and settled for the night in the verandah of the small village school that was an hour's walk from the temple. Atmananda always walked at least an hour after the evening meal.

CHAPTER 5

DIVINE DESIGNS OF LIFE

Before dawn, Atmananda set out to take a bath and perform the morning rituals. The school where he had stopped for the night was quite far from the river. So, he took a bath by drawing water from a well and sat a few yards away to perform his rituals. When the village women started to come to fill their pots from the well, Atmananda and his group got up and walked away.

They walked for an hour. The protruding root of a massive tree on the path was not so clearly visible in poor light and Atmananda, who was walking ahead of everybody, tripped over it, fell, and injured his right leg. He could not get up or walk. His followers lifted him up and carried him to a clearing near the path. They made him sit on a flat stone. He was bleeding, and they did not know what to do. Atmananda asked them to get some leaves of a very common wild plant, which he then crushed to a paste and applied on his wound. There was no cloth to bandage it with, so he removed his towel, which was the only cloth he was wearing other than the loincloth, and tied it over the crushed leaves.

Atmananda could not walk because of the excruciating pain. His followers offered to carry him, but he refused. He sat on that stone all day. There were no houses in the vicinity, and the path had only a few travellers. If they walked back a few kilometers, they would reach the village where they had spent the previous night, but Atmananda was stubborn. Hunger never bothered him, but his followers needed to eat. Some of them expected Atmananda magically to get them food, as he had done before. But nothing happened.

One by one, the men started grumbling, standing away from Atmananda, out of earshot. Said one of them, "If our Guru could materialise food for a priest, why can't he do that for us?" Another added, "My vision is getting blurred, I can barely see." A third wondered, "Is our Guru testing us?" "Are you sure he materialised food the other day, or did we imagine it?" "He did. We all ate." "I am sure he has no such powers. It is probably the temple, Lord Krishna, and the priest that made it possible. If he had such powers, he would not allow us to starve. Why can't he materialise food for us now?" "If he has the power to know our minds, he should know that we are hungry. Why isn't he doing anything about it?" "Is he meditating, or sleeping, or pretending to sleep just to fool us?" "He never asked us to follow him. He will never ask us to leave. It is entirely up to us to stay or to leave." "What is his plan? Is he going to sit on the rock until his leg heals? That may take weeks!" That was a scary thought for all of them.

It was almost midnight. None of them had eaten anything. No one had a clue about what lay ahead. Some of the followers decided to go back towards the school. They started walking but the forest path was dark and scary. They feared snakes and the nocturnal animals. They stopped and returned. Atmananda seemed to be sleeping, seemingly unaware of all that was going on around him. Manu and Ramakrishna sat on either side focusing on their Guru who was always seated in their heart centre. They did not feel any hunger. The other seven were in total confusion. Some of them tried to lie down and sleep, but the bizarre sounds from the jungle, their piercing hunger, and the fear of preying animals severely affected their ability to sleep.

Finally, a few hours before sunrise, Atmananda woke up. He asked Manu for two sticks, used them as crutches and walked forward. His hungry, confused, sleepy followers reluctantly followed him. After they walked for about an hour, they came upon a well that had been provided by the king for the comfort of the travellers. They drew water, drank, washed, bathed, and some even washed the clothes they wore. Atmananda cleared his wound, applied more leaves, and tied them to his leg using the same cloth again.

There was no food to be found anywhere. It was a long period of fasting. After performing his morning rituals, Atmananda started walking again. As always, he never told anyone where he was going or how long he would walk. He just walked. Seven of his followers had only one thing on their minds –food.

Sunrise brought out colorful birds from their nests, flowers bloomed, and the forest path looked pretty and heavenly with various flowers, dew drops and the sun's rays decorating their path. But only Manu and Ramakrishna could enjoy this.

The others were looking for fruits, leaves, roots, or even seeds that they could eat to quell their hunger. Atmananda walked on with his crutches. He never asked or cared how his followers felt. He never asked anyone to follow him as he was an *Avadhoota*, very introverted and a complete loner. Finally, it was noon and seven of the followers were tired. The group soon reached a stream coming down through the forest and flowing towards the river. They washed their tired feet and faces, and drank lots of water.

Atmananda sat under a tree and closed his eyes. Manu and Ramakrishna sat next to Atmananda, connected and dissolved into his heart center.

The seven confused followers moved away from them and started a discussion. The leader of the group, and perhaps the hungriest of them, Amara, said he was leaving. "I don't see any end to this journey. I cannot live on an empty stomach like Manu and I am convinced that Atmananda has no divine powers. He is just an ordinary wandering monk."

Another concurred, "I agree. Atmananda has no spiritual powers. At the temple, I am sure, those vessels must have been powerful and blessed, and performed that miracle."

A third one added, "I too cannot remain this way. He is not concerned about us. He only thinks of himself. After all, what exactly have we learned from him so far?"

The fourth pronounced, "This is true. Why do we continue to walk with him? It is always walking an uncertain path, and we get no training. He teaches us nothing. He confuses me to the point of frustration. I am leaving too."

"I am also leaving too. This hunger is not worth all the trouble."

Amara said, "Friends, he is just an ordinary man. He fell, he was injured, and he cannot heal himself. He cannot feed himself or others. He is helpless. Can't you see? He is an ordinary man. We are deluded if we think he is otherwise."

Finally, they concluded that Atmananda was just an ordinary

wandering monk with no extraordinary powers or knowledge, and made preparations to leave. They decided to bid Atmananda goodbye and approached him. But Atmananda, Manu and Ramakrishna, were sitting with their eyes closed, deep in meditation. The seven did not have the patience to wait until they opened their eyes. They just walked away.

Thirty minutes later, they saw a tree bearing delicious fruits. They plucked and ate as many as they could and packed a few for the rest of their journey. After eating and resting for a while, Amara said, "See, Atmananda does not even have luck on his side. Only after we left him, we found food. We starved the whole day and the whole night, looking at him and hoping that he would move. We made the right decision. We are free now, and lucky to have found food." Everyone agreed.

Atmananda, Manu and Ramakrishna came back to terrestrial reality soon after the group left them. Atmananda tried to get up. Manu held his hand and helped him. Atmananda got his crutches and started walking. Ramakrishna said *"Gurudeva*, I shall fetch the others. They might be sleeping somewhere nearby. Please kindly wait for a while." Without looking, Atmananda said without any emotion or concern, "They have left us. Let us move on."

Barely ten minutes later, they saw a small house belonging to a farmer. When they came close to it, the farmer's wife, a young woman, came out of the house, invited them in, and asked them to be seated. She offered them water and freshly cooked food. They all ate heartily. Atmananda blessed her *"Anna Daata Sukhi Bhava!"*[26] She was happy when she heard these words. She told Atmananda

---

[26] *May the one who serves food always be happy and in abundance*

that she was pregnant and sought his blessings for a good and healthy child who would make their lineage proud. Atmananda blessed her, *"Tathasthu!"* (So be it)

She then requested them to relax, have the evening meal and stay the night over, and accept their limited facilities. Atmananda politely refused and decided to walk on. The farmer's wife also offered some plant medicine for his wound. He politely refused that as well. When they started walking, the woman was at the gate with folded hands expressing deep reverence for Atmananda. Before they turned the bend, Manu looked back to gesture a final farewell. When he turned back, he did not see the woman, the house, or the cattle. There wasn't a trace of inhabitation. It was only thick forest that blocked the rays of the sun. He could just see the forest path stretching behind him.

As always, Atmananda never looked back. He kept walking and both Ramakrishna and Manu noticed that Atmananda was walking without the crutches. There was no sign of injury on his leg! They wondered what the reason for this divine drama was, and concluded that it was to shake the tree and shed the dry leaves, dry of spiritual conviction. Atmananda always said, "Conviction is essential when one chooses to walk the path of liberation." Perhaps conviction is more essential than faith. Passion and fearlessness are just the by-products.

One leaf from the life of Atmananda ends here.

CHAPTER 6

HOTTER THAN THE RAGING SUN

The following chapters in this section are an account by Mahendra Manu, one of Atmananda's close followers, who was instrumental in collecting details and spreading awareness about the great Guru.

I shall narrate the stories about some of *Gurudeva's* followers such as Srinath, Raghavacharya, Kalikananda, and me. I have also outlined some experiences and anecdotes of *Gurudeva* that open a window into his glorious stature. *Gurudeva* was like a flowing river. Before joining, each follower had travelled a considerable distance in their spiritual journey along their paths based on their constitution. *Gurudeva* facilitated their orientations – bhakti yoga, jnana yoga, etc. and subsequently, they moved ahead on their chosen path.

Gurudeva neither had any habits nor was he particular about food. He mostly ate whatever he got, never going in search of food or to gather *bhiksha*. Some places provided *bhiksha*, but he would say, 'Let's walk'. Some of his followers wanted to stay back and have the *bhiksha* but *Gurudeva* didn't care, so people seldom brought food to him. Even if they brought food, he would take a look at it and then feed birds or cows or he would feed whoever was around, but not eat anything himself. There was nothing much to do for *Gurudeva*. He didn't need any service.

Among the followers, Srinath was one who rendered the most personal service. He was like *Gurudeva's* shadow. He had joined *Gurudeva* before me and was with him until his *mahasamadhi*. Srinath had never talked about his past, but someone mentioned that his father had remarried and his step-mother was not very happy with her stepson. He spent most of his time sitting quietly, not doing any work, and always in meditation. His parents thought that he was wasting his life and would not be able to support himself after their death. They threw him out of home, so that he could find a job and support himself. Having left home, he did not care for much and could be seen sitting near a shop or in the park or some other place in isolation.

Some time later, a passing *Avadhoota* told him, 'Your path is the sky.' Since he did not have any initiation, he would keep sitting and staring at the sky. His whole meditation was being the sky, nothing else. He only needed one sentence as a means to connect. His mind was connecting to the sky continuously. The sky means expansion – a blue sky, a cloudless sky. Over time, he spontaneously shifted into *shyambhavi mudra*[27], and he expanded beyond the body. It was during this time that he met his Guru, Atmananda. He was sitting near a shop and staring at the sky, as was his usual practice when *Gurudeva* walked past him. *Gurudeva* just looked at him, didn't say a word, but with his eyes indicated that he should join him. Srinath immediately followed *Gurudeva* and never left him. He saw the sky in *Gurudeva* – his Guru had the form and the vastness of the sky. All his life, *Gurudeva* only gave him his presence – no guidance. When Srinath found the Master, he realised that when the *Avadhoota* told him that his path was the sky, he meant that his Master was the sky, without boundaries.

---

[27] *eyebrow center gazing gesture*

He would be sitting like a statue, almost like *Gurudeva*. He was an introvert and rarely spoke. Whenever anyone asked, 'When will *Gurudeva* wake up?' or 'Is there something you can do?' he would stare back blankly. So, he was completely ignored by everyone for people realised that there was no point in talking to him. They would tease him and make fun of him. But that did not bother him. Whatever *Gurudeva* asked him to do, he did it promptly without thinking whether it was the right time, right place, or the right situation. No questions asked, and no thought or reasoning before carrying out the command. If *Gurudeva* had asked him to jump off a mountain, he would have. He was a personification of obedience.

Usually, *Gurudeva* never performed any rituals. However, sometimes he would light a fire and make some offerings. It would be for someone in some part of the universe, but he never explained why he was doing it. For instance, he would take food in his hand and offer it to the fire because someone was probably hungry somewhere, or something was meant to happen elsewhere. Once, during one of those rare occasions when *Gurudeva* was performing a ritual, he asked Srinath to take a bath in the river and come back immediately. The river was overflowing, and it was hazardous to enter the river since one would just get swept away by the surging waters. That did not deter Srinath at all. He just jumped into the river and was pulled into the gushing waters. He was dragged many kilometres away before he could manage to swim to the river bank. From there, he ran all the way to reach *Gurudeva* just as he was finishing the ritual. People asked him if he was mad to jump into a river when it was in full spate, but he did not answer, he just smiled.

When *Gurudeva* sat under the tree before taking *mahasamadhi*, Srinath also sat under there. Their consciousness merged, and he became like a shadow of *Gurudeva* by the time *Gurudeva* left the body. *Gurudeva* had taken over, removed whatever karma was left in balance, and had dissolved Srinath. Soon after *Gurudeva* took *mahasamadhi*, Srinath also left his body in about two weeks. Just as *Gurudeva* had done before taking *mahasamadhi*, he also sat under the tree and stopped eating and drinking. By that time, he must have reached high levels of *samadhi*[28]. But no one knows. Since he never articulated, never displayed himself, never tried to prove anything.

Gurudeva had another follower, Kalikananda who had tremendous suppressed anger like a volcano inside him. *Gurudeva* kept him close to himself without permitting any eruption! He had met *Gurudeva* in Varanasi. He didn't travel with *Gurudeva* further and settled down in Varanasi. He followed *aghori*[29] practices centered on the Divine Mother. He was daring and fearless and a good *sadhaka*. This suited his orientation and he had been engaged in these practices before he met *Gurudeva*. He moved to the cemetery and engaged in intense practices. He became very powerful and acquired many siddhis. Eventually, Kalikananda became a proper *Avadhoota* like *Gurudeva*.

Then there was the *brahmin* priest, Raghavacharya, who followed our *Gurudeva* for a brief period of time. This was when I had joined his group. Raghavacharya was around sixty years old and hailed from the southern region of Andhra Pradesh or Karnataka. He was also a wandering *sadhaka* who found it convenient to follow *Gurudeva* for a while. He was well versed with the scriptures and was one of the few people who understood *Gurudeva's* state of an *Avadhoota* and sometimes explained its nuances to us.

---

[28] *Higher states of consciousness*
[29] *an intense and radical form of spiritual practice*

When people gave Atmananda money, he would typically give it to someone next to him and ask him to buy something for everyone. On one such occasion, he gave me the money and asked me to buy food for everyone. There were twelve to thirteen people in our travelling group at that time. The money was sufficient to purchase dry rations and vegetables for cooking a meal for everyone. I had managed to get almost twice the quantity that one can usually buy with the same amount of money and was very pleased with my achievement. I handed over the material to Raghavacharya who was assigned the task of preparing the food. He was very disciplined, punctual, and always insistent on doing the right thing. He was puzzled by the amount of surplus food. He enquired how I managed to get so much food material for the amount of money given to me by *Gurudeva*. He even asked me if I had taken some provisions without the vendor's knowledge. I assured him that I had not stolen anything but had legitimately bargained with the street vendors to get the most material for the given money.

He was upset and told me that *Gurudeva* never negotiated with poor people as a rule. On the contrary, he would take less and give them more money than was due. He would also help them sell their wares. These people were poor and were merely earning just enough for sustenance. They were not accumulating money for pleasure, leisure, or luxury, but were eking a living from the daily sale of produce. Hence, *Gurudeva* felt that exploiting them was wrong. Raghavacharya also emphasised that our *Gurudeva* was a true *Avadhoota* and was never concerned about the future. Hence, getting more than what was required for the current meal displayed a lack of faith in the Tradition that always provides.

Raghavacharya insisted that I return the excess food to the street vendors. I was embarrassed and reluctant to go back and do it.

Raghavacharya said if I was a true devotee of *Gurudeva*, I ought to obey his instructions. I thought about it and decided to go and return the excess material; it would be the right thing to do. The vendors were surprised by my gesture. They asked me to keep the provisions since they loved *Gurudeva* and considered it an offering to him. I informed them that as per the law of *dharma*, I could only take what was due. As per their *dharma*, they could offer it directly to *Gurudeva*. I knew that they would not be able to come to meet *Gurudeva* as they could not leave the market. They reluctantly agreed to take the items back, although they had given them for *Gurudeva* in all sincerity. This was a learning lesson for me, I decided I would not bargain with small street vendors hereafter.

Once, a group of us including Srinath were travelling in Tamil Nadu, in south India. At this time, *Gurudeva* was mostly silent. We came across a Shiva temple and decided to take darshan of the Lord. We walked along the corridor and reached the sanctum sanctorum of Lord Shiva. There were several smaller temples in a circular structure outside it. Just as we were about to enter, *Gurudeva* asked us to stop and to follow him. He headed to the entrance. We came across an old abandoned *Shiva* kept on one side of the corridor. It was an ancient structure and was not well maintained. *Gurudeva* instructed all of us to bow down and take Lord Shiva's blessings. Someone asked if we should go to the sanctum sanctorum and offer our prayers there as well. *Gurudeva* tersely replied, "Not required. The Lord of the temple met us here."

As we were walking out of the temple, some people working in the temple asked us why we worshipped only the old Shiva *linga*. *Gurudeva*, as usual, did not say anything. We explained that we were following our *Gurudeva's* instructions. The people from the temple told our group that this was the original Shiv *linga* of the temple. It had been a while since they had installed the new Shiva *linga*[30] and performed its *prana-pratistha*[31]. Not many people knew about this. We now understood why he mostly sat outside the temple when he went to pay respects at big temples. Rarely did he go inside. We realised that when an *Avadhoota* visits a temple, the Lord of the temple comes out to receive him where it is suitable. *Gurudeva* preferred not to disturb the deities. In this temple, Lord Shiva probably wanted to meet *Gurudeva* at an isolated location. We realised that our temples are not merely places of worship but places of power and rejuvenation. Further, *prana-pratistha* is a real process. Those who have the vision to see will see and feel the presence of the deity. That is why we should respect our Hindu temples.

Gurudeva also said, "No hearts connected to consciousness will starve for presence." I have experienced this truth many times. Once, before I started wandering with my *Gurudeva*, I got entangled in an argument with a group of people over a trivial matter. I was about to get beaten up because of my aggressive attitude. I had only met *Gurudeva* only twice until then, over a period of a few years. As usual, he had shown indifference, rather, my ego considered it indifference instead of it being a test of endurance, and I had decided not to meet him anymore.

When this particular incident happened, the young ruffians were all set to beat me up. Suddenly, I saw *Gurudeva* walking in and with a firm voice said, "Stop, this is my follower, leave him alone." The people who were trying to beat me froze and then retreated. *Gurudeva* looked into my eyes and said, "Mahendra, come." I have no idea how he knew my real name. We never spoke, and I had

[30] *A divine symbol of Lord Shiva*
[31] *a ritual where the energies of the presiding deity are induced into the idol*

never given him any personal details. Anyway, he started walking, and I followed him. That was the first step of my journey with him. I never left him after that. It amazes me when I think how he came to be present at that spot during my critical moment. Later, I realised that his seeming indifference is only a mask. He is well aware and well in control of everything that is happening around him and beyond, especially in the lives of people who connect with him with love and honesty.

Gurudeva was an epitome of freedom. Listen to him in profound silence. You will hear his words echoing from deep inside. "When you think you are something, it is ridiculous. When you say you are nothing, that is ridiculous, too. When you realise you are nothing, you start experiencing freedom. Beyond personal identifications and frames lies the truth of existence."

It is beautiful to watch someone who wants nothing from earth, while walking the earth. We start to look with total detachment and even indifference towards the desires people who we see around us, or who have come to our *Gurudeva* for blessing them with money, name, fame, possessions, etc. *Gurudeva*, detached as he was from himself, would sometimes look at them, and sometimes ignore them. He deliberately wore the robe of a powerless, often eccentric, ordinary *sadhu*, which must have saved him from various greedy people.

One might think that proximity to a powerful *Avadhoota* like my *Gurudeva* meant that we got to discuss deeper levels of spirituality all the time. On the contrary, we hardly spoke about spiritual matters. I found it to be the same when *Gurudeva* met other powerful Masters. They discussed nothing spiritual. To me, the meeting of two Masters felt like two suns merging to give more light. No medium or words were needed. If you get a chance to stay with liberated Masters, make sure that you observe, but don't imitate them. Imitating them only gives us certain character traits or habits. Observing them provides us with detachment and awareness of perfect love in action.

ATMANANDA'S WORDS OF WISDOM

Rarely do we get to discuss something spiritual with *Gurudeva*. It sometimes happens as a reflection of someone's visit. Once he said that Buddha had said, 'The human tongue is more dangerous than a sword as it leaves lasting wounds. The tongue injures people more than a sword and the injuries are harder to heal.' We could understand that most of life's calamities are created by relative truths or partial truths translated by prejudiced and speculative minds and articulated by our boneless tongues. This reminds me of various beautiful things that Buddha has said which perfectly suited our *Gurudeva's* level of existence.

"The most distant place for us is our past. No amount of money or time can take us there."

"The biggest, highest and tallest mountain in this world is human lust. Nothing is more difficult to conquer for the human mind than lust."

"The hardest thing to keep in this world is a tiny promise. Things are easier said than done. If promises are not delivered, man takes more lives too, to complete it. Hence promises are quite detrimental. If unfulfilled, it increases karmic weight."

"The quality that makes one feel lightest in this world is humility which comes out of maturity and awareness. There is nothing lighter to mind than humility. When man chases name, fame and fortune, this is lost."

"The closest to us is death. Death is closer to us than any human relationship and is the only unavoidable relationship."

"The easiest thing to do for liberating oneself in this world is to spread the message of our loving Guru while spreading love with our very existence unconditionally. Your personal wealth has nothing to do with it. If you are afraid to talk about your Guru who gave you himself, you are a hypocrite. Grace will not enter your doorway. Hypocrisy prevents grace."

One day, after he spent time with an aloof, wandering *sadhu*, *Gurudeva* said, "We all are liars. We are lying all the time. Whenever I say I am Atmananda, I am lying. This body is called Atmananda. I am not. Whenever people talk with identifications, all of which are temporary, they are lying because whatever is temporary is not the ultimate truth. Look around you – no animal will tell you that it is a bull or a monkey. They are not bound by their incarnations. We are so eager to maintain our ego and identifications. Whenever we begin to articulate who we are in terms of terrestrial existence, we are further and further detaching from the original truth.

Hence, we must realise that we are all liars, glorious liars who love to maintain those lies and are even proud of it. I am not an *Avadhoota*, I am not even Atmananda. These are all identifications that society has given me for its own sake about my state and form. This is its need and not mine. I am free. Likewise, we identify ourselves with fleeting emotions and make them ours. We are not our emotions either. We are free. Until this is understood, there will be pain."

On another occasion, when a village head came to see *Gurudeva* with some *dakshina*, he asked him to talk about his Guru. *Gurudeva* just looked blankly at the sky and said, 'How can I ever praise the glory of my Guru? I can never fathom him. Nobody can know him. My limited intellect cannot measure his dimensions. It is only his grace that gets revealed within me as an awareness of his presence. I am far too insignificant to know his stature. Nothing can describe him. He is truly unfathomable.'

He stopped, thought for a while and continued, 'He is hotter than the raging fire. Cooler than the coolest breeze. Brighter than a million suns. Faster than flashes of lightning. Louder than a thousand drums of thunder. He is more innocent than a newborn child. He is purer than the purest. He is action in inaction. He is my mother, father and all the kin put together. He has no father, mother, beginning or end. The whole manifested universe is nothing but a mole on his glorious face. He is unfathomable. He is free. He is not bound by the universe and the universe is not bound by him. He is freedom. He is bliss. He is myself.'

That sums up the stature of my *Gurudeva*. I humbly submit this at his Lotus Feet.

CHAPTER 7

BORN OF FIRE

Gurudeva was unbound and free, neither bound to anything nor detached from it. He was in everything. He treated a human and a non-human with equal respect. He had command over the weather and the elements, which he seldom displayed. He would walk in the rain and thunder while we knew that he could either choose a shelter or even stop the frenzy of the rain. When we pestered him to wait until the weather cleared, he would say, 'Do not disturb the elements.' I later realised that we should not interfere in the eternal flow of nature, even if we have the power to do so, and also to keep our internal elements in harmony for a good life without excesses.

Gurudeva was once bathing in a river along with his followers. Standing completely naked facing the river, he was washing his few belongings – a loincloth and a length of cloth that served as a towel. He usually tied the cloth around his waist. He owned nothing else other than a vessel and a small cloth bag. One of his five followers, who was next to him, said, 'Maharaj, people are watching you.' *Gurudeva* turned around, looked, and laughed, 'To see what?' He muttered, 'Foolish people. Senses drag their mind, and they are total slaves of senses. What can they see? Nothing!' Unaffected, he washed his clothes, tied the wet clothes around his waist and climbed up to the river bank. He sat down on a rock, away from people, faced the rising sun, and meditated, totally absorbed and oblivious to the movements around him. Time went by. *Gurudeva* continued to meditate.

As the day progressed, the rock started becoming hot. *Gurudeva* was still in his state of *samadhi*. His followers stood around him until the external heat became unbearable, and the fire of hunger started heating them from within. Finally, one of the followers who was called Panduranga approached *Gurudeva* and whispered in his ear, 'Deva, the rock is burning hot. It may affect your body. Please get up.' *Gurudeva* slowly opened his eyes and looked at his followers who were struggling to stand barefoot next to him, unable to bear the heat of the rocks.

He smiled, 'If you are born from fire, no Sun can burn you. I am born from fire.' Then he stood up and started walking. A few steps later, he turned to Panduranga and said, 'Be the fire. That is the secret. Nothing can ever burn you. Nothing in life can dampen you – this is the unquenchable fire of the spirit, the fire of our tradition, the white fire!' Panduranga could not understand, he humbly requested his *Gurudeva* to explain. *Gurudeva* casually said, "Your body is made of elements. Be one with the elements when you are in your body, and you will remain in equanimity with nature. Be one with all elements and they cannot hurt you. Only when you alienate yourself from the very elements that you are made of, does your body suffer. Imbalance in elements causes diseases. So beware!"

Once Gurudeva was walking with a few people through a forest pathway between two villages. Gurudeva had been invited to speak at a small temple in the next village. The temple had a clearing like a ground in front of it, with a river next to the ground. It was a small temple near the river with no wall or much paraphernalia. It had a podium where people used to give discourses. The discourses were attended by the people from the surrounding villages. The temple was on the other side of the forest pathway. A fire had broken out in that area and the place including the forest pathway, was still smouldering. A follower requested Gurudeva to avoid crossing the pathway since they would get burnt. Gurudeva said, "Don't worry. Follow me." and walked through the pathway. They followed him and crossed over to the other side safely. When they looked back, they could see burning embers and fire all over the pathway. They wondered how they managed to cross the pathway without getting injured.

He had no need for food because he had no hunger. However, he took responsibility to arrange food for the people who were with him He would somehow ensure that food was available. Sometimes, people observed that he manifested food whenever it was unavailable.

At other times, he would create a dearth of food for a few days to test the people following him and create circumstances for those who were not ready, to leave.

Usually, Atmananda was not affected by the elements. But when it is inconvenient, he could stop anything, He had stopped rain many times, especially early morning rains. He always took a bath in the morning, irrespective of the weather or natural conditions. Usually, he took a bath alone. Unless invited, his followers never took a dip with him. Sometimes, he would signal at them to join and they would enter with him. Sometimes, it would be raining heavily and the river would be swollen. He wouldn't care. If he decided to take a bath, he would take a bath. He would ensure that he took a minimum of three dips and come out. People around him would be afraid that he would get washed away. Some would say, "Don't go. It's dangerous."

He would ignore them and proceed despite the warnings. He did not like being controlled by people and their fears. When he would enter the river, the rain would drizzle and the water would be calm almost like a tub or a pond. He would dip, wash his body and come out wet and completely drenched. As soon as he stepped out, the torrential rain would resume, the river would start rushing past, flooded with whirlpools and floating debris. It would the same as before. This surprised many people and they wondered, "Was this real or an illusion? Did he take a bath?" These questions would come to their mind. He was very understated and never made a show. Those who observed keenly would notice. The rest would be blissfully unaware of what happened.

I was also very fortunate to get a glimpse that Gurudeva existed well beyond the boundaries of earth. That left me in awe. One evening at a sanctuary near a forest clearing, all were asleep. I had left Gurudeva near the fire that he kept burning whenever he could. He would sit there the whole night looking into the fire. Fire is a symbol of existence in non-existence, as it easily converts any matter into ash. Where Gurudeva was sitting, I saw that it was just fire. There was no form of my beloved Gurudeva. There was just fire, a mild fire. I realised at that moment that Gurudeva is definitely not the finite body. He could easily convert himself into any of the elements that constituted the body. At that moment, he had dissolved all elements and had become just fire to talk to the external fire.

These stories reveal the nature of true saints who need nothing but are fully contented. People are never satisfied - no contentment or satisfaction. Here we have someone who's breezing through life with no demand, fully confident like a king. He doesn't care. He walks free, but at the same time fully conscious. He has control over the elements and has controlled his own mind. Unlike, a ruler who is a slave to his own greed, lust, temptations, desires, and so on, Atmananda is a true emperor who enlightens people and raises them to his stature.

SECTION 4

The Eternal Wings of a Grand Tradition

*"In the lap of a Grand Tradition,
life eternally flows."*

CHAPTER 1

AN ENCOUNTER WITH AN AGELESS SAINT OF THE HIMALAYAS

Two *brahmins* in their early fifties from the banks of river Nila in Kerala recounted this story. They discovered an ageless saint on their pilgrimage to the Himalayas. After visiting many shrines, they reached Badrinath where they met this saint. During their stay in Badrinath, they visited the saint several times, conversed with him in detail, and collected random fragments of his story. He did not narrate his life story chronologically but cited many incidents from his past as examples to prove his point during their conversations. This provided them with enough details to paint a broad picture of his life and journey, starting from his childhood as a young boy called Raman. There are three parts to Raman's life journey: The first part – leaving his home town, meeting a *brahmin* priest and staying in his house for a few years where he learnt Sanskrit and *mantras*. The second part – meeting Atmananda, and the third part – leaving Atmananda and the lone journey to Badrinath.

It was afternoon, and the Badrinath temple was closed after the midday rituals. The two *brahmins* were tired and hungry after the long journey. The high altitude, low oxygen, lack of food, and general fatigue made them feel quite ill. The temple would open only four hours later. A guard, recognising them as *brahmins*, guided the weary travellers to the nearby house of the temple's chief priest. When they arrived at the priest's home, he had finished his lunch and was about to have his afternoon siesta. Still, he welcomed them and enquired about their trip. They briefly spoke about their journey and their intention to stay in Badrinath for a week. The priest asked them if he could assist in any way. They hesitated to tell the priest that they were hungry and tired. They politely declined, saying that they would certainly contact him if need be.

They got up to leave so the priest could rest. As they reached the door, he called them back and said, "There is an old saint who belongs to your hometown who lives nearby. Would you like to meet him?" There was no place they would find anything to eat, and they had nothing else to do. Hence, they decided to spend some time with the saint until the temple opened for worship. The priest requested one of the guards to guide them to the saint. The guard took them to the banks of river Alakananda. Badrinath is at the height of twelve thousand feet, nestled in the mighty Himalayas. Covered with a thick blanket of snow in winter, the cold is biting. The visitors were shivering despite their winter clothing. As they crossed the bridge across Alakananda, the guard looked down at the flowing river and exclaimed, "There he is!"

They could not believe what they saw. A lean old man, wearing only a loincloth, was bathing in the freezing waters of the river. It was impossible to bathe in the river at that temperature. They reached the other side of the river and waited for the saint to complete his ablutions. He seemed least affected by the freezing waters, the cold breeze, or the extreme weather conditions. He was walking barefoot over the stones in the water as though it was a bed of roses. As he approached them, the guard explained that the two *brahmins* were from his hometown and were sent by the temple priest to meet him.

Saints usually have nothing to do with their life before taking *sannyasa*. However, the saint smiled and beckoned them to approach. His loincloth dripped icy water. He had a stick in his hand and a *kamandalu* pot that was filled with water from the river. He looked at them. His eyes were sharp and penetrating. He looked very old with his flowing white hair and white beard, at least a hundred years old. Yet, his eyes shone youthfully. The guard took their leave. The saint started walking and asked the two of them to follow him. They reached a small hut. The saint entered, asked them to come and be seated. They sat on the floor, which was surprisingly warm.

He looked at them and asked, "Are you thirsty?" They both said, "Yes". He gave them a few drops of water from his pot and asked them to drink. They thought that this was some kind of initiation or purification. But, as soon as they swallowed those few drops of water, they felt something shift in them. They no longer felt cold and thirsty. Then he asked, "Are you hungry too?" They said that they were hungry as they had not eaten for many hours. He smiled and again gave them each a few drops of water. They swallowed it. Suddenly, their hunger vanished, and they felt sated. They were greatly surprised.

Even though a saint whom they had previously met had taught them a *mantra* to conquer thirst and hunger, it had not been very useful for these seekers. They said, "Lord, you have effectively conquered the need for eating and drinking. You have demonstrated your divine powers to us. Tell us, who are you? You belong to our hometown. What is the purpose of our meeting? Why did we meet? We are both curious to know more about you." The saint laughed and said, "I believe you have been chanting certain *mantras* to control the urge for food. What happened? Why couldn't you control your mind through your practices?" They knew that he could see everything; nothing was hidden from him. "Yes," they replied, "we have been chanting the *mantra* focusing on the respective *chakras*. But our mind was wandering, and we could not make much progress."

The saint laughed again and said, "If you walk up the Himalayas one step at a time, your body will get accustomed to the changing oxygen levels and the weather situation at each level. Why are all of you trying to speed up in your powered vehicles, when all matter needs time to settle into your system? Everything needs duration and space to provide the maximum benefit. Everything needs time. Unfortunately, most people are in a mad rush, searching, chasing something, and they do not even know what that is. How can you achieve spiritual progress? Patience, flexibility, adaptability, acceptance, determination, the dedication to one single path of your choice, and the consistency to follow it against all the odds, are vital for success in spiritual pursuit. Most people change their Guru, rather than change their thinking." He laughed.

They understood that he was referring to their impatience in the spiritual journey. They had been meeting many saints and sages trying to speed up their *sadhana* while ignoring the critical aspect, their capacity and eligibility for higher learning. They had not been concentrating on developing this essential factor. Instead, they were following their shifting mind, falling at the feet of many saints, expecting quicker elevation without any hard work or the removal of their internal trash of lifetimes! Since their capacity and eligibility did not grow at the same pace as their travel, they had not made much progress. Most *mantras* or *sadhanas* that they had picked up on their journey did not ensure any advancement either. They had met many saints in the past, but this old saint truly fascinated them.

Swamiji said, "Drop what you know. You are carrying a heavy burden of undigested knowledge and age-old *samskaaras*."

"*Swamiji*, what can we drop?" the two priests asked.

"Drop everything. All that you need will be yours, anyway. You 'need' nothing. All that you think you have, you do not have. It will all wither away sooner or later. All that you give away, you will always have. Spirituality never ends with one incarnation of the soul. It continues through time and space, as long as it should. You are covering yourself more than necessary. Shed your coverings. Do not hide; do not hide your real face. Be bold enough to be yourself. You will experience reality. When clothes become an addiction, we become unnatural."

They paused to digest the hidden meaning behind the saint's answer before asking, "*Swamiji*, who will protect us from this cold and *tamasic* ignorance?"

"Existence!" replied *Swamiji*. "Are you feeling cold now?" he asked them. They realised that they were not feeling cold at all. *Swamiji* continued, "Who is protecting you from the cold now? The same existence will protect you from *tamas* and ignorance too. You are not the doer."

They contemplated those words, and still feeling insecure about their future, asked, "*Swamiji*, we feel afraid to shed anything at all."

Swamiji laughed. "If you are afraid, go home. You are just infants. You need protection. Spirituality is not for you. You will need more maturity to earn spirituality. Fear has no meaning here. Fear cannot exist here." *Swamiji* paused for a while and continued, "You are hiding your fears within your clothing. Escapism is the opposite of spirituality. The two cannot co-exist."

Swamiji looked at one of them straight into his eyes and said, "Family tree is becoming thinner and thinner; no offspring; conducted many rituals to beget a child; everything in vain; *kaala sarpa dosha!*"[32]

Traditionally, *Brahmins* have worshipped snake gods along with many other deities. Almost every family used to have a temple for snakes in their yard. With nuclear families, people became less religious, or grossly ignorant of reasons behind the patterns of worship, and worship abruptly stopped. The adverse effects of this lack of connectivity started appearing in families in the form of unnatural deaths, lack of children, lack of marriage, and disharmony in relationships. Similarly, family deities were once a part of every family. They did not appear by themselves. The ancestors brought them for protection and grace. The ancestors of the family invoked and installed the deities to protect them, their heirs, their property and wealth, in return for the promise to honour and respect them at all times. Hence, the deities can be compared to guests. These customs were handed down through generations. When subsequent generations stopped honouring them and taking care of them, it was like insulting one's guests by removing their bedding and resting space. Many families can still experience the repercussions.

---

[32] *severe curse of the snake gods*

He asked, "But *Swamiji*, what is the reason for *kaala sarpa dosha*?"

Swamiji said, "Ingratitude, my son. Snakes on earth are of two types. Earthly snakes that are gross and predominantly *tamasic*; and divine entities who took the form of snakes for agility and isolation. You will never mess with a snake, right? That is why they chose that form. Humans have been closely associated with the divine entities that exist in the form of snakes. We have co-existed with them for a long time. We used to respect and worship them. They have their *loka* (realm or sphere of existence). They have come here out of compassion for us, the ignorant ones. They brought us to higher awareness and showed us the dimensions of the Supreme Father in three aspects - *srishti* (creation), *stithi* (preservation) and *samhara* (dissolution). They introduced us to the power and force behind these three aspects of our existence – the Trinity. They showed us the path of higher spirituality. They also protected us, as they protect and support the deities that they introduced to us.

We gave them a special place in our garden, close to nature, with the promise that we would not disturb their peace and, in return, they would bless us with a good life. Subsequent generations went back on our promises and destroyed the noble snakes and their abodes. We cheated them and killed them. We destroyed their homes and built our houses on them. We started to suffer their pain and agony in our lives, in our families. Whenever we hurt someone by our thoughts, words or actions, we hurt ourselves. We get hurt more with the violence that we unleash, deeply within our consciousness and life. This is called *kaala sarpa dosha*. We have systematically abused and destroyed all beings that showed us the true path and quite sadly, have consistently glorified those who are just glitter to our eyes! Higher snakes represent the protection and presence of divinity on earth.

Lord Vishnu rests on Anantha, the serpent. Lord Shiva has snakes as his garland. Vasuki, the snake king, was used, instead of a rope, to churn the ocean of milk for *amrit* (the celestial nectar). No celestial rope could have equalled Vasuki's strength! The snake represents both the *Kundalini shakti* (divine feminine energy) that lies dormant in every human as three and a half coils, as well as the movement of the sun and moon *naadis* up towards the *sahasraara*[33]. They represent flexibility and ascension. Snakes have an essential role in our spirituality. They brought us the highest wisdom and performed the duty of protectors. The usual signs of *kaala sarpa dosha* are childlessness, a fewer number of children, divorce, lack of marriage, and marital problems. We need to respect snakes. Continued ingratitude will pull us down further."

One of the *brahmins* asked him, "*Swamiji*, you belong to our home town. Do you have family there?"

Swamiji thought for a while and said, "No family, but I used to have some friends. Perhaps you might know them." *Swamiji* mentioned the names of a few people and their family names. Their family names were familiar to the visitors. It dawned on them that these people had died a few centuries ago, and their fourth or fifth generation descendants were currently part of those families. They were shocked to realise that *Swamiji* was born in 1600. He was almost three hundred and seventy years old! They told the saint, "*Swamiji*, these people who were your friends are no more now. Their fourth and fifth-generation members are our contemporaries." *Swamiji* thought for a while and said, "Well, I am an old man. Sometimes, I forget the speed with which time moves. I am glad their lineage continues." He mentioned it so casually, as

---

[33] *the crown chakra – the energy center at the crown of the head*

though his longevity was something ordinary. The visitors could not believe it and continued to stare at the old saint with mixed emotions.

Swamiji asked, "You are *brahmins,* isn't it time for your evening rituals?"

They looked at each other. They had not been following the *brahminic* rituals sincerely. They were sure that *Swamiji* was referring to their insincerity in adhering to the *dharma* of their inheritance. *Swamiji* said, "Being born in a *brahmin* family is like marrying *dharma* by choice, beyond one's *karma.* You, as *brahmins,* have inherited the *sattvic dharma* of serving society, imparting knowledge, and elevating the consciousness of mankind. If you do not follow your path, what other paths will you follow? *Swadharma*[34] is very important for everyone. *Dharma* is as important as *karma.* Never forget that *brahmanism* should be nurtured through purity of thought, word, and action as well as selflessness and non-violence in all aspects. Being born in a *brahmin* family or wearing a sacred thread will not make you a true *brahmin.* Live as one, in all sincerity."

There was silence. The saint said, "Go now. Take a bath and worship Lord Badrinath. Come back tomorrow, and we shall talk again." They reluctantly got up and left. Amazement filled their minds. They did not feel any cold, hunger, or thirst but felt wholly rejuvenated. They no longer felt any fatigue.

Many questions churned in their mind. Who was this remarkable saint? From where had he come? They decided to return to know more.

---

[34] *one's dharma by birth*

CHAPTER 2

THE INEVITABLE JOURNEY TO THE HIMALAYAS

After the two visitors left the old saint, they were in a daze, lost in thoughts. They did not speak to each other for a long time. The saint had subtly inspired them to follow their *dharma* and stick to one path to attain spiritual progress. He performed, in front of them, great siddhis without any pretension, pomp, or splendour. He made no effort to impress them, nor did he expect anything from them. All the attractions from the material world which they could offer him were of no interest to this semi-naked saint. "Is he a saint of the *Navnath* tradition?", they wondered. It did not matter which path he followed. It only mattered where he had reached. He had indeed reached 'home' or was very close to it.

They managed to find a place to stay, took a bath in the *Tapt Kund* (hot water spring), and attended the evening prayers. They were functioning in a semi-conscious state. Their mind was elsewhere. They felt as if they had found the teacher they had been seeking since several lifetimes. Many thoughts crossed their minds. They mused. Would he accept them as his disciples? Were they eligible? And what about their family back home? It is not easy to detach from the world. The mind wants to, but one's responsibilities compel one to lead a worldly life. Everyone cannot be a *Siddhartha*[35] to be able to abandon one's family in search of the truth.

With their minds in turmoil, the travellers managed to sleep for a few hours. Despite the bitter cold and the strange environment, they felt very energetic without sensations of hunger or thirst. It was magical. At around 4 a.m., they heard sounds from outside their room, sounds of people walking and chanting. They also got up, took a dip in the *Tapt Kund* again and felt much better. They went to the temple for the early morning worship. At daybreak, they started walking towards the saint's dwelling. When they arrived there, he was chanting some *mantras* and performing a fire ceremony. They waited until he finished. After the rituals, he invited them to sit near the fire to warm and purify themselves in its proximity. They bowed down to the fire, took some sacred ash from it, and reverentially applied it on their foreheads. They were keen to hear of the saint's journey from the south of India to Badrinath in the Himalayas and imbibe some wisdom.

To break the ice and initiate a conversation, they asked, "*Swamiji*, during winter, Badrinath is usually covered in ice, do you continue to stay here or do you go down to the lower regions of the Himalayas?" *Swamiji* laughed, "What have I got to do with the elements? Why will they bother me? I go nowhere. I am an old man. I stay here. How can any ice dampen my fire?" He pointed to the fire before them. They understood the hidden meaning. The fire that he referred to was the fire of spirituality. Ice, for him, was a distraction from his path. No distractions could conquer his single-pointed, dedicated, spiritual life, because the single force that creates all distractions, the Mind, did not exist in him! He was

---

[35] *Gautama Buddha's name before he renounced and left home*

always in a 'no mind' state. Thus, Maya or delusion could not exist, either. He was in total control of himself and the external elements. It was clear that distractions had no room in his life.

They thought about how people chase rainbows, and when they get closer, it is nothing but water vapour! People have always been falling in the trap of mirages. Here they were, before a saint who had nothing to do with illusions, distractions, delusions, or rainbows. He sat there in his old body like a rock or a pillar on the path of spirituality, laughing at those who chase images and words and get lost when both images and words decay and disappear. What a world of pomposity, such wasted lives! How many lifetimes have we chased rainbows and stayed ignorant of our folly! God alone knows!

They asked, "*Swamiji*, how did you reach here?"

Swamiji laughed again and said, "How does it matter? Everyone has a story as you do. No two stories are alike. All stories are insignificant as every life is inimitable, distinct, and unique, and lives keep flowing through time into eternity. The past of this body has no value for me or you, just like your past. If you can carry something from me now, at this moment, do so. I am here to give. This moment is your only reality."

They didn't know how or what to carry, as they didn't know their requirements or their capacities. They mused, "What a situation! Here is a saint who is capable of giving us everything we would ever need, he is asking us what we would want from him, and we do not even know what we want! If Lord Badrinath Himself came before us and offered a boon, what would we request? This is the naked truth of our existence; we do not know what we need."

Finally, they said, "Bless us, *Swamiji*, so that we do not fall into traps on the spiritual path."

"*Tathasthu!* (So be it)", said *Swamiji* and continued, "Abandon dependency on siddhis, as though they do not exist at all; as you may gain them when you progress spiritually. Respect siddhis and live without any attachment towards them, and you will stay liberated. Siddhis often bind a person and prevent his spiritual elevation. The lure of siddhis can also instigate, in your mind, the presence of the eight most powerful and extremely dangerous enemies of human existence, and especially on the path of spirituality. Those are *kaama* (terrestrial ambition), *krodha* (anger), *lobha* (greed), *moha* (attachment), *mada* (lust), *matsarya* (competition), *ahankara* (pride), *asooya* (jealousy). They are like invisible cancer that usually binds and destroys human beings from within. Always beware of these enemies. Always stay rooted in truth and non-violence in all aspects of your life, and keep supreme faith."

Swamiji's story follows.

CHAPTER 3

GO TO THE NORTH.
DO NOT LOOK BACK.

On February 23, 1600, on the banks of the elegant river Nila in the southern part of India, in a small house, at around midnight, a baby boy was born. He was called Raman. His parents were poor *brahmins*. He was to be their first-born and only child. Raman's father was a priest in a nearby temple. It was a small temple, and his income consisted of nothing more than a single meal or a few coins, which the worshippers offered him. He and his family had to subsist on very little food and no money. He had a tiny house with a mango tree and two coconut trees in the small yard. They somehow managed their life that way, as Raman was growing up.

The child had never been exposed to any luxuries, which the neighbourhood feudal lords of their community enjoyed. Raman's mother used to customarily visit the affluent families during celebrations or festivals, and they would give her some food and clothing. Being a true and *sattvic brahmin*, Raman's father would get up at 3 a.m. every morning, take a dip in the nearby river, go straight to the temple in wet clothes to preserve the sanctity of the temple and its deity. The temple was just a narrow lane away from his house. One morning, while he was climbing the stone steps from the river, he felt a slight pain in his chest. He ignored it and continued walking up, but before he could reach the temple, he collapsed and breathed his last. Since it was very early in the morning, there was nobody around. Hence, no one saw him fall. After dawn, news of the death of the noble priest spread. Raman was a little over three years old when his father died.

The child knew that something terribly wrong had happened in his house, but did not quite understand the depth or the implications of the tragedy. He saw his father 'sleeping' on the floor, watched by many. He could not understand why his father was sleeping during the daytime; this was something he had never witnessed before. He also could not understand why all of them were watching his father while he slept. For him, it meant nothing, because his father slept every night, just like he did, and nobody had been quite concerned about it thus far. It was quite different for his mother. With the sole breadwinner of their household gone, she did not know what she would do. Raman saw that his mother was weeping. She looked inconsolable. He slowly walked towards her and touched her hand. She hugged him and cried even more. She kept repeating, "Your father has gone forever. He has left us alone!" Little did Raman know that this was the beginning of a grossly uncertain life for both of them.

His father looked peaceful in his sleep. They had kept his body on the verandah of their house. The priests came and took his father's body a little distance away from their home. They had cut some branches of the mango tree to make a wooden frame, and had put his father's body on it. They bathed Raman, made him do some rituals and finally placed his father's body in the fire. Raman watched all this with no understanding of what was going on. He was quite disturbed when he saw his father's body caught in flames. Raman could not understand why his father, who was only sleeping, was being burnt. Deep sorrow welled inside him, and he burst out crying, even though he was too young to digest the gravity of the situation.

Many neighbourhood uncles and aunts who came to the funeral, tried to console him and his mother and expressed a lot of love before going back to their homes. They invited him and his mother to come to their homes after the customary mourning period was over. Soon after the death of his father, he and his mother started experiencing further poverty. There was no food at home. Being a *brahmin* woman, it was difficult for Raman's mother to find work, as social customs did not permit her to work in non-*brahmin* homes. It was not easy.

At that time, the caste system was prevalent in India. *Brahmin* women were not allowed to be seen in public, let alone work outside their homes. Likewise, people of other castes, especially those who consumed meat and fish, were not allowed to come near *brahmins*, who chanted *mantras* and performed rituals and systematically worshipped the deities in their own homes as well as in temples. The *brahmin* families also kept the sacred fire alive in their houses through generations. The system of untouchability between castes was introduced to preserve the sanctity of temples. Temples had deities or idols that were installed with sacred rituals that ensured *prana* existed in them, and their power had to be maintained. The power of the deities was maintained and enhanced through prescribed methods of worship and *mantras*.

The flesh of animals was considered as dead, without any *prana*. Dead organisms were contradictory to *mantras* and defeated their very purpose. That is why *brahmins* kept themselves away from all those people who consumed flesh. For the same reason, some people were not even allowed to enter into temples. Rigid systems were made to ensure the sanctity and power of the deities in temples, and priests who were well educated in the proper worship pattern were chosen to perform their daily worship, which usually started during *brahma muhurtha*[36]. Priests were also expected to maintain high purity. Later, systems were abused, and untouchability became caste-based and discriminatory.

Raman's mother did not know what to do. Being born a *brahmin* became a curse for her. Those of other castes did not have any problem getting work in the paddy fields or as household maids at the houses of the wealthy landowners. She did not know how to make ends meet and bring up a small child. She visited relatives who lived in their neighbourhood. None showed any concern or any sincere intention to help her, except allowing the mother and son to join them for a meal if it happened to be mealtime. After a few visits, she stopped doing that. It did not do them any good, and it amounted to even more humiliation. She was worried about Raman and how he would feel. It was obvious that nobody would help them. All their offers for help during the funeral were false, and it became clear to her that they didn't mean it.

She still maintained some hope and tried to contact all their relatives, who lived near and far, through a farm worker who lived close by. This man was a good man, but since he was of a lower caste, he had his limitations. He was not even allowed to look at her or talk to her face to face. As was the custom, she always stood behind the door or the wall while conversing with him. He was sincere and always carried her letters to her relatives and also got back the replies from them. None of them wanted to help her, and

---

[36] *The time between 3 a.m. and 6 a.m. - the time of Brahma (heavenly time) – considered ideal time for spiritual practices*

everyone offered some excuse for not being in a position to help her and her son. A few sympathetically sent her some food or old clothes. This was only one-time assistance but, life had to go on.

The farmworker always brought Raman a fruit or a sweet whenever he came to their house. Even though it was not allowed to eat the food prepared or touched by a person of another caste, Raman and his mother were too poor and too hungry to care. His sincerity and love were unconditional and unmistakable, which deeply touched them. A few weeks after her husband's death, a distant aunt came to visit her. She was like a wandering monk who did not stay in one place for a long time. She was respected by society. She was in a distant place when Raman's father died, and when she heard the news, she decided to visit them. She was saddened by the plight of this family and deeply disappointed that all the other relatives turned a blind eye towards mother and son. She promptly took the initiative, talked to a wealthy local family and got Raman's mother a job in their house as domestic help.

Raman's mother began work there immediately. Since the wealthy family was from her community, it was acceptable. Raman also accompanied his mother to work, as she could not leave the child alone at home. There were many people in the house and many children too. They were good and kind people. Raman and his mother were treated well. They were given sufficient food, and nobody bothered them. When his mother was busy the household chores such as cooking, washing, or cleaning, Raman played with the other children of the house. They even shared their treats and toys with him. Raman and his mother finally found peace and happiness. It was a big relief for them after the uncertainty that they faced after Raman's father's death.

One day, the lady of the house announced to all the servants that her daughter's marriage had been finalised. She distributed new clothes to all of them and asked them to dress well on the day of the wedding. They were thrilled by this gesture. Raman also got new clothes. He was thrilled. He went running to his mother to show her his new possessions. She hugged him and wept in joy. Little did she know that this event would be a turning point in their lives.

As the date of the wedding approached, guests started arriving. The domestic workload increased tremendously. One day, as Raman's mother was cleaning the rooms on the first floor of the huge mansion, the bride's mother asked her to come inside her bedroom and have a look at the gold and precious stone jewellery purchased for the occasion. This was the first time Raman's mother was seeing such splendour and riches. She gave her a diamond necklace to hold. She marvelled at its beauty and resplendence, admired it, appreciated it and handed it back to the bride's mother. Not once did she feel that she too should have some ornaments like that. Raman's mother was a pious and level-headed woman. She knew the reality of her position. She neither craved for jewellery nor earthly riches. She went off to complete her chores.

Soon after lunch, she heard a great commotion in the house. People were rushing here and there. Someone said, "The diamond necklace is stolen!" She had touched it and felt it, so she knew that it was a precious one. They searched the whole house. They even called the police and questioned everyone, especially the servants. They even took some of them to the police station and beat them up to get to the truth. They took Raman's mother too, for the mother of the bride had told the police that Raman's mother had held the ornament in her hands for a few moments. She tried her best to convince everyone that she had not taken it. They checked her thoroughly. They checked her house. She was threatened, abused, and humiliated. "Where have you hidden the stolen material", they kept asking her. She cried and cried. She begged them to believe that she was innocent.

The necklace was not found. Finally, in frustration, they gave up. But the suspicion continued. A day before the wedding, she and Raman were asked to leave the house. She lost her job! She could not believe her fate. Raman could not understand what was going on, but he could figure out that his mother was in terrible distress. His innocent mind thought that she was crying because she had no gold jewellery to wear. He tried to console her as best as he could by telling her that when he grew up, he would work hard and buy lots of gold for her. This made her cry even more. It was not gold that she craved, it was just two meals a day for Raman, and that was all she wanted in life. She never cared for herself. How could she tell this to Raman? How could she make this child understand? She refused to sadden the young boy's heart and wiped her tears and pretended to be happy.

After the wedding, the elders of the community who supported the rich landowner decided to punish Raman's mother for stealing the jewellery, for they firmly believed that she had it and had cleverly concealed it somewhere. They issued a diktat, "Nobody should give this woman a job, food, or support of any kind. Nobody should give her medicines or clothing. No physician should treat her. She is hereafter excommunicated from society." All hopes had vanished. That day Raman's mother wanted to end her life, but she could not think of killing the six-year-old Raman. She decided to survive and keep him alive. Nobody in the village would assist an excommunicated woman since that could get them excommunicated. Fearing the wrath of the powerful landowners, none dared even to offer them a glass of water, let alone allow her to work in their farms or houses.

She started becoming weaker. She and Raman survived on whatever was available in their little property. They had no money and no support. Nobody even looked at them. This was more torturous than imprisonment for them. The farmworker who used to help them could not help them any more because of the excommunication order. He was helpless and angry, but he had his own family to consider, and he was afraid that his bold actions might adversely affect his wife and children. Everyone stayed away from them. Raman's mother started getting weaker and weaker and fell ill. Since no physician would treat her, she could not get any medicine. Despite that, she tried to collect fallen seeds and fruits from their yard and made at least one small meal for Raman every day. Raman also helped her as best as he could.

Her health deteriorated further, and she was too weak even to stand. She crawled slowly from one room to the other. Raman was too young to lift her. Still, he tried his best to help his ailing mother. Raman's mother knew that she would not live long. One night, she called Raman to her side. Raman saw tears rolling down her cheeks. She hugged him and said, "My son, I will leave you soon. I am sorry. I cannot stay in this body any longer. I am going to the place where your father has gone. But I cannot take you with me. I have always taken you wherever I have gone. Now, I must go alone. I will die soon. When I die, you alone will not be able to burn my body, as you and our relatives did, when your father died. You are too young. You have no money, and nobody will help you. If you can, drag my body up to the yard, push me into the pit there, and throw some soil on it. If you cannot do that, just leave me here, take this stick and this cloth sack, and walk towards the North."

"Go to the North. Do not look back." Those were the last words of that poor, innocent, and pious woman. She closed her eyes. Raman hugged her and put her head on his lap. He rested his head on her face. An hour or two passed. The boy thought his mother's face felt cold. She was straining to breathe. He poured some water into her mouth. She drank a little, and the rest of it spilt out of her mouth. She looked at his face one last time as if blessing him, and she passed away. Raman sat next to her, hugging his mother's body till dawn. He did not know what to do. He had become an orphan. There was nobody in his life anymore. He got up and sat on the verandah looking outside. Birds were chirping in the yard. Grazing animals looked at him. Did they comprehend his sorrow? He hoped and wished that someone would look at him. Nobody looked at him or even at his house. He cried and cried. Nobody cared.

He went back inside. He saw his mother's body again. Again, a wave of sorrow passed over him. He hugged her and cried. Finally, he decided to do what his mother had asked him to do. With great difficulty, he dragged the body of his mother, which had become very stiff by then, to the edge of the door. Somehow, he dragged it out of the door and into the sand outside. He was sobbing non-stop. As he was attempting to drag his mother's body through the sand, the farmworker saw him. He could not believe his eyes. He was shocked to see this young child struggling in the yard. He terribly agonised when he suddenly realised that the pious woman, his neighbour who he always respected had passed away! Agony tore through his heart along with deep guilt of not having been able to help them when they had needed it the most. Now it was too late. He said to himself, "Let the rich villagers excommunicate me, kill me, I don't care. I must help this poor lad."

He rushed in and helped Raman to move his mother's body to the pit that she had mentioned. He brought a pickaxe and covered her body with soil and damp earth. Both he and Raman sat there looking at the grave for a while. Soon, Raman got up, went inside their house, took the stick and the cloth sack entrusted to him by his mother. He opened the cloth sack. He cried again when he saw that his mother had packed some raw rice, a few coins and a few loincloths for her son, despite their abject poverty! This was her only savings! Finally, Raman wiped his tears and came out. The farmer was waiting outside. He said, "Come with me. I will look after you. I will take you home." Raman thanked him and told him what his mother had asked him to do. The farmer listened to Raman's words with tears in his eyes. He knew that he could not make Raman change his mind. He loved his mother so much. He would not do anything contrary to her wish or command.

As Raman was about to leave, a messenger came running towards him and asked, "Where is your mother? The landowner's wife wants her back in her household. They finally found the missing necklace. It had fallen in a narrow space between two beds. When they pulled the beds out for cleaning, they found the necklace. The landowners have removed her ban and excommunication. She is now welcome in their house. You are welcome too." Raman stared at him and gently smiled. He pointed towards the grave of his mother and without any emotions, said, "There she is. She cannot go back to their house anymore. She has gone forever." Raman looked one last time at their little home. He bowed down at the grave of his mother and walked towards the 'North', never looking back. That little boy Raman was the three hundred and seventy-year-old saint sitting before the visitors in Badrinath!

CHAPTER 4

THE JOURNEY TO LIBERATION

Raman's path was clear. The loss of his mother had created a huge vacuum within him. Before dying, Raman's mother had given him a definite destination and a firm purpose in life to be fulfilled in the days ahead. He had firm faith in his mother's words. So, he decided to walk towards the North. Where was North? The Sun rose on his right side and set on his left. The way in front of him was his path. He knew nothing else, and he needed to know nothing else. As he took his first tiny step on the path of Ultimate Liberation, the guiding Masters took ten steps towards him. This is always the case. Once the conviction, determination, and dedication are absolute, the Masters, God or Universe will help to complete the task.

Raman walked the whole day, and by sunset, he found the verandah of a seemingly unoccupied house, near a village path, and decided to spend the night there. There was a well in the compound. He saw a bucket and understood that the well was usable. The local villagers were probably drawing water from this well. He washed his face and drank some water. He did not feel any hunger even though he had not eaten anything since his mother's passing. He sat on the verandah, looking at the setting sun.

An old woman appeared before him. A toothless smile brightened up her wrinkled face. She also looked like a wanderer. She sat down next to Raman and asked, "What are you carrying in your cloth?" Raman said, "Some rice, some coins, and a couple of loincloths." She said, "Let us cook the rice." Raman opened his cloth sack and put the rice in her bowl. She went towards the well, washed it, put some stones together for a makeshift oven, took some dry sticks and dried cow dung that was lying around, put them under the bowl. She then lit it with a matchstick. Soon the rice was fully cooked. They shared it. The old woman gave Raman the major portion, which was not much, and she ate the rest. They also shared the skimmed rice soup.

By then, the sun had set, and it was quite dark. A partial moon lit the sky. Apart from Raman and the old woman, there was nobody else in the vicinity. The old woman swept the verandah that was covered with dust and dry leaves, spread on it the several rags that she carried, and invited Raman to sleep next to her. For a moment, Raman felt that his mother was calling him. In the darkness, the old woman's voice felt like his mother's. Raman lay down next to the old lady, who said, "I could not find anything to eat the whole day. You were hungry too, but you gave me all that you had. Bless you, my son! You will never starve in your life. My words will never go wasted. I bless you."

Raman was already quite tired and drowsy. He slipped into a deep sleep, like a trance. The last few sentences that he heard from the old woman went straight into his subconscious mind, as an assurance, as well as an important direction.

"Never allow dust to settle on your consciousness. Be alert. Be aware. Inertia always lurks around the corner. It is not always easy to sweep away the dust, especially if it piles up. It may take lifetimes. You may not see me ever again. But, remember, your mother is with you. She will protect you until you reach your final destination. She is guarding you now, and she will guard you until you are in safe hands or the realms of the Almighty. She is postponing her further lives for your sake. She is a divine soul. She knows who you are and the purpose of your birth. She has decided to walk with you till the very end. You will not see her, but you will feel her presence at times. She sent me today. She will send many more, more powerful than me, to assist you in your journey. It is a divine collaboration."

These words always remained with Raman as reassurance during uncertainty. When he woke up in the morning, the old woman had disappeared. Little girls were playing in the courtyard, and some women were drawing water from the well. He got up, went near the well, and asked for some water. A plump woman looked at him questioningly, but without speaking a word, poured water into his cupped palms. He washed his face and mouth. He took some leaves from a mango tree and brushed his teeth. When the women and children left, he bathed, washed his loincloth and wrapped a fresh one. He saw a mango within reach. He plucked and ate it. He took the loincloth that he had kept for drying, folded and packed it in his cloth bag and walked towards the north again.

His journey was quite smooth, as he got assistance constantly and miraculously, whenever he needed it, apart from an incident where a greedy merchant tried to get Raman to work in his shop. This merchant gave him some food and then trapped him as domestic help. He kept away Raman's cloth bag that contained his loincloths and the few coins that his mother had given him. This was the merchant's way of making sure Raman stayed with him. But a fight broke out in his neighbourhood and caused chaos. Raman saw the opportunity and ran away from this entrapment, without his belongings. Fate took away even his paltry earthly possessions from him. He walked empty-handed towards the North.

One night he slept in a temple rest house that provided free accommodation for travellers. The middle-aged temple priest saw this small lonely *brahmin* boy, and out of pity, took him home. The priest lived in a small house near the river. After his service hours as the temple priest, he used to teach the Sanskrit language, the scriptures and *mantras* that are used during worship to the *brahmin* children of his neighbourhood. At that time, he had about seventeen students. Raman joined as the eighteenth student. Raman stayed with the *brahmin* priest, helping him and his small family that consisted of a pious wife and a beautiful daughter, with their household chores. He always accompanied the priest everywhere. He attended classes without fail and in a few years, Raman became well versed in Sanskrit and the scriptures. He could also perform worship, and many times, when the priest, his teacher, was unwell, he conducted the rituals in the temple so systematically that all the devotees loved and respected the boy.

Every day, Raman woke up along with the *brahmin* priest at 3 a.m *(brahma muhurtha)* and went with him to the nearby river to bathe and complete the morning rituals performed by *brahmins*. The river was wide but quite shallow near the bank. They chanted together and bathed in the river along with many other *brahmins*. They washed their clothes and hung them for drying, on strings tied to poles or pillars of the post-bath worship sheds, a few steps from the riverbank. All the *brahmins* chanted *mantras* together, creating beautiful vibrations all around in the early hours of the morning. The priest and Raman would then proceed to the temple to light the lamps, bathe the deity, change its vestments, decorate it, and perform the regular worship. This was done without fail every day, come rain or shine. By the time they completed it and opened the temple doors for the aarati, the temple hall would be filled with devotees.

Raman had not lived with his father for a long time, for he had died when Raman was very young. Therefore, he had not experienced the lifestyle of the temple priests. Here, living with his teacher, Raman learned how the *brahmin* priests lived, and experienced the pure and pious way the whole family existed, totally surrendered to the Tradition and the Lord. He never heard them quarrelling or imposing themselves on each other. Their young daughter always behaved in a dignified and selfless manner. He never saw them advising her or training her. She seemed to have picked up the qualities spontaneously, as part of her upbringing. He saw that wandering monks or beggars never left their house without food, clothes, or money. They considered everyone as guests who are representations of God, and gave them whatever they had or could part with.

Deep harmony firmly rooted in spiritual conviction and faith prevailed in the whole household. This gave Raman stability in his formative years. They always treated Raman as part of their own family. They never displayed any discrimination. He never felt like a stranger there. He was given full freedom in the house, and they shared with him everything that they had. They were not rich in terms of wealth, but their hearts were filled with richness, which is much more valuable and has more permanence.

The priest and his family always woke up at 3 a.m. and always went to bed at 9 p.m. They had their dinner at 7 p.m. They only ate *sattvic* food made of grains and vegetables grown above the ground, nurtured by the sun. They never consumed any roots or the bark of plants or trees. They had a cow and a calf at home. They treated the bovines as family members, gave them a lot of love and care, and always made sure that the calf got sufficient milk to drink before they milked the cow. The calf was always untied, free to scamper about, and could drink its mother's milk whenever it wanted.

They never sold the cow when her milk ran dry. Instead, they served the cow with the same dedication and care, with gratitude for the selfless service that she provided. Raman learned a very vital lesson in the expression of gratitude towards all beings and to take no creature for granted. He understood that each being, when showered with love, produces pleasant vibrations, which harmonise the atmosphere in homes, especially those where love prevails in abundance. The well-being of all creatures on earth gets reflected in the whole earth and beyond. It removes emotional blockages, and grace flows abundantly.

After five years of living with them, Raman's education was complete. He decided to continue his journey. The priest and his wife invited Raman to stay with them for a few more years. But Raman had already decided to continue his journey to the North. It was the Lord Himself, in the form of a beggar who had come to the house and told Raman, as he was handing over cooked rice to him, "Son, it is time to travel again. This is neither your abode nor your destination. It is time to leave this place." Raman told them about this incident and his vow. They accepted his decision without much ado.

Raman had cultivated a mango plant in their garden. In five years, it had grown into a fruiting tree and bore some mangoes. He washed five mangoes, put them in a plate, and placed it at the feet of his teacher, saying, and said "Master, this is my *gurudakshina* to you. I am indebted and grateful to you and your family for all that you have given me – food, shelter, knowledge and above all, unconditional love towards a poor, homeless child. This mango tree will grow, and so will your riches. You will have no dearth of anything in life."

The priest blessed Raman and hugged him. Bidding adieu to the lovely family, Raman started his journey towards the North once again. Raman's prediction or blessings indeed came true. In later years, the priest and his family inherited a huge fortune, and the priest's daughter also found a very pious and wealthy husband. They lived their lives happily ever after. But this turn of fortune did not affect their behaviour; they continued to lead a life of simplicity, surrender and gratitude to the deities they worshipped. The priest continued his work in the temple and did not stop educating children.

CHAPTER 5

THE MASTER SEEKETH THE SEEKER

Atmananda Chaitanya said to one of his constant companions, *Swami* Chidananda (who was earlier known as Manav), "A boy who belongs to the place where the great oceans merge, has reached the Konkan land. We must meet him." *Swami* Chidananda asked Atmananda, "How is it relevant to us? You never go in search of followers!" Atmananda laughed and said, "He is relevant to the Tradition. I am not just a man; I am the Tradition." Chidananda had learnt not to ask questions, but grasp all knowledge through practical lessons given by life and the Guru. That was how the Tradition worked. Still, he blurted out, "Which Tradition?" They were walking. Atmananda suddenly stopped, turned, and looked straight at Chidananda's eyes for some time. Chidananda shivered at that intense gaze, and he started sweating. He sensed a very strong and intense power like Lord Shiva Himself. He became paralysed. He felt his third eye burning and bursting. His spine became hot.

Atmananda spoke in a calm, deep voice, "The *Navnath* Tradition! Lord Krishna called all higher beings before he left his physical frame and told them that the purpose and message of his *avatar* must continue. He chose nine people as its messengers. They are the nine Narayanas. 'Narayana' means 'destination of man'. Lord Krishna, Himself Narayana, summoned the nine Narayanas, who were projections of Himself, to his presence and ordered the formation of *Nath Tradition*. Thus, Krishna expanded Himself from one to many. They became the *Nava* (nine) *Nath* saints. They are Matsyendranath, Gorakhnath, Jalendarnath, Kanifnath, Gahininath, Bhartarinath, Revananath, Charpatinath and Naganath. Lord Dattatreya is the primordial Master, who started the Tradition.

The purpose was the continued preservation of *dharma*. Their realm of action is the whole universe. Each *Nath* Master displayed profound wisdom and a distinct, unique character that made people wonder if they were indeed part of the same *Nath* tradition at all. Some stressed on yoga, others on silence, or devotion, knowledge, faith and patience, purity, non-violence and faith at all levels. The *Nath* Tradition is like a grid. In seeming diversity, there is extreme unity and purposefulness. All *Nath* Masters operate as one entity, one breath, even though each Masters displays a different method. There is extreme oneness and also diverse expressions. Some of the saints of the Tradition chose to burn themselves like candles, giving light and purity to the chaotic world. This is their mission.

They decided to settle fifteen thousand feet high in the Himalayas, in caves, hidden in the ice, away from human eyes. They recycle their semen backwards through *yoga siddhi* (power of yoga), and they glow like glowworms. They are luminescent. They silently send soothing energy to the whole world. They are intense. When it is time to shed their bodies, they walk towards a nearby pool, withdraw their soul, cell by cell, to the top of their head, and remove themselves (their soul) from their bodies. They shed their bodies in the water. They always choose *mahasamadhi* in water.

They only live for the world, not for themselves. Their prayer is 'May the whole world and its various beings be saved and elevated, except us.' They sacrifice their lives for the world, unassumingly, expecting nothing in return, not even gratitude. Some saints of the Tradition choose to be among people in the marketplace, like you and me, to demonstrate the *dharma* of existence. Most *Nath* Masters do not have any formal Master guides. They are chosen and guided by the Divine, purely based on their eligibility. Thus, there is no initiation. The common man cannot understand or appreciate this truth. He will miss the grand message too.

All of us are distinct and inimitable. Each *Nath* Master displays a different aspect of life and living. They are usually polite but can be extremely rude at times. They are here only to serve a specific purpose. All are extremely powerful, and at the same time, completely unassuming. Only those who have the eyes to see it will recognise them. It is very difficult to recognise an unassuming *Nath* Master. Even if one recognises them, it is very difficult to follow them. If one follows a *Nath* Master, it is very difficult to get anything from him, unless one surrenders and dissolves oneself completely. Others will just see and will never understand or benefit.

Our Tradition is an open river. There are no initiations. None with selfish motives can enter this river. They will get killed and thrown into the mud. Only good souls and true believers can enter this river. A *Navnath* Master will travel the seven worlds and seven oceans to find and rescue a pure soul. Eligibility is the only criteria. Eligibility is achieved through purity. Purity is achieved through conviction, commitment, and consistency. The Tradition is created to spread the message of true love, beyond all boundaries, and preserve the ultimate *dharma* of existence."

This message was drilled into Chidananda. He stood there in a trance-like state for hours. When he came out of his trance, it was late at night, and there was nobody around him. He understood that Atmananda had gone towards the Konkan. He walked the whole night, as fast as he could, in that direction. By morning, he found Atmananda and his entourage and joined them. Even though he saw Chidananda walking towards him, Atmananda did not acknowledge or pay any attention to him. This was typical of Atmananda. One glance was equal to a ceremonial welcome. He believed not in formalities, but discipline. Discipline as a walking stick on the path of purity.

Three days later, Atmananda and his group reached Konkan. Atmananda and his people kept walking until they reached a huge banyan tree. There were many men, women, and children sleeping on the brick platform under the tree. It was daybreak. Atmananda saw Raman, he went straight up to him, touched his third eye, and said, "Wake up." As though hypnotised, Raman got up. He stared at Atmananda's eyes for a minute or two. Atmananda sat down. Raman fell at his feet, held both his feet for a long time and kissed them repeatedly. He recognised the Tradition more than the saint. He had not physically met Atmananda before. He found the Tradition in the eyes of the saint. It was unmistakable.

Raman travelled with Atmananda and his followers for five years. At Varanasi, he called Raman and said, "You must leave now. You have to go up North. You have all the siddhis. Never display them for fame or power. Never display them in front of sceptics or people of power for recognition or money. Do not be 'visible' unnecessarily. Be visible only to those who come with purity and faith. Do not interfere in people's future. Stay in their present. Guide in the present. You will become a great Master and a beacon of light of our Tradition. Your invisibility and invincibility will be your strength. Usual karmic beings will not recognise you.

Those who recognise you will be of our Tradition. They are eligible. I will be with you always.

Always be aware of your spine, especially the thin string that runs through the spine linking the poles of your consciousness. That is your stairway. Lures of the flesh are unavoidable. But I have given you the wisdom and awareness to see beyond. You will not be affected by the flesh, both your own and others'. Both will be well within your control. In extreme conditions, self-indulgence is better than entanglement. Entanglement leads to karma. *Karma* pulls you down. Women are unique creations. They represent *shakti,* the creative dimension of *Parabrahma*. They are powerful yet fluid. They are flexible; they have multiple dimensions. They should be revered. Indulgence is not a sin. If it becomes entanglement, it binds. It prevents liberation. Emotion attached with entanglement prevents liberation. Anything that prevents liberation is sin for the soul. Be aware."

Raman was eighteen years old. He was at the doorstep of youth. He began his ultimate journey in total renunciation. Step by step, he went higher and higher into the Himalayas. Due to the grace of the Tradition, nothing affected him. Nature provided him with food and water. He learned through his consistent practices to stay beyond the elements and their requirements. The body is made up of elements that have been put together for a purpose. It is disintegrated when the purpose is completed.

At Badrinath, Raman became a complete renunciate. He met many Masters. Many guided him and protected him. He stayed there thereafter, invisible to the human eyes until the two travellers discovered him. He was centuries old. But age did not matter. He could live forever if he wanted to; and leave the body, if he so desired.

This is what the travellers understood from their communion with the ageless saint who had no name, no address, no possessions, no identities. In a world where people are competing to carve images, this saint lived as a strong reminder that we must leave back everything here when we finally depart. We cannot carry earthly conquests or possessions with us to other dimensions. A liberated existence is truly worth it.

SECTION 5

Atmananda Leaves…
…Atmananda Lives

*"What the pupa calls the end of the world,
the Master calls a butterfly."*

CHAPTER 1

GLIMPSES OF THE *AVADHOOTA*

When I, Mahendra Manu, look back upon my time with *Gurudeva* Atmananda, I can never claim to have really understood him. Initially, he seemed to be full of contradictions, absurdities, and inconsistencies. But when I started accepting it all as part of his character and stature, I began to accept him without judging. Most importantly, he displayed no insecurities. I started seeing his uncanny authenticity, uncompromising conviction, and inconceivable profundity when I started seeing him without the lens of judgement. Acceptance without conditions made a drastic difference in my own thinking process.

He asked me to focus on myself instead of focusing on him. It was intriguing. He used to say, "Form might lead to delusions. The same applies to expectations." I was beginning to be aware of that. So, I stuck with his recommendations or teachings, rather than his form or personality. Nevertheless, his actions and activities were certainly influencing my character. Detachment from all things around me was settling in without me being aware of it. Fears, as well as insecurities, rapidly vanished too. Looking back, in a way, I was subconsciously imitating him. In this context, I would like to quote a few of his teachings, which could be considered as silent initiation.

While walking through a forest area, we cautioned him of the possible attack of wild animals. He said, "If this 'dead' body becomes useful for the survival of another being, why not? Consider it as better use of the body than using it for indiscriminate consumption of the wealth of Mother Earth." *Gurudeva* always considered his body as 'dead' and spirit as 'life'. He used to say, "My life is not the body. It is now in the body but not affected by the body or even the existence of it. Being unconditionally available is the initiation in the path of Liberation. Conviction is the *dhuni*."

Once, sitting by the fire, I saw our Master staring at the flames intensely as though speaking to them. Suddenly while staring into the fire, he seemed to tell someone, "I have no more incarnations." We heard that. We waited for his next words. For a long time, he kept staring at the fire. Then we heard him speak again, "My next incarnation will be sophisticated. I will hide myself behind the garments of that time. I will confuse the world with my attire. I will shake minds with my character, style, nature, methods and habits." He spoke no further. When we got a suitable opportunity, we asked *Gurudeva* about his next incarnation, but he did not bother to answer. We gathered that he was talking to someone in the fire or through the fire, or in a divine communion with the invisible Masters.

An *Avadhoota* always remains unfathomable. *Gurudeva* often spoke to himself or beings that we cannot see. He used to stare at something and speak to it as though it were a human being. Once I saw him speaking to a fallen, dry piece of wood! What I heard was, "I have to come back. So, it is better to leave quickly to come back. Is it painful? Oh, no! Pain is only in the association. I am the consciousness of an atom and this mountain. No shell can give me pain. Pain is with the shell. I am not my shell. I must give myself. I must stop being 'I'. I have kept this body and all that is connected to this body away from the marketplace. Now, I must keep all of them in the marketplace. I will offer my next body to the lions (worldly people) to feed upon. If that is the command, I will." I often wondered who was this 'I' this perfect *Avadhoota* was talking about. Later, I understood, that he was referring to his state, perhaps his human dimension that we could see, or a certain aspect of his state, but never the personality that we usually refer to as 'I'.

"I am the consciousness that existed in the atom. Then I expanded to become a cell. Then I became a fish. I came in everything that walks, crawls, swims, and flies. I am also the medium (elements) they thrive on. I am the non-attachment that exists inside every shell. I have taken millions of lives. I have felt and experienced the pain of separation of each mind from its body identification every time. I have felt the pleasure of liberation after each body too. When a bird comes to liberate a worm, when a tiger comes to liberate an incarnation, each time when death comes to liberate an existence, I shed the garb of illusion and I become complete consciousness. I am the consciousness of the eater and the eaten, yet I have no birth or death. Birth and death happen as ripples within my consciousness. I remain complete and immortal always."

One day *Gurudeva* said to us, "It is no use following me. You are wasting your time with me. Even I do not know where I am going. I know I have nowhere to go. You are not like me. You have places to go to. So, do not waste your time with this foolish wanderer." We were perplexed by these words, but we understood their meaning only after some time. Initially we thought that our Guru was asking us to leave. But his later actions revealed that he wanted us to think, to be aware. When he said we had 'places to go to', he meant our desires for material gratification. He had no desires. He had no place to go to, every 'place' was him. We still had desires. This meant, if we chose to follow him, let it be without other desires and with only one aim - liberation. A liberated being becomes everything visible and invisible. For my Master, 'He' is the final home. His journeys, if at all, are all inside the home of his consciousness. There is no outer journey through the senses and mind for him. This was a strong reminder for all of us.

At one point, *Gurudeva* slowed down and started showing signs of detachment from everyone, as if preparing to leave his body. He did not leave the shade of a banyan a tree for a week, and was staring at the sky all day. He lay there without eating, drinking, or sleeping. All of us concluded that he would soon be leaving his body, and that was a painful thought for us. Our anxiety grew day by day. One day, *Gurudeva* spoke: "You fools! Why are you so anxious, upset and crying? You are upset because I may leave this 'dead' body. I am ashamed that you have understood nothing by walking with me all these years. Death is inevitable for everyone, but not the soul. The soul never dies. I will never die because I was never born. All that is born will die. This is the truth and there is no tragedy in it. When my work is over with this body, I will leave it.

I am not the body and nobody can hold me back. You will also leave your respective bodies just like I will, someday. Crying over a dead body is the silliest and stupidest thing one can ever do. When I die, do not put my body in a tomb. Burn it and give the ash to the rivers that bathed it and nurtured it all these years. There should be no visible trace of Atmananda. I will come back again in another body to fulfil every wish of everyone who connects with me. When I come back, I will come back only for the sake of *dharma* and will have no boundaries or barriers. It will have nothing to do with this body that people call Atmananda." *Gurudeva* made this very clear and started his wandering pattern again when he felt better. We understood that he had wanted to give us an important lesson in life.

We rarely saw any emotion in *Gurudeva*. He always existed in his own world. One day, as we were walking past a small-town market, we heard a local leader giving a speech, attended by an audience of about a hundred people. Guruji did not wait to hear the speech. He abruptly walked past them without paying any attention. *Acharya* Shankar, who was with us for a few months, hailed from that town. After a while, when we sat down to rest, Shankar told *Gurudeva*, "Guruji, the man who we saw speaking to a crowd is a popular leader of my village. He is doing many things for the poor. But he is intolerant about saints, and always speaks of saints and monks as lazy, useless people. He even tries to prevent temples from giving them food or shelter. On the one hand, he is serving the poor, but on the other, he abuses harmless monks."

Gurudeva responded by saying, "He is serving only himself and nobody else. All his moves are calculated for his own advantage. When he pretends to serve the poor, he is looking for their support for his popularity. He keeps them poor that way. Monks have no value for him. He pretends to be secular, but when it comes to defenceless monks who have nothing to do with him, it doesn't suit his own motives. Only a subtle heart will see the peace that these monks spread on earth. By not needing anything, they are leaving a message of contentment in this world of greed and political manipulation." *Gurudeva* seemed a bit angry about what was happening in the hypocritical world around him.

Many people thought *Gurudeva* was indifferent. His ways were unfathomable. Most times, he ignored many people who had walked with him for days. He did not even acknowledge their presence although they had spent a lot of time around him. Sometimes, he just gazed at them for a while without speaking. At other times, he spoke seemingly unimportant things. This caused many people to become disillusioned and leave. Thus, he screened the deserving from the undeserving. He was unfathomable. Those who saw only his body, character, or behaviour, never understood *Gurudeva*.

Not all questions deserve answers. The spiritual states of humans are the answers to many questions, and so is their silence. What I understood is that questions and answers are more often than not just a mind game. This is the way the mind feels important. A 'thinker' is often a prisoner of his mind. The greatest thing that one can achieve in one's lifetime through detachment is silence from thoughts, for which acceptance is the key. Karma brings thoughts, words, and actions along with emotions, and those very things created karma too. Silence is a good answer to many questions.

Gurudeva said, "When awareness rises above all the deeds (thoughts, words, actions), it transcends the states (waking, dream, deep sleep). When awareness transcends states, it merges with consciousnesses. When consciousness rises above witness-hood, it merges with the soul. When the soul rises above witness-hood, it merges with the supreme consciousness. Thus, the unit becomes the universe. Man becomes God."

CHAPTER 2

MANU BREAKS HIS 'SILENCE'

Mahendra Manu started talking to his students. They had been pestering him to talk about the *mahasamadhi* of his *Gurudeva*, Atmananda Chaitanya, the divine merger of his soul with eternity. He was a little reluctant because he could not easily explain it. Finally, he put his thoughts together and spoke to them.

"My beloved children," he said, "yesterday, you asked me how I could keep my inspiration always alive, without boredom, and live a disciplined life dedicated to my Master. The answer is simple. When we firmly decide on a positive ideology or a purpose for living, when we totally believe in our purpose, when we have firm conviction that it is worth dedicating an incarnation for, we will not be affected by pleasure or pain, and nothing external or internal will shake us. The clarity and purity of our supreme purpose itself will keep us strong, determined, dedicated, committed, and continuous. Conviction, Clarity, Consistency, Continuity, and the Courage to live it, without doubt or comparison, are the secrets of my self-inspiration.

Soon after my *Gurudeva* left his body, I was confused. What next? Then I realised that the Guru himself is my path as well as my destination. His state is my goal. He had blessed me with a pure goal without my knowing it. He was the completion that I was looking for, and my goal was to merge with the ocean of consciousness that my *Gurudeva* represented. To need nothing while having everything is spiritual emperorship. So, I decided to dedicate the rest of my life to speak about the glories of my great Master, and thus make him live in people's awareness forever.

When I talk about my *Gurudeva*, it becomes my *sadhana*. It integrates me into his consciousness. It elevates my awareness. It establishes peace and contentment, and a feeling of a great life well lived beyond the lures of mind. Thoughts of my *Gurudeva* are a constant reminder that I am integrated to him. My destination is his stature as pure consciousness. This shelters me from all adversities and always keeps my frequency high in awareness and stable in disposition.

The world is exactly what we are or how we perceive it. Our world is our extension. In this world of extremely binding illusions, my Guru is my shelter. No rain can drench me, no fire can burn me, no season can disturb me, and no condition can deviate me from this resolution. The only vow that I ever took in this lifetime was to dedicate my life to my *Gurudeva* against all odds. This is also my spiritual practice. All we need in one lifetime is a positive purpose. Once you believe in it, that itself will lead you until the end.

I do not get stressed. I do not get bored. I am neither affected by anything around me or inside me, nor by anybody's opinion or criticism because my conviction for my *Gurudeva* is unshakeable. This conviction is my inspiration. This commitment is my reminder. I know that I do not exist. He exists through me. I keep myself clean and empty so that he can continue to express himself through me.

The mind often ridicules the truth and brings in doubt. Doubts enter the mind only when we are slack in our faith, or when we are occupied with adverse mental states, delusions, and situations. We should keep ourselves protected from all this. When we start doubting, we must reinforce our faith and conviction and remember our pure purpose of this lifetime. Reinforcing our faith will completely eliminate doubts.

When our minds are integrated into the supreme consciousness beyond forms through the form of our Master, elevation in awareness happens spontaneously. When we are steadfast, we stabilise in that awareness. When stability happens, dissolution begins. When dissolution intensifies, we become one with the Master. At first it is no separation in the mind (the mind is the only faculty that creates separation), until we realise the true state of no separation.

It is due to the sheer grace of my *Gurudeva* that I can speak to you about this incident etched in my memory. Let me narrate to you the toughest and most difficult thing for me to ever express - the final days of my Guru, Atmananda Chaitanya. It was the most dreaded moment for all of us. First, I shall express the event as I experienced it, when I did not know its significance or subtle aspect at all.

Gurudeva was always with Srinath who was like *Gurudeva's* shadow, having no separate existence. Srinath certainly knew much more than us about Atmananda's needs, heart, and intentions, but he never spoke or explained anything to anybody. *Gurudeva* hardly talked to Srinath who was like *Gurudeva's* pet dog who demanded nothing and was always happy to serve him. The rest of us, who were still dominated by our thinking minds, were only watching random scenes of a drama without knowing the whole story.

As I have said earlier, *Gurudeva* became more and more withdrawn towards his end, especially after the forty-eighth year of his incarnation on earth. We suspected that he could be leaving his body. But we were never sure for he always had his hyperactive and relatively inactive phases. He was only forty-nine and still too young. Often in the past, his followers had seen him in a trance-like state for several days, without food and water, and suddenly he sprang back to life and resumed travelling.

Thus, when he slowed down this time, we assumed it was a temporary phase. We had no idea that that these were his final days on earth. He was sitting right here, at this same ghat. He sat under this banyan tree. The tree could probably tell us many more secrets about my beloved *Gurudeva*. Only the silent can hear eternal truths. Those who speak only talk their mind. I was still my mind at that time.

CHAPTER 3

PREPARING FOR THE EXIT

Mahendra Manu continued. "I remember that it was a Thursday. *Gurudeva* and the rest of us arrived at the ghat. First *Gurudeva*, and then later all of us bathed at this very same ghat. *Gurudeva* brought out a begging bowl that we had not seen before. He kept it on the ground and covered it with a cloth. He asked all of us to sit down and served us sumptuous food. None of us had ever experienced this. He put his hand into the begging bowl under the cloth and produced many delicious varieties of food items.

We could not see the bowl for the cloth covered it. This was the first time we saw this aspect of our Guru. Usually, he was disinterested when it came to food. So this surprised us greatly. I can never explain the taste of that food. It was truly heavenly. No one, nobody, not any living human could have cooked anything like that. It was doubtlessly celestial food. *Gurudeva* did not eat a thing. We requested him to eat with us but he shook his head.

He did not say anything. As you know, we hardly spoke to our Master. What can we say to a perfect *Avadhoota* who is in total control of not only his body, but also the elements that constituted his body? That was the last of our terrestrial interactions with *Gurudeva*. We were unaware of it at that time. *Gurudeva* never explained anything, anyway. We always had to guess and gather.

He looked intently at all of us, into our eyes, as if giving us blessings or transferring something from him to us, one by one. We were seven of us. He came to each of us, looked into our eyes for a few minutes, and then walked away from the river bank to this Banyan tree.

He sat at this spot where I am now sitting, facing north, just the way you see me now, in the same lotus posture. All of us sat around him as you do now. *Gurudeva* sat like that with his eyes raised to heavens for many days. We sat for some time and afterwards took turns to be with *Gurudeva*. He was wholly absorbed into himself and probably did not even knew whether we were there or not.

Only Srinath sat on the other side of the tree. His back was against the tree trunk. He faced south, like Lord Dakshinamoorthy. Srinath's spine was aligned to the tree trunk, just like *Gurudeva's* was aligned on the other side. They both sat still, a reflection of each other. The tree united their bodies, if not the consciousness. We were all amazed at the stature of Srinath, the silent one, who asked for nothing nor articulated anything. He was the most unassuming one amongst all of *Gurudeva's* followers and the one who can be truly called a disciple. He was always one with his Guru, as though he was the very personification of our aspiration.

Gurudeva sat like this for almost a week. To be precise, seven days and ten hours. At one point he called us, assigned us various tasks, and sent us away. When we returned after completing those tasks, which I shall mention soon, he was not in his body anymore. We did not know when he had left. Only Srinath was with him at the tree. It was Srinath who told us he had left. He knew we wished to know, and obliged us in very few words. He alerted us and said that it was time we cremated his body, as per his wish. *Gurudeva* had said 'No remnant of Atmananda should remain on earth. Everything should be returned to where it is taken from. No name or form should be preserved. Atmananda is never born and will never die.'

I distinctly remember two incidents that I was lucky to witness. It was perhaps on Monday, four days after *Gurudeva* started his penance under this tree. Towards midnight, when all of us were fast asleep around the tree, I sensed the presence of someone. I was curious and also worried about *Gurudeva* getting disturbed. I got up. What I saw was amazing. A glowing, radiant saint was sitting in front of *Gurudeva* and both seemed to be communicating without words.

The saintly figure had flowing white hair and beard and a very peaceful, calm look. the scene was enchanting. The saint seemed to be giving some instructions or permission to our *Gurudeva*. Soon, the celestial figure dissolved and vanished. I cannot say for sure if this was my imagination or it was real. Looking back, I believe it was Guru Shantananda, Atmananda's Guru, who had come back to tell his favourite disciple that it was time for him to exit the mortal coils. My limited awareness tells me so. To me, Guru Shantananda seemed one of the twenty-one *Shweta Rishis*[37].

The following night, I saw a similar vision. This time, I saw a group of saints around *Gurudeva*, and he was communicating with them. Again, everything was non-verbal. All of them were very radiant and looked very young, perhaps in their thirties. *Gurudeva* resembled them. The same facial features and beard. It was almost like a family reunion. I believe they were the nine great Masters of

---
[37] *the council of the pure white sages who are considered the twenty-one pillars of Earth*

the *Nath* tradition, the *Nava Naths*. They seemed to have come there to honour and appreciate our great *Gurudeva*. They also stayed with *Gurudeva* for some time and then dissolved into thin air.

While this was happening, the whole place was bright, as though lit by a thousand suns. The tree was illuminated. When I looked at Srinath on the other side of the tree, he looked transparent, like he had no body; he seemed to be made of air and light. For a moment, I could only envy his state where he had already transcended to the level where he came into the aura field of these celestial beings. I also realised that Srinath and *Gurudeva* had merged into one.

I always felt Srinath would stay on earth only as long as *Gurudeva* did, that he would not stay longer than his Guru in the body. He had already become the shadow of his Master. When the body leaves, naturally the shadow also leaves. These thoughts came much later though, and not while the event was happening. I decided to stay awake, to watch over my *Gurudeva*, and to witness these celestial beings come and go.

Their vision itself was elevating me to greater levels of inner silence, which that even my practices were unable to deliver. Perhaps my *Gurudeva* was giving me all that I could handle, and much more, before he left his body. Nothing spectacular has happened ever since."

CHAPTER 4

THE FINAL GOODBYE

The students listened attentively as Mahendra Manu spoke.

On Wednesday evening, *Gurudeva* called us and gave us some tasks to do. He sent all of us, except Srinath, in different directions. Srinath was not even part of our conversation. When we asked *Gurudeva* if we should wake Srinath, he shook his head. We were all happy that *Gurudeva* had called us, we presumed that he had decided to end his weeklong penance, and everything would be normal now.

He gave me six coins and asked me to get firewood from the nearby village. I thought that *Gurudeva* wanted to do a fire ceremony to signify the end of his penance, during which he had stayed without food or water, and not even attended to a call of nature. Six silver coins was a lot of money to buy firewood. I was very happy to get a bullock cart load of firewood.

When I returned with the wood, I saw that my beloved *Gurudeva* had already left his body! This was Thursday morning. I was extremely dejected. I grieved. I felt that my whole world was burning, and that I was burning in it. I had no interest to live without the presence of my beloved *Gurudeva* on earth. I cannot explain in words what I felt. I sat alone and cried my heart out. I am sure that the others were equally affected. I couldn't see, for tears blurred my vision. I could not believe it, I hoped that *Gurudeva* was still in a trance and would wake up and start walking anytime.

Gurudeva's body was radiant and subtle as always. He seemed to be sleeping. It took a while for me and others to realise that *Gurudeva* was indeed gone. The only one who seemed unaffected by *Gurudeva's* departure was Srinath. *Gurudeva* never tolerated unnecessary display of emotions. So even we calmed down. I felt lonely and abandoned, like an orphan. I neither knew where to go, nor what to do. While we stood immobile around the body of our beloved *Gurudeva*, the silent Srinath took charge.

He instructed the bullock cart driver to move *Gurudeva's* body to the cremation ground over there. He first got all the wood unloaded at the cremation ground, then he used the cart to bring a priest from the neighbourhood temple. Next, he assembled all the materials that we had all brought, everything that is required for a cremation as per Vedic system. I could not even imagine how *Gurudeva* had arranged everything for his own cremation, he had even left us sufficient money to hire a priest. Srinath performed the ceremony on behalf all of us.

Before noon, *Gurudeva's* body was consumed by the funeral pyre. Everything happened so fast. It was a very tough day for all of us, this day of the departure of our *Gurudeva*, our pillar, our support, our everything. Srinath seemed completely unaffected. After the rites were over, he came and sat under the tree. The next morning, he got up before sunrise and performed those prescribed sacred rituals that a son does for his father. None of us understood all of that. Srinath was quiet, he didn't speak or discuss anything with us, he just proceeded with the customary rituals, as though he was used to it.

Two weeks quickly went by. There was a lot to be done. After two days, we took our *Gurudeva's* ashes and as per his wish, immersed them in the sacred river. We also provided food to some passing monks and priests with whatever money we had. All the customary rituals were completed by the fifteenth day. Srinath sat in meditation under the tree without food or water all these days. He joined us only for the mandatory rituals. We started discussing our life ahead, and what we should do.

We decided to go our separate ways. I wanted to stay back here where my *Gurudeva* left his body, to be of assistance to children like you, if they came to me in search of the precious, like I did at one time. The others made their own plans. On the morning of the seventeenth day, everyone was ready to leave, everyone except me and Srinath, who did not participate in this discussion. He was still sitting under this tree with his eyes closed.

My companions decided to wake him to bid him goodbye. When they touched him, they found his body cold. He was no more! Sixteen days after *Gurudeva* left, and after completing all the necessary rituals for the Master, the disciple also left. When we shifted his body and laid it on the ground, we saw a small pile of silver coins on the spot where he had been sitting. It was just enough for a decent cremation, the customary rituals, and the feeding of the poor. We couldn't comprehend where this money could have come from, for we knew that he had very few clothes and possessions, and certainly no money.

My companions stayed back for another twelve days until all the rites and rituals were done for this great disciple of *Gurudeva* as well. I must tell you that Srinath was to *Gurudeva* what Hanuman was to Ram. I was extraordinarily lucky to witness this divine company, collaboration, and existence.

After everybody left, I was alone. Despite the vacuum, I never felt alone. My Master had given me everything that I could handle within my capacity. I still remember his words: 'It is not in sadhna, but in integration, that the highest is achieved. It is not merely in practice, but in awareness that elevation takes place.' This became my truth. I was thinking, talking, and living the consciousness of my *Gurudeva*. I never felt any separation. In fact, I felt his presence more than ever before.

He made me. Without him, I would not exist, except as a useless 'mental' animal with no awareness. He rescued me not only from my detrimental gambling habit, but also transformed my random existence into a purposeful life. I exist only as a shadow of *Gurudeva*, and I know I cannot come anywhere close to Srinath in his devotion to *Gurudeva*. I know this very well, because I am still my mind. I have however, given as much of myself as I could, to the wish and will of my *Gurudeva*.

The story of Atmananda does not end here. I continued to live here and met a few people who told me about my beloved *Gurudeva* after his passing. I shall relate those to you one by one.

CHAPTER 5

A NAGA *BABA'S* ACCOUNT

A couple of months after the *mahasamadhi* of my *Gurudeva*, I started serving in the nearby temple in the mornings in return for food. Every day, I received sufficient food for one meal by the grace of my *Gurudeva* – sometimes uncooked grains and pulses, and sometimes, cooked food. One afternoon, I had returned from the temple and was cooking rice and pulses in a pot by the ghat. A middle-aged Naga *Baba* reached the ghat for a bath and rest. I invited him to share my meal. He graciously agreed to eat with me. We shared the meagre food and chatted about various things after we had finished our meal. The conversation soon drifted to Atmananda when he enquired about my Guru. This Naga *Baba* had not heard about *Gurudeva* before. But he said that he had met my *Gurudeva* and conversed with him. This surprised me because, at that time, *Gurudeva* hardly spoke to anyone. I know this because I had been with him! The Naga *Baba* recounted two experiences which I feel inclined to share with you.

The First Experience of Naga Baba

The Naga *Baba* recounted, "I was sitting on that stone after bathing, and I saw a *sadhu* in a loincloth walking towards me. When I offered my respects, he returned my gesture with a respectful nod. There was nobody else at the ghat other than us. I had previously seen him sitting with his eyes closed under that banyan tree. Thus, I knew he lived nearby. He entered the river. The current of the river was much stronger than it is now. He waded over the stones into deeper and deeper waters. I shouted and said it was dangerous to go further. He turned and looked at me, nodding in acknowledgement, and stopped. I closed my eyes and continued my chant. A few minutes later, when I opened my eyes and looked, there was no trace of him. He couldn't have finished his bath and left the ghats so quickly, walking over the rocks on the riverbed. Where had he disappeared? I could not understand. Later, while leaving, I did not see him under the tree either.'

I asked the Naga *Baba* when this incident had occurred. It turned out that it happened precisely the hour when we were cremating Gurudeva's body. How could *Gurudeva* come to the ghats and bathe here, while his body was being consumed by flames elsewhere?

I asked the Naga *Baba*, "Did you ever see my *Gurudeva* with a begging bowl?" The Naga *Baba* said, "No. He had nothing in his hands." My mind was still on the begging bowl that he had produced out of nowhere and given us all a sumptuous dinner before he prepared himself for his *mahasamadhi*. We had not seen that bowl before. Nor did we see it again. There were no possessions around him when he attained his *mahasamadhi* under the tree.

The Second Experience of Naga Baba

The Naga *Baba* continued, "My Master had left his body a long time ago. I had questions regarding my practice, which I felt was not leading me to higher awareness. My mind was getting involved. I did not know who could help me. One day, this question bothered me so much that I wished to leave my body. Suddenly, your *Gurudeva* walked in and sat beside me. He said, 'Stop doing everything now. Integrate instead. Your Master has not left. He remains as a promise and a principle. Connect to the principle. Stop doing everything.' This was like a command to me. Seven days and seven nights, I sat in the same place, totally unconscious of myself. I did not know when your Gurudeva who gave me this experience left my side. When I returned to the consciousness of my body, my mind had died completely. All separation had disappeared. I could see my Master in everything. I became fully aware that neither life nor death could affect who I am. I became complete. Now, as we talk, I realise that your Gurudeva had already left his body when he delivered this experience to me. It overwhelms me."

The Naga *Baba* left me in awe. He left me with the understanding that my *Gurudeva* is still alive and working. Only his body had gone. He has not gone. I just wished and hoped that he would come and give me his celestial darshan. The Naga *Baba* said, "We must never judge such a Master. We cannot, and we should not. They are one with God, and they only follow their dharmic duty beyond the frame of social expectations." We sat for a while, sharing more memories of *Gurudeva*.

To sum it up, the Naga *Baba* said, "See how clean and clear his life has been. He lived a perfect life, all the four dharmic stages of life that are defined in our scriptures - *brahmacharya* (bachelor student), *grihastha* (householder), *vanaprastha* (seclusion) and *sannyasa* (renunciation). He was totally surrendered to his Master as a *brahmachari*. He learned from his Guru with humility and gratitude, and thus showed us how a true disciple should be. He first practised, and then he preached what he learned, walking the length and breadth of this blessed land called *Bharat*, without expectations, and without gathering any burden of possessions or positions. He guided and took care of his followers just as a householder takes care of his family. Then he detached from everything, even speaking and communicating, and wandered as a perfect *Avadhoota*, transforming lives on his path, again without expecting anything from others, or polluting himself. In the end, he existed only in God-consciousness, completed everything that he came for, and left without any difficulty."

This new awareness of my *Gurudeva* always keeps me inspired.

CHAPTER 6

PRESENCE FROM THE BEYOND

A Divine Healing

Sometime after my beloved *Gurudeva* left his body, there developed a severe problem in my spine. My back hurt and I had to lie down most of the time. I'd never wanted to depend on anybody, but due to this debilitating condition, I had no choice, but to rely on my disciples for help. I couldn't meditate, do the evening rituals, or perform any of my daily rituals. One day, I was sitting on a rock by the riverside. My disciples sat some distance away from me. Due to the excruciating pain, I felt so helpless that I wept. I wondered what to do.

I said, "*Gurudeva*, I surrender, I cannot handle this pain anymore. I don't want to be dependent on anyone. Please allow me to walk into the river and leave my body and end this life." As soon as I spoke these words, I felt that somebody was stroking my head, a hand was on my *sahasraara*. I turned and looked around, but there was no one. I first thought I was hallucinating, but a short while later, I could definitely feel the warmth of a masculine hand massaging my lower back, where it hurt.

I felt dark energy leaving my body and pure bright energy entering in. It went on for a while. Since I was quietly sitting on the rock and looking at the water, my disciples thought I was meditating, and they did not disturb me. Nobody there knew what was going on. This lasted for some time, and I was in a trance. Finally, when it ended, I got up and realised that I was fully healed. When I surrendered to my beloved *Gurudeva*, he came in the subtle energy form and performed the healing. This compelling experience confirmed that *Gurudeva* was still around even though he had left his body.

Traces of Existence

Gurudeva was like the water element, always going with the flow. After his *mahasamadhi*, I attempted to create a likeness of his image so that I could remember him. I used all my sculpting skills to create a statue and I installed it on the bathing ghat where I used to take my daily bath. This allowed me to be in his presence and I worshipped him every day. I kept in mind that *Gurudeva* had said to us that he did not want any trace of his existence to remain on earth. He wished to be cremated and his ashes dispersed in the holy rivers.

A few years later, the river was in spate and the water level rose. It took the statue away, leaving no trace of my *Gurudeva's* existence, just as he had wished. Following this incident, I consecrated a set of *padukas*[38] in his name and installed them at the ghat. My *Gurudeva's* power was evident, because the water from the river would gently touch the *padukas* and recede. The same river washed away the tall statue never flowed over the *padukas*.

Amar's Story

Before the statue was washed away, I had a visitor who came to the ghat inquiring about it. He was a tall *jatadhaari*[39] carrying a

---
[38] *sacred footprints of the Master*
[39] *person with long braids of matted hair*

danda[40]. He looked and behaved like a typical *Avadhoota*. He said that the locals had told him that I was the sculptor who had carved the statue. He had come to ask me whose statue it was, and my relationship with him. I introduced myself and told him that the statue was of my *Gurudeva* Atmananda. As soon as he heard the name, his eyes lit up. "This is the guru who changed me. I am what I am because of him." And then he proceeded to narrate his story.

He introduced himself as Amar and said he came from the eastern state of Assam. When he was still in his twenties, he had visited Varanasi as a pilgrim. My *Gurudeva* also happened to be in Varanasi then. During those days, *Gurudeva* was still speaking publicly and engaging audiences. He allowed people to come to him and ask him questions. Amar happened to hear *Gurudeva* in Varanasi and was fascinated. He finally found someone whose words resonated with him. This is what he had been looking for all his life.

He had not planned on meeting *Gurudeva*, nor did *Gurudeva* invite him to accompany him. When *Gurudeva* started traveling, Amar followed him. Just like that. He was like a stream, flowing wherever *Gurudeva* went. I suspect he started getting a bit too comfortable. After a while, *Gurudeva* got very upset with Amar, for no apparent reason, and asked him to leave the group immediately. This happened when they were crossing a forest. Nobody asked why *Gurudeva* did that, and neither did *Gurudeva* explain his decision. Amar was left back in the middle of the forest. He was alone and had no idea where to go.

The first thing he saw when he started to walk was a corpse being cremated close by. Amar became extremely fearful. He asked the

---

[40] staff

people who had come for the cremation where they were staying. They said their village was behind the hill. Amar asked them if he could go with them for he was very frightened to be by himself. They told him that he could not come along with them because they were mourning the death of their chief. Since they could not cook for others until the mourning period was over, they would not be able to entertain any guest. So, they left Amar there, right in the middle of a graveyard!

Amar realised he had so many fears to conquer. While these are considered normal fears for anyone, his fears had been masked until now. All his fears came up one after another rather– the fear of starvation, the fear of being alone in the forest, the fear of loneliness, the fear of darkness, the fear of spirits, and so on. He despaired. It became unbearable for him. He felt that it was better to end his life than go through this trauma. He decided to end his life by drowning in the river that flowed next to the cremation ground.

With these thoughts, he entered the river. He felt the cold water touch his feet. He continued to walk and the water reached up to his waist. He kept walking for what seemed an eternity. He realised after some time that the river seemed different, for the water level wasn't rising. Then he noticed that he wasn't walking at all, he was lying by the riverside. How could that be? His only conscious remembrance was entering into the river; everything else seemed a haze. It seemed like someone or something had pulled him out of the water and put him in a meditative, trance-like state.

He got up and meditated by the river. He was still in a trance. The beings from the burial ground were only interested in him if he was functioning consciously. But since nothing was consciously affecting him, all these beings started leaving one by one. All he could see was that there was a fire, and all these beings were walking into it and burning themselves. He had visions of many people leaving his body. Just like a soul leaves the body, he was relieving a lot of dead bodies from inside him. He was witnessing them leave. He was allowing it to happen, and it happened. He was just a witness. There was no motion.

Nothing mattered to him anymore. He let go and burnt all his fears. He could feel that all of them were gone, leaving him empty. He sat there without any fears. He felt that there was no time or space. He sat empty and vacant for many days. He survived hunger, thirst, and all his conscious fears. From a human context, he must have sat there for a very long time. Then finally after a few weeks, he got up. It was almost like his body was not there. He was in a subtle, etheric state.

He could see himself as a crystal; everything was passing through him, within him, around him. Everything was visible to him as pure crystal. When he finally started walking, he could not feel his feet touch the ground. It was like he was dead. He then met a saint with a silvery beard and an ecstatic look on his face who asked him, "Do you think Atmananda left you in the forest to die?" Amar replied that it didn't matter because he had already come out now. Then the saint said, "He made you himself."

Amar's shift in consciousness had happened almost overnight. Nobody had taught Amar to meditate. All this just happened to him. His consciousness shifted when he started walking into the river. Then, everything that followed was a trance. The saint's statement was a reminder to Amar that he was still alive, and that he had arrived and reached the state of an *Avadhoota*. So, he became an *Avadhoota* almost overnight.

The moment I heard Amar's story, the first question that came to my mind was, "Amar, you had it so easy. *Gurudeva* made it very simple for him. Why didn't *Gurudeva* do this for me? Why did I have to toil so much?" Amar answered without my asking, "Mahendra Manu, you had to be with him till the end. You exist to sing his glory!"

That was the difference.

CHAPTER 7

WATCH AND WITNESS THE COWS

Once, a middle-aged person named Ramappa accompanied our group. *Gurudeva* did not have the habit of acknowledging, welcoming or receiving anyone who chose to walk with him. He probably did not even notice. Guruji did not like conversations. We have seen Guruji watching cows or other animals intently for hours. We used to tell each other that Guruji was liberating them with his eyes. He looked at animals with more attention than he looked at humans.

On one such occasion, a week after Ramappa joined us, Guruji was gazing at a group of cows in a field. Ramappa went close to him and said, "*Gurudeva*, my desire in this life is to reach higher levels of *samadhi*. Bless me and help me." Guruji did not reply for some time. Later, he said, "Watch and witness the cows." That was it. He said nothing else. He got up and started walking. Ramappa sat there and began to watch the cattle. When we were leaving with *Gurudeva*, we saw that Ramappa was intently observing the cows.

Many years later, after Guruji attained his *mahasamadhi*, I had the good fortune of meeting Ramappa quite by chance. Ramappa by that time had attained great spiritual heights. I did not recognise him. I was returning with a few companions from the north of Bharat, after our annual holy dip in the Ganga during the Kumbh

Mela. We happened to spend night at the ashram of a saint whom we had never met before. Since ancient times, it is the tradition in most ashrams to host Kumbh pilgrims without any expectations.

The chief of that ashram had a flowing white beard. He invited us graciously. In the evening, after dinner at sunset, he gave a discourse to his disciples. It flowed somewhat like this:

"*Gurudeva* asked me to observe cows and walked away. (When he uttered these words, I thought this might be Ramappa) I considered this as a *diksha*[41] and sat at the same spot where *Gurudeva* sat and immediately started practising. In the beginning, I saw only the forms of cows. I saw only their activities.

Every day I did the practice that *Gurudeva* had initiated me into. A few days later, I could recognise individual cows that grazed in that field. Soon, I started seeing their characteristics and traits. I started noticing how they behaved. I saw their behavioural differences as well as their hierarchy.

They never seemed to be in a hurry. They were always peaceful. They ate only what they needed. They were very patient. They never complained or made any unnecessary sounds. They accepted their surroundings and realities without any complaints. They were tolerant. They never grumbled about the rain or excessive sunshine. They were consistent in what they did. They never showed signs of boredom. I learnt many things from them – concentration, acceptance, consistency, commitment, contentment, no complaints, and above all a stable mind, peaceful to the core.

---

[41] *initiation*

I realised that *samadhi* states need all these qualities. *Samadhi* itself is a state of stillness of the mind, and these animals taught me that. Night and day, I sat by that grazing ground and watched them. When these gentle beings wandered, I followed them. They became my Gurus. I learnt the great secrets of life from them. Everything begins with acceptance. I understood why my *Gurudeva* always watched animals and sat in a meditative state. He was witnessing the states of *samadhi* that nature displays through every plant, tree, leaf, and through all living beings. I also realised that they did not eat after sunset; they ate all day only after sunrise. They followed the sun. I surrendered myself to the sun and the sun became my Guru too."

Ramappa's explanation now convinced me that he was referring to my Guru too – *Avadhoota* Atmananda Chaitanya! He had given enlightenment to many through a casual word or sentence. Here I would like you to understand one important point. My *Gurudeva* in his usual unassuming way taught Ramappa, and through Ramappa many others, an important technique – Practicing Awareness.

Usually, Gurus initiate their disciples into *manana* (contemplation), *dhyana* (meditation), or some rituals to reach levels of *samadhi*. Here, *Gurudeva* taught awareness by observing the cows – which is neither *manana* or *dhyana*. Cows have no anxiety over their future, nor any regrets about their past. They have no prejudices or fears, explained Ramappa. They were always in the present, in tune with their body and nature with total acceptance. This is an essential lesson in spirituality. Being in the now, being in awareness, being in a space between *manana* and *dhyana*.

When Ramappa paused in his narration, I introduced myself and told the audience that I was there when this incident occurred.

Ramappa was moved to tears. He got up and tried to prostrate at my feet in deep reverence for my Guru. I did not allow that. Instead, I embraced him. We both could not contain our tears of happiness. We held each other for some time.

Then I spoke, "Ramappa, I am so happy to see you, not just because you have attained higher levels of *samadhi*, with the grace of our *Gurudeva*, but because you are imparting and explaining the unorthodox methods of our *Gurudeva* to your students too, and thus are keeping his memory alive. Not many understood our *Gurudeva*. He has given such impactful guidance to thousands, maybe not through a discourse, but by a mere utterance, a nod, a glance, a sentence, or his life example."

A person asked Gurudeva how to develop *saboori* (patience). He pointed to a dog in the distance and replied, 'Look at that dog.' The dog was sitting next to a drunk alcoholic. At first, he felt insulted thinking that Atmananda had called him a dog and left Atmananda's group. Later on, after Atmananda's group had left the place, he happened to observe the dog. He saw that the dog served the master with patience all the time. The dog constantly followed his master everywhere – whether he went to the alcohol shop, lay drunk on the pavement, wandered aimlessly, and so on. The dog patiently followed his master irrespective of whether he was angry, upset, abusive, violent, and so on. No matter how his master treated him, the dog patiently stood by his side. The person understood and inculcated patience through constant observation of this dog. Atmananda delivered the needful in one cryptic response. He didn't sit down with the person and explain the meaning. He just threw the rope and went. The person guy took time to understand the deeper significance behind Atmananda's casual statement. But once he did and followed it, he found his answer.

He gave the rope to everybody in a casual way. Those who were observant caught it and used it to move ahead in their spiritual path. We are fortunate to have living examples like you that followed his seemingly casual guidance and attained the highest. Sadly, not even five percent of people who came to him understood it or caught that thread. They just moved on in life. They missed the bus. But Gurudeva always delivered. Our Guru has left his body, but he had insisted that his body should not become a burden to earth. He was formally cremated."

Hearing about the death of Atmananda, Ramappa's smile vanished, and tears filled his eyes.

I continued. "Also, *Gurudeva* had written nothing for posterity, except what he wrote in our hearts and minds. Ramappa, today I am happy. When I hear our Guru's words through you, I feel so happy and proud. He allowed us to walk with him and, through his life, he taught us invaluable lessons. A perfect *Avadhoota*. He was always so centered and stoical, he displayed no emotions, never complained or cried. He existed without existing. He lived without living. He always was and always is with us."

Ramappa said with tears in his eyes, "I just wish that I do not fall again into the lures of this world." "When you are under the protection of a Master like Atmananda, you never need to worry about any fall in spirituality, I replied. "There won't be a state of *yoga bhrashta*[42]. Atmananda, as a Guru, will never permit that. Our *Gurudeva* was seldom understood because he hardly expressed himself. His life was his message. If people did not understand his life, they did not understand his message either.

---
[42] *fall from grace*

I had noticed that he observed animals very keenly. He spent a lot of time doing just that. He often forgot time, weather, hunger, thirst, and sat watching the animals, insects, and birds. Now, with your narration, I get a clear insight as to why he was observing them, and what he concluded from those observations. He taught us the greatest of philosophies – acceptance and surrender. Thank you."

We embraced again with sincere and heartfelt emotions. I was genuinely happy to see Ramappa, primarily because he had reached a high level in spirituality, and also I was touched by his gratitude for our Guru who had made all this possible. We stayed that night and left the following morning after breakfast served to us by Ramappa's disciples. Ramappa did not consume anything between sunset and sunrise. We did likewise, and decided that we would hereafter eat before sunset.

We bid goodbye to Ramappa with this comforting thought that a true teacher never dies; he stays as a thought, a teaching or a reminder through different minds, well beyond his death. Atmananda's body was cremated. Neither were there any statues or monuments nor any books about him. This was his guidance to his followers. It was as he had once said, "I will walk the earth as if I never walked at all, leaving no injury or residue." Yet, he lived through his followers. The ones he enlightened, lit the fire in others. That fire is Atmananda's continued living presence on earth.

"I will walk the earth as if I never walked at all, leaving no injury or residue."

- Atmananda

THIS BOOK IS A WORK OF FICTION

SECTION 6

Teachings of Atmananda

"You gave me this life. You gave me this breath.
This life belongs to You.
I do not exist.
Only You exist, my Supreme Lord."

CHAPTER 1

MEMORIES OF A WANDERING MONK

Each word of a Master who is established in silence is like celestial nectar – precious and rare. *Gurudeva* communicated through a glance, gesture, or nod, and avoided using words as much as possible. Words are often diluted expressions of powerful thoughts. But during his younger days, *Gurudeva* used to communicate with people through speech. He even conducted spiritual discourses, as well as individual discussions with a lucky few. I was fortunate enough to meet *Swami* Kripananda, a wandering monk, who was with *Gurudeva* during that period for just a few weeks. I, Mahendra Manu, mention *Swami* Kripanandaji's reminiscences about *Gurudeva* in this and the following chapters.

"Atmananda used to talk about integration as the most important *sadhana*. Integration means a conscious merger with the consciousness of the Guru. His consciousness was vast and unfathomable. As with all powerful Masters, the expressions of his incarnated appearance conveyed nothing about his consciousness. Only those who had the power to witness the vastness of his consciousness could integrate into it. When I, Kripananda, complained that I could not understand how to integrate, Atmananda said, 'Integrate into the visible, and reach the invisible. Integration matures and stabilises only with the invisible.'

"I connected to his form and started serving the form with a firm resolution that I am serving the formless. In other words, it was me, quintessentially the formless, serving the formless. This was integration to me. I followed him for a few weeks like this, until one morning he said, 'I want all of you to leave me. I am going to observe silence and isolation.' Thus, he left us and walked alone into a forest, barefooted and bare-chested. *Gurudeva's* exit forced me to integrate into his formless aspect. That made me Kripananda.

I was enchanted to hear this. I understood that the Master is continuing to give me all that I needed through many mouths, and my heart filled with gratitude. Each word about my *Gurudeva* was celestial nectar for me, directly delivered from heaven. I also understood that *Gurudeva* insisted that activities or *sadhana* cannot give us higher elevation, as much as integration can. Integration needed perpetual conscious awareness. That meant staying alert and being aware of who I am. This also meant that I am connecting all my waking hours to my true form, the formless, which is the form of my *Gurudeva* as well. How wonderful! This was celestial nectar indeed!"

I asked Kripananda, "*Swamiji*, I have heard that *Gurudeva* revealed his wisdom in his younger days. May I humbly request you to divulge more details about Guruji's revelations?"

Kripananda obliged by sharing *Gurudeva's* insights that he had garnered from that period. "When a student is ready, the teacher appears. A teacher cannot deliver anything to a student who is not ripe, not ready for knowledge. The whole universe comes together in the creation of true spiritual Masters. The whole universe is their operating plane. There are no walls or boundaries. The great Masters existing in various planes of the universe operate on one rhythm and purpose. They are all one.

There are multiple forms, because forms are needed to express. But, beyond all the forms is one single entity, one creator, one creation, one purpose. The biggest and most substantial creation of our Father was relativity. Along with relativity occurred duality, time, gravity, and space. Everything was ready for grand expressions to take place. Expressions took place, and are still taking place at every level, at every moment. There is no negative or positive in the absolute sense. All are just expressions of the grandeur of relativity.

Father never really 'created' anything further. His creations created many things further. Father arranged the creation objectively, just like our soul objectively aids the daily creation of our personal realities. Shiva and Shakti potential existed in each single creation. The Shakti aspect that moulded beings, using consciousness as the sub-stratum, created all that could be created.

Creation continues unabated. Creation also has its duration. So dissolution also happens simultaneously. On the one hand is creation and on the other, dissolution. When these two aspects are established, existence also comes into play within that duration between creation and dissolution. Creation itself has its dimensions. Characteristically diverse, but essence-wise, one.

Father made the first of creations, and those creations made further creations. So, even though the same consciousness was at work, the awareness levels of the new creations and their further creations were of diminishing nature. Some created only dependents or slaves, just like we create walking and talking robots. They had no specific identities. They kept binding restrictions on them so that they remained bound and enslaved. They had specific breeding patterns and gestation times, while higher beings multiplied at will for a specific purpose and dissolved at will when the purpose was fulfilled. The relatively lower beings operated on limited awareness and more on instinct.

Every creation does have the inherent dimension for achieving the Father's consciousness. But entanglements, inertia and lack of awareness prevent them from seeing beyond. When the veil of ignorance is lifted by the grace of Gurus, visibility becomes constant. The path becomes well lit. Understanding the divine will, relishing in divine stature, higher entities assume tangible forms in various corners of the universe, to guide those who need to be guided. They do this out of compassion. On the earthly plane, most have only terrestrial needs. They sway with karma. Those who are ready for elevation will get elevated. Even to salvage one such soul, a higher being may arrive. Everyone has value. Each one is valuable."

Swamiji then proceeded to recount a dream that my *Gurudeva* had related to his travelling group at that time, which included Kripananda. *Gurudeva's* narration is described by Kripananda in the following chapter.

CHAPTER 2

A DREAM OF REVELATIONS

It was raining all night. I was lying down under a tree, in deep slumber. At one point, I felt an expansion, such that I felt I was expanding beyond my body. It was a strange feeling. All my identifications of this life left me completely. It was not this life. It was some other life. I was simultaneously a witness and a participant, as well as a recipient of many answers from my 'Father'. The dream follows…

A group of us were descending onto a world of water. I heard my elder saying to my Father, "This is an untouched world. We can create anything we like because water completes the balance of elements. This place has rich space, air, water, fire, and land (earth). We can create anything that can stay and regenerate in water, space, and on land."

Soon, this discussion started spreading all over our ship that was stationed above the planet. We could stop and move into any space, at any time, at any speed. Using sharp energy beams, we could manipulate any type of matter on our path either by levitating it, reducing its mass, or disintegrating it. We had travelled far and wide. Our ship itself was our world as we lived on it for several human centuries. There was no concept of time, nor aging. Our people positioned themselves spontaneously. Their age depended on their purpose. A child could remain a child for as long as the child and its parents wanted it to be a child,

The elder spoke. "We shall descend here. We shall first create some zones for us to live in, rejuvenate, and operate."

Our energy is levitational. Our communication is image transfer or non-verbal. We look, we establish eye contact and the transfer happens. The best of our elders can do this without eye contact.

We descended and landed on a surface. Please remember, there was only water, space, and nothing else on earth. We peacefully roamed about on many parts of the earth, travelling at the speed of thought. Our people separated and went to many places. As the elder suggested, we built houses first. Huge houses in the shape of pyramids. They were built over underground water using energy created by the movement of water. The energy was levitational. We used stones, connected them to energy and levitated them, put them in place, and in no time, we created our spaces. Good spaces that would help our creative work. We were here not to enjoy, but learn. This world was our school. We were here to express our creative skills.

The elder called all the creative heads and said, "The spaces[43] are perfect. The air flow is good. Good for creation. Water supports them. Create those things that can survive with air and water, and will perish without it, unlike us who can survive without anything. Energy is precious. Hence use it wisely. Install energy in each creation that will support that creation as long as the creation is in a good condition. The operating system can be a virtual receiving

---

[43] *pyramids*

point. It can have multiple functions such as feel, analyse, decide, handle instincts, as well as express its inherent character. Keep boundaries for the sake of consistency. This composition can be called beings.

Each being should have a distinct character, constitution, and duration. Each type can be called a species. Each species should have its capacities to reproduce its own species and thus survive time, but still within a time frame. Water[44] should be the carrier of energy in their bodies and when it is lost, the embedded energy leaves that body. Keep fire[45] as the motivational factor that motivates and regulates frequencies inside the bodies. Let the fuel be subtle energy that travels through *prana* which will maintain, recycle, and rejuvenate the system. Let the structure of body be the structure of the cosmos, microcosm contained in macrocosm and vice versa. That would be the unit structure. The forms are up to you.

First, we shall create the basic harmless, non-destructive forms and then based on its structure and character, we shall create the regulatory forms. Everything should be adaptable to the nature of this place. Even the destructive forms should not create imbalances, i.e., one should not wipe out the other, instead they should regulate each other instinctively. This structure should apply to all realms, such as earth, water, air. Instinct should be the tool for survival and continuation of the species, and should be based on necessity for these two. Instinct and innocence should be combined, except when you provide in some species, advanced analytical ability that is beyond instinct.

But beware, unless they segregate these two, they will have the

---
[44] *in this context, blood*
[45] *heat*

potential to bring havoc to the balance of our creation and even this platform. It is your responsibility. If you create advanced beings who can think, plan, and execute, then some of you need to be here to guide, nurture, and protect them too. You can certainly interact with our world, but your responsibility would be to ensure the well-being of this world. Beings may consider you and worship you as Gods. Your responsibility is to ensure that no negativity enters them. Guide them always, to maintain their highest potential, which is our potential. Nurture them to our level of awareness.

Numerous beings were created by our people and by me. We all created, based on ourselves and our abilities. Some created beautiful beings. Some small beings. Some big beings. Some only created for water. Some created for water and air. Some created beings for water and land. All beings were interdependent. Everything managed the other. This was a beautiful and peaceful creation spree. We all wondered at some of the creations. The most beautiful part was 'giving life', and making that process automatic when species had to continue. We automated the process. We also gave the option for 'upgrading', which I consider as evolution based on repeated existence, location, and necessity. These options made the difference along with survival instincts.

It doesn't end there. It was not only us, or the beings from our world that came to this realm. Following our tracks, beings from various worlds came. We were not ownership-oriented. But some others were. Some of them started manipulating our creations. They manipulated the intelligence of the most advanced of all creations – Man. We had only installed the capacity to love, care, nurture, and be selfless in that creation. But they installed multiple other inferior options such as ownership, possessiveness, hatred, revenge, anger, jealousy, pride, and many other things. They were cunning. They used the forms of our creations.

They worked subtly in our creations and made them reject us so that they could have total control on this land. For us, this land was not so important. There were many lands possible. But whichever land we had been to, these beings with negative attitude came to destroy all that which we created. We couldn't manipulate or bribe our creations. We gave our creations the wisdom to discriminate between good and bad. If they got deluded, all they had to do was turn to us. We would help. But they usually took our creations so far away from us that they could not find their way back for a long time.

We remained as creators forever as we are beyond birth and death. Many from us also lived here in the form of man to experience and guide mankind to freedom from binding of this land, from compulsive births and deaths. Originally, we had not created a species in entrapment. This happened only through delusive manipulations of beings of that nature. Instinct did not provide ownership. Lack of ownership means lack of traps. Instinctive existence is always a liberated existence. Beings live, experience, and leave. Simple. Ownership made the whole difference. It is manipulative thinking. This is falsehood for us. This is the story of how liberated beings became trapped beings. This is how they lost their way.

Moreover, the manipulative energies also accelerated the evolution of species. This created imbalance. Our structure was perfect. There were no more lions than a school of deers could handle. Their appetite was also different. Manipulative beings created voracious appetite by manipulating intelligent beings. The false identifications, supremacy, ego, and desire to control were all manipulations. They were not true. Awareness of perishability, no ownership, live and let live, use instinct more than emotions, ego and pride... these were our original contributions to the human species. The accelerated evolution process, the insane utilisation of natural resources, control over most species by one species, use and abuse of their breeding processes for selfish gains, a life based on tastes and not necessities – none of them were from us.

We only created spaces that were regenerative and rejuvenating. Therefore, we created pyramids on earth. When manipulative beings multiplied and started using our energy sources for their manipulative work, we chose to close access to them for everyone. Therefore, you lost access to our spaces on earth. Manipulative beings were controlling almost all centres of rejuvenation and regeneration on your land, thus denying access to mankind to realms of creative, higher awareness. We foresaw this and we closed access to higher energy zones that we had created for our purpose. Some of us carefully choose and still exist in higher energy realms of your plane even now, which are usually mountain tops or deep crevasses of your land which are not easily accessible to your kind.

Ours is a respectful world. A world rooted in justice, where injustice is not even an option. Justice is not a burden for us; it is our way of life. Others come first. Respect comes first. Understanding, appreciation, and love come first. This is our world. Insignificance of oneself is what we practise. Thus, justice is always maintained. We do not destroy, kill, or manipulate any being. We assist if needed and we nurture every being, in whichever world we visit. We still live in this world as options of higher good for the deluded masses. Aggressive, manipulative beings created deluded systems compatible for manipulations. They attacked and annihilated the truthful and the kindhearted to maintain their greedy structure.

They killed the people who we supported, branding them as evil while they masked themselves as good; they even wore the mask of God.

They controlled, annihilated, manipulated, and even destroyed all the species that used instinct more than intellect, using aggressive technology. The examples are all the non-human species on earth that are bred and killed for food and pleasure. Those were the species that were originally unaffected by any intruders because they lived only on their inherent instinct. They manipulated those with the capacity of awareness by overemphasising the mind[46] over awareness. They worked on their dimensions on mind from higher possibilities to lower dimensions of binding fears, sins, concepts, opinions, interpretations and analyses. This completely eclipsed the basic instinct and inclinations connected to the species.

We gave mankind the awareness to become one of us, and to connect with our world, a world based on kindness. But the manipulative beings bound men to limited intellect and restricted their evolution to the possibility of coming close to our awareness. The original human potential was our awareness. But their controlled human state became lateral and to that of terrestrial dimensions against the originally programmed potential of absolute awareness to the level of becoming creators. They were trained to see diversity instead of harmony and unity. They saw separation instead of unification.

Manipulative beings created regressive awareness from that of the original progressive awareness to absolute dissolution into consciousness that we had created. In progressive awareness, the secrets of creation as well as the reasons for reincarnation,

---

[46] in this context emotions

irrespective of the world of incarnation, was always crystal clear to every being because they always remained closely linked to the source or the fundamental of creation, which in human terms is called the SOUL. The manipulative beings, through regressive awareness, made the human species mere minds, removing even the ability to appreciate and allow instincts connected to every species naturally. They made the human species unnatural and disconnected from everything, including themselves. This was the easiest way to control and manipulate further.

We can destroy all these in a moment. But we cannot use violence. We only defend. We do defend. We do protect when called upon. But we do not reduce our frequency like they do. We do not manipulate for our advantage. We do not need any favours or advantages from anyone. We are complete by ourselves. We sincerely represent the qualities of our Creator – unconditional love and kindness without expectations. There is no suffering in our world. Suffering is a manipulative emotion, a tool of control, and so is fear. There are no fears in our world. Suffering, denial, sins, fears, guilt, debts, and so many such things are totally manipulative by nature. They are not from us. They are used in this world to control beings.

Freedom and kindness are our methods. Forgiveness itself does not exist in our world because there is nothing to forgive. We do not do anything apart from acts of kindness. All emotions such as forgiveness, jealousy, control, human laws, and religions based on sins and forgiveness, are not from us at all. There is nothing to forgive and nobody is eligible to forgive. We know what to do, how to do, and how to exist harmlessly. All the other matters including multiple flavours of emotions, social structures, options by law, bindings and control, sins and prisons, are all products of manipulative existence.

Neither do our beings talk about rights, nor do we talk about responsibilities. We have only functional duties which we chose as per our constitution. We chose our position in our world accordingly. A few beings with the same duties perform in the same way as the other without competition or comparison, multiply at will and need. A creator can become a thousand creators as per need, and then dissolve once the need is completed. We do our best and we do not take ownerships of our creation because the basic ingredient of our creation, the energy which you term as the soul, is not ours.

The installation of the soul in a creation is the technique that we have learned which helps to create beings. Every creation dissolves itself after a few experiences on this plane. Rights belong to the delusive mind. It is the same with responsibilities. Duty means being functional. Righteousness is our law. You call it *dharma*. We have given our own nature to our creations. Those who could recognise it, are called *Avadhootas*. They are close to our realm. They usually have nothing to do with this land, even though they exist here as our beacons.

We do not have do's or don'ts. If at all, whatever is selfish is a 'don't' for us and whatever is selfless is a 'do' for us. There are no sins because we do not have any do's or don'ts. There are no heavens nor hells. In fact, our plane of total freedom is heaven. Hell could be that of total binding and control through fear. That could be your world too. The fear of retribution, heaven and hell are manipulative. The concept of a punishing God is not from us. We do not have such Gods. We do not have any fears either. If you have any Gods who will get angry because you do not obey them, they are created by manipulative beings. We do not have them, nor do we create them. We have many beings who assist, help, and guide many beings in many realms. They are also not Gods.

Godliness is possible. God is the supreme being. There is only One. We all are sustained because of that One. We have no birth or death. We create ourselves out of pure being and dissolve ourselves if there is no need. Usually, we do not dissolve ourselves because of the service we do in the universe. We only create pure beings in our capacities. We also have parasite beings that cling to our creations for their existence. They are not from us. We have no parasites in our realm. We have only pure, absolute beings.

Manipulative minds are not interested in the process of creation and maintenance of a species. Their method is fear, control, manipulation, and annihilation. They, like any parasite species that they nurture, just use and abuse whatever we have created for their own advantage and pleasure, which is of a sadistic nature. Since they did not create it, they have no pains in annihilating anything. Creation is a painful process. Annihilation is effortless. This is why we had to annihilate, not only abandon, our power places such as pyramids because they would have used it shamelessly to manipulate and annihilate whatever we had nurtured.

Not all creations on earth are ours. There have been many like us from other zones who had the power to infuse 'souls' in inanimate objects and make them work in a specific programming for a specific period. They did not need physical bodies made out of elements for their expressions, just like us. They could make, maintain and discard bodies at will and remained the same with or without the body. The induced, infused souls did not have that capacity. If they lost a shell (body), they either took another one (another laborious process of womb and birth) or wandered body-less for a certain time. The totally helpless also stayed in some bodies because they couldn't create their own.

Dependency is the way of manipulative beings. Ours is non-dependency on anything. We give food to the body just like you water your plants. Manipulative beings use dependency to the level of subtle habits and fears of losing certain things that you depend on in life for certain gratifications. They could be unnecessary things, in an absolute sense. Nothing would happen to life if those things did not exist. Dependency is the trap. Next is deprivation of those that you depend on. Deprivation leads to craving. Craving leads to crime. Crime is connected to sin and punishment. Thus, the trap becomes a noose.

Creations get stuck with existence over many incarnations. This was not our original plan. Our plan was to leave the creations with absolute freedom of liberation at will, death at will, just like us, and work easily towards no dependency, through perfecting awareness beyond dependency. In this case, the mind and intellect were just tools for experiencing life. They were not binding factors. There was nothing to learn, analyse, or remember. In the flow of experiences, which is based on acceptance and unconditional love, it was just a pleasant flow like a smooth, cool breeze. This could be called heavenly.

Dependency was defined through denial, as I said earlier. The favourite subjects were food and sex. Instinctive sexuality for the sake of continuity of species had been our plan. In this plan, humans mated just like animals do. Nakedness was natural in that context. Covering up was a suggestion of manipulative beings. Through covering bodies, the differences were more pronounced.

Differences were just on the surface; inside all were the same. The differences accented the illusion of variety, further binding, and further dependency. Sexuality was as natural as breath. As was food. We were not dependent on food because we were not dependent on the element-based bodies. We could exist in and expel our bodies at will. We created more of ours at will and by necessity. We could create an army at will.

On this plane, it was not possible, and that was also used by manipulative beings to control people. The harder the creation, the more was the possessiveness, especially if awareness was low. The effect of hard-earned was used by manipulative beings to create that effect. We did not have the aspect of sexuality in us, and for that matter, the love of our plane was never conditional or subjective. Love was our nature. We had no other emotions. Food was another binding tool, as I mentioned earlier. Mainly sugar and salt. Taste buds were bound by sugar or salt or both. This also caused craving for it. Craving meant memory and binding. When food and sex stayed in the mind of beings, they became bound. To top it, deprivation caused craving. Craving was bound by morality. Morality was connected to sins. Sins were connected to punishment. Sin > punishment > guilt > fear > control. This was the story of manipulative minds.

In our world, none of this existed. If we wanted to experience any human emotions, we could either create a body for it, or feel through an already available body, without manipulating it. Remember, life was just a series of experiences. All experiences were feelings. Some you termed as good and some bad. We did not have anything good or bad. There were no sins or punishments in our world. There was only righteousness for a larger purpose – being our complete selves."

I woke, I heard and saw it all very distinctly. I heard the voice speaking very clearly to me. I arose with the lightness that only Absolute Truth can provide.

CHAPTER 3

VISIONS OF THE DARK SIDE

Continuing the revelations from *Gurudeva's* dream, Kripananda then elaborated on *Gurudeva's* thoughts on the factors that keep human beings in bondage. "On the one hand, there are external factors induced by the manipulative beings, and then there are internal factors that are part of existence, necessary to run this show of duality. Understanding these guiding words from *Gurudeva* will allow many a spiritual seeker to recognise and navigate the obstacles that arise to block progress in spiritual evolution."

When Masters operate from a level of purity, they feel and work at a very different level. They want to give everything possible to everybody. They don't look at someone as good, bad, or to be avoided. For them, everything is the same, everyone is the same, which the world does not understand. Why? Because the world is always biased. As the world plays with duality, it sees some things as good, and others as bad. When Masters operate at a level of purity, they exist outside duality. Hence, it is very difficult for Masters to stay in this world or to be in the body.

In contrast, most people exist in duality and are hence influenced by many things, situations, and energies around them. In fact, only fifteen percent can be seen by them with the rest being invisible!

There are broadly five types of influencers who keep us in relativity or relative darkness. All of them are highly influential and very much involved in our day to day life.

Please know that all these influencers and levels are a creation of God itself, but they have a different nature.

1. ENERGIES

Energies are not *atmas*. They have an existence as energies, not as beings who can create a body. They can be termed as personified flavors. Their nature is similar to bacteria or parasites who depend on other beings and express themselves and work through them. These energies connect to that part of you which they can thrive on. These energies connect to your energetic sheaths (physical, pranic, mind, wisdom, bliss) and occupy the appropriate sheath(s) as per their requirement. They have nothing to do with the person. It is the activity that gives them strength. They survive only through feeding on tendencies such as alcoholic or sexual addictions, violence, abusive behavior, etc. which make them stronger. They make the victim think that these tendencies and urges, which get stronger, are the victim's own.

These energies are very subtle and not spirits of other beings. Just like a seed that knows exactly where to germinate, these energies know where they can grow and on what they can feed. Suppose you have feelings of enmity towards somebody, energies of a similar nature enter you because they can feel that this is the right place for them to stay, grow, and express themselves. These energies can enter you just like bacteria enters your body. You won't even know. They can exist forever. Their existence is not connected to one life, but can go through multiple lifetimes.

2. WEAK/LOST CONSTITUTIONS

These are constitutions that are so weak that they do not have the power to create their own bodies. These constitutions should not be confused with energies. They have no perpetual existence and can be liberated but they don't know the way. They are lost.

Why don't these constitutions have bodies? They had no elevation while they existed in the body. They had no connection to a Master or to God. They did nothing elevating like *sadhana*, chanting, praying, etc. to increase their frequency. They were preoccupied by terrestrial life and emotions, hence are now stuck in that realm only. There are many such 'terrestrial' people. In case of a 'usual' or normal death, it is easier to take birth because it is part of a cycle. However, sometimes it is possible that they take an existence without a body. This is because they may have lost the body, but have everything else – desires, wants, etc. – remaining dormant. Then, they find a suitable body to fulfil these desires. In 'unusual' death (suicide or murder), this possibility is enhanced since it is not part of the normal cycle.

The lost constitutions also function similar to energies. They will give you thoughts as per their own desires. For example, "have alcohol" or "make love". The victim will feel that these desires and urges are their own. Society will also look at it as the victim's action or desire, because the victim is all they can see. Society then judges the victim as an alcoholic, a bad guy, a gambler, etc.; but where is all this actually coming from? No one knows.

These constitutions don't know how to take birth. They don't know the path. The main cause for these constitutions to be bound to Earth is ME and MINE. Who can they easily enter? People who are emotionally imbalanced and negative in nature - people who are addicted, constantly complaining, criticising, judging, being angry and/or negative.

We must also understand that performing *sadhana* does not secure us from these lost constitutions. It is still possible for certain constitutions to enter, but they are good in nature —constitutions of seekers. These good constitutions have unfinished work and may not have been able to take a body for some reason. Hence, they find a suitable body to finish their own *sadhana*. This is how their path becomes clear. They may influence the victim into thinking that (s)he is doing the wrong *sadhana* because it does not match their own. Purification practices need to be done to be clear of such constitutions too.

Why? Because the lost constitution will influence the victim to perform actions that are required for its own progress. For instance, imagine a person who is doing *sadhana* on Krishna is occupied by a constitution who has already done *sadhana* on Shiva. The constitution will influence the victim to believe that (s)he will achieve nothing by doing *sadhana* on Krishna. It may say that this is an illusion, and the victim must do *sadhana* of Shiva by going to the cemetery. This victim may be disillusioned. They may feel that they wasted their whole life up to now. They may wonder what is the point of living. They will be lost and searching. This may even lead them to commit suicide. This is how wandering souls work.

How do these constitutions (both negative and positive) occupy your body? There will be many souls wandering in places where acts of violence and negativities were committed, such as cremation grounds, cemeteries, battlegrounds, murder sites, etc. For these constitutions to enter, a person needs to leave the door wide open. This can easily happen through negative actions and emotions, judgemental behaviour, arrogance, jealousy, ego, and all such attributes. When one goes to such places unprotected and uninsulated, they can easily enter and occupy you. If you are very powerful or completely surrendered to a Master, they won't come near you because your aura field is extremely powerful. They will be unable to penetrate it. Once they occupy the victim, the victim may get totally confused. Some even commit suicide!

3. ENTITIES

Entities are beings like us, with a function, but they are without a body. Some of these beings are from outer space. They stay as energy forms and function like parasites by latching on to their host and experiencing through them, mostly to the host's detriment. In this aspect, they are similar to energies. Unlike energies, they have a form like a cluster. Entities do not have any agenda for liberation – they do not want to leave earth because they are happy functioning the way they do. In this aspect, they differ from weak/lost constitutions who are looking for salvation.

Living in the parallel universe, these entities are induced as they may not be directly sent to you or called by you. They can come to you by somebody else's connection with you. They may be transmitted through sexual intercourse, proximity, strong emotions like alienation, sympathy, etc. For example, if somebody who is handling these entities is constantly thinking about you, then the entities will get attracted to you. Neither are they sending the entities, nor are you inviting them, but the entities get attracted to you, indirectly, and come along because of the traffic of thoughts reaching them. The entities want to see you and look at you. This is how they reach you.

They are not as interested in the experience or sucking the energy of the host as they are in controlling or possessing the host. They feel an ownership towards the person they are attracted to. It is not love, but a feeling of jealousy, anger, and possessiveness. Hence, if they feel that you are getting connected to something or someone, they will try to block it. Because this connection will not give them complete ownership of you. They will put negative thoughts and hatred about it in your mind. You will feel that it is your own genuine intuition – the inner voice telling you that "all this is not good for you", or "this person is not good for you". But it is not so for these thoughts are planted into you by them.

People have felt this with their Master. They may have had no bad experiences with their Master, but they still feel that the Master is not good for them. Also, these entities run away as soon as they come near a Master, and then everything is as it should be. But they attack again when you are vulnerable.

4. BEINGS CONTROLLED THROUGH BLACK MAGIC

These beings have a selfish nature and aim to trouble or destroy you. They can create disturbances in your life even if you may not be in their realm. People can control these souls and beings through sadhanas and then send them at their will to disturb you. They can do it for money or for mischief. The people that control these souls also do it to prove that they are more powerful and superior than others. They perform *havans* and use practices that are violent in nature, such as blood sacrifices, to attract beings and souls of the same negative frequency. Once these beings are attracted, they are kept possessed and then used against somebody.

5. A REAL BEING WITHIN YOU

This is the original being that took this incarnation to experience life through this body, based on its karmic agenda. Some of it could also possibly have been inherited from the family where it takes birth. This inherited karma is not completely owned by the original being. Whether good or bad family karma, the original being takes its own share and distributes the rest amongst other family members. When it gets married and goes into a family, it will also share their inherited family karma and it becomes a bigger mixture.

Other than our real being, we have to cleanse and purify ourselves of all these other parasitic influencers on a daily basis. It can change your destiny. How? When you remove all alien energies from your energetic sheaths and all interferences from your life journey, your own destiny becomes apparent and it is like bright sunshine. Generally, one feels clouds and darkness because of all these influences. Also, because of these influences, the impact of one's own destiny is increased manifold. Once they are removed, the impact is also removed and one feels immensely light.

If we intend to make ourselves available to serve, we need to understand all this clearly. Broadly speaking, there are two types of saints. First are the wandering kind that live away in the Himalayas, and are not visible to most of society. These saints who are invisible to society are not doing much in the world. They do not indulge in any pleasure nor have any wants or desires. So, they are not interesting to these entities, because the entities seek only those who handle emotions.

The second are the saints that live in society to cleanse it. They do *havans, sadhanas,* chanting, healing etc, to first cleanse themselves and reach a level of purity, and then cleanse society from these entities.

This is very important to understand. Why? Because when you are on a spiritual journey, you have a great responsibility, to yourself and to the world. Your *sadhana* is a way for you to reach the highest point. Everybody's *sadhana* is different. Whatever is your main work is your *sadhana*. This is how progress and purity happen. People separate *sadhana* and work, and then it just becomes like washing hands and feet superficially. There is no actual cleansing and purification happening. It becomes clean for some time but then again you have to wash. There has to be a lifestyle of purity to remain there. Always be pure and reach the purest. Whatever you do should be your *sadhana*.

Let's take an example. For a cook, cooking food is his *sadhana*. Instead, if you make him sit and meditate, that won't work for him. His real *sadhana* only happens when he is cooking. Work, for him, is worship. You should be fully occupied in your *sadhana*. The more you practice with purity and selflessness, the more you get elevated. This will also then become your *dharma*. You are giving back to Mother Earth in the form of *dharma* and, in the bargain, you are getting purified.

People tell a Master to take care of someone who is not well, or who is in the hospital. Even though the Master may be physically elsewhere, (s)he seems to take care of the ailing person. How does that happen? The main secret is to remain completely pure and uncontaminated, otherwise you cannot leave, or you cannot reach anywhere. That is how much power a thought holds when you are working at that level of purity. Just one thought and it happens.

Now the last point and the most important point. What do these influencers do when they come to you? First and foremost, they see where the source is and then try to disconnect you from the source. Suppose you consider a Master as the path or gateway, they will try to close this gateway and disconnect you. Those who are deeply connected to a Master are more difficult to disconnect because there is a ring of protection. They create a negative thought or notion in your mind about your Master to disconnect you from the Master (your source). Then they work on you. If they don't disconnect you, they cannot work on you.

They try and enter at your weakest moments, especially the ones that are possessive, and try their best to disconnect you from your Master. They will put thoughts like – he is just an ordinary human being, he is eating, drinking, sleeping, etc. First, the divinity aspect is completely nullified and you feel that the Master is a common person. They'll say, "Why do you want to associate with this Master? He is doing this… he is doing that…" More and more such thoughts come, and then you completely separate. You are confused. You feel doubt, that is the first step, then confusion, then you get disconnected, and then they work on you completely. After that, they do not have much interest in you. Let's say, you want a new phone that is in the showroom. You pine for it, you long to have it. Once you have it, you are not interested in it anymore. Then you hanker for a newer version of the phone. The old one is now forgotten. This is the same way they get entertained.

The influencer's job is to make you feel that there is too much light, so you draw the curtains. This will disconnect you from sunlight and bring you in relative darkness. Their work is almost done – they have to bring you to relative darkness to create full darkness. Once you are in darkness, you stay there for a long time and it is difficult for you to come back to light. If you have ever gained grace on your journey, then there is a strong chance that a Master will come and pull you out of the darkness. This can only happen while you are struggling. If you are holding on to faith, it means you have not yet gone against the Master. But once you become negative and go against the Master, which is the entities' main aim, then it is very difficult. So that is what they create, this is how they make you act against the source, against the sunlight.

The second illusion that they make you believe is that the sun is not permanent, it is only available for a while. They create an illusion that what you are connected to is not permanent; instead they are the ones who are permanent, darkness is permanent. Remember, if darkness is created, it remains forever. To maintain light, you have to do a lot of *sadhana*. Once you stay in darkness, it becomes your comfort zone. You become *tamasic*. *Sadhana* becomes difficult and insignificant for you. They also twist the teaching. They even make you negative towards God. "Is God permanent? Is God omnipresent? Where is this God you are talking about?" These are the kinds of thoughts they subtly plant.

People nowadays question even Masters. They say the people with Masters are writing about the obstacles they overcome. They question why the Master created the obstacles. They hide the fact that the person's karma created the obstacles that the Master is removing. They make it sound like the Master created the obstacle and is then removing the obstacle himself. This is the illusion they create. People creating such doubts are completely in control of entities. These are the kind of parasites we have to deal with and purify.

How do we know if we are operating from a level of purity? When there is complete contentment. Uninterrupted, uncontaminated contentment.

When you feel totally content and peaceful without any hidden agenda. When your contentment and peace are not conditioned, and you feel bright all the time, it is a clear sign that you are operating from a level of purity. Sometimes it is also possible that this feeling of contentment is induced by the energies and entities, just to make you feel that you are at the right place, but in that case, this feeling of peace and contentment will be temporary. A sense of permanent contentment, without any agenda, is what decides your level of purity. Don't confuse yourself.

This can only be done by continuous self-purification and awareness. Chanting also helps. The Gayatri *mantra* is a very powerful tool against all these beings. In our tradition, the *mantras* of Lord Hanuman are very effective. So are those of Lord Narsimha. A Master's Gayatri works very effectively as well. Finally, the Kavachams (Devi Kavacham, Shiva Kavacham, Anjaneya Kavacham among others) are very powerful.

CHAPTER 4

CHHAYA VAIRI AND THE GOODNESS FACTOR

Kripananda then proceeded to explain *Gurudeva's* thoughts on the internal influences that keep people in delusion. Kripananda said, "Atmananda used to talk about *chhaya vairi*. He used to warn people 'Beware of *chhaya vairi*'. Initially I did not understand what that meant. Later, he himself in one conversation, without asking, revealed its meaning."

This is *Gurudeva's* explanation in his own words:

"*Chhaya* means shadow. *Vairi* means enemy. The shadow enemy. *Chhaya vairi* is your twin brother. It is your shadow. It is born with you and will die with you. It thrives on your insecurities and weaknesses. It should never be underestimated. It may remain unseen at times. But, remember, the shadow is always with you. Wherever there is light, there is also shadow.

Chhaya vairi obscures the positive and highlights the negative in people. It can even create ideological warfare in the world. It will, it will. It will thrive on death and destruction. It will thrive on obscuring goodness, using the masks of social systems, manmade laws and systems, religious dogmas, science, economy, and so on. *Chhaya vairi* attracts all that is destructive towards it and makes people believe they are doing the right thing. *Chhaya vairi* makes people shout, "Kill the noble men, release the thieves."

Chhaya vairi manipulates minds to its advantage. It will control politics. It will control minds. It will create artificial freedom and comfort zones. It makes people believe in temporary happiness. It will bind people to sensory pleasures. All types of negativities, addictions, and bindings are its allies. It will create an illusion to make the wrong look right. It will obscure all the karmic and dharmic laws and create an illusory, pseudo-moralistic world. Karmic law has fulfilment as the basic reason for incarnation, and dharmic law has unity and balance in life.

Chhaya vairi is the child of Kaliyug. It is the shadow of the current time. The strength of the era is its strength too. Just like the soul is present in all incarnations, human and non-human, *Chhaya vairi* is also present in all humans. It is reasonably silent in other beings. It needs the platform of the intellect to function, because its mode of operation is through illusions, make-believe and transitory, artificial contentment. Humans are constantly deluded that they are happy and free, and it binds them to their mind.

Liberation, brightness, truth, innocence, unconditional love, compassion, kindness, goodness, and such matters are enemies of *chhaya vairi*. Weaknesses and vices are its strength. *Chhaya vairi* uses the mind more effectively than the spirit. Spirit or consciousnesses keeps the mind alive unconditionally, while *chhaya vairi* uses minds to achieve its purpose. Anger, hatred, jealousy, revenge, lust, greed, pomposity, ego, pride, the need for approval and applause are all allies of *chhaya vairi*. Manipulating external entities are its friends. *Chhaya vairi* will also use religions to find its way into the hearts of human beings, using fear and control. Liberation is taboo for *chhaya vairi*. It needs binding to survive.

Chhaya vairi will make us ridicule simplicity and adore complexity. Material richness will even influence simple things like truth, ethics, and compassion. Profits will supersede kindness, love, and ethics of coexistence. Making us believe that might is right, it will first ridicule and then exploit the weak and helpless.

It will create indifference towards cruelty and violence in people's mind. It will make qualities such as unity, harmony, and tolerance insignificant and will make humans believe that anything is right as long as one wins in the material world. It will thrive on inequality and will do everything to maintain it. It will use complexes as a tool for suppression of humanity and will use all tools to create that insecurity in the minds of people.

Chhaya vairi makes people believe that vices are tolerable. It allows corruption, selfish accumulation of material wealth, exploitation, and manipulation for success in the material world. All this is considered true success. But it is the opposite of truth. Ill-gotten wealth by unfair means has a short life. It gets depleted as fast as it comes, through oneself or one's family members. Whatever materials we earn here, or which we did not bring with us when we came here, are not legitimately ours.

What is truly ours are the experiences from it, and also the desires because of it. Our material bank balance is ours only until our death, after which the account holder changes. Our spiritual bank balance on the other hand is ours forever. Our spiritual bank balance grows and our spiritual wealth multiplies with acts of kindness, selflessness, compassion, etc. Spiritual well-being associated with the company of great Masters also ensures a stable spiritual bank balance. The spiritual bank balance begins with our inheritance brought forward. The good deeds of our ancestors are carried forward and added to our spiritual bank balance.

Just like an inexperienced gambler depletes his material bank balance, a person with wicked ways will deplete his inherited and earned spiritual bank balance, and will soon fall into horrific debts that take several lifetimes to clear. They spend up whatever they have brought forward from previous lives. Additionally, they also spend up whatever they earned through a few acts of kindness. In this way, they deplete their spiritual account. Remember, a spiritual bank balance is the only account that continues beyond boundaries of births and deaths.

Chhaya vairi makes them feel that a 'being against' attitude is alright. It obscures the depletion of the spiritual bank balance. Once everything is lost and the person is under heavy karmic debt, *chhaya vairi* simply abandons him, and he has to handle his own karma created by bad actions. Thus, through indifference, selfishness, greed, and bad karma, the vibrational frequency of earth will substantially reduce. More and more such beings will relentlessly exploit. Finally, when there is nothing left to exploit, the whole species will perish. Human and non-human co-existence will become history.

Indifferent humans rooted in sensory pleasure are ruled by *chhaya vairi* and will care for nothing. They will wipe out species, flora, and fauna and will replace it with mock, artificial materials to pander to their ego. *Chhaya vairi* will use ego and religion to rule. Chhaya is shadow. Shadow is dependent on form. Form is truth. But shadow is relative, it is an illusion that assumes far more importance than truth. When *chhaya* (relative truth or even illusion) becomes more important than form (truth), humankind will degenerate. Pious and noble people will be killed and those who have material possessions will be regarded as great people. They will be honoured by rulers and laws. Laws will bend for them. Rulers will serve them. Justice will wait at their doorstep. *Chhaya vairi* will have the last laugh.

This hidden enemy walks with us from birth till death, waiting for us to fall, in order to conquer us. There will be wars based on ideologies. Religious inquisitions will kill more people than diseases. Religious dogmas will destroy humankind by alienating them from the one basic truth *Aham Brahmasmi*, which means the soul is eternal and divine. All of us are walking with one guiding principle, *Tat Twam Asi*, which means we are the true consciousness that we are looking for. Now, we have to find it and realise it.

But religions may obscure that principle for a longer time and destroy goodness by alienating the believers and the non-believers from each other. We will even see competition in religious beliefs. When religious leaders compete, the followers will fight. Supremacy will be measured in terms of power to control and use minds.

People will use their talents to diminish and destroy the other, rather than to create peace and harmony in the world. They will use all their powers to strangle the truth and exterminate those who believe in the unity of consciousness and harmony. They will obscure the truth and truthful people using mundane and insignificant subjects like sex and money, by cunning use of morality to put someone down. *Chhaya vairi* works through minds this way. It will make someone believe that being against something or someone is the right thing.

Never for a moment do people realise their fall in frequency because of that. Acceptance and contentment are the signs of a spiritually mature human being. Concepts, prejudices, anger, hatred, jealousy, and revenge are signs of instability, insecurity, and ignorance of truth. But, *chhaya vairi* makes them feel as though they are soldiers. When they fall in frequency, *chhaya vairi* simply abandons them. It uses and throws people. We can expect ideological warfare based on such belief systems sooner or later.

So, what is the remedy? The goodness factor!

The goodness factor is the selflessness factor. It depends on one's unselfish contribution to the world. It should be contribution without expectations. Governments especially should function on one factor, the goodness factor. The more one contributes individually, positively, the governments should reward with no taxes, and free healthcare, education, travel, etc. Governments should adopt all those who are good. Politics and positions should also be based on the goodness factor. All assessments, rewards, and recognition should be based on the goodness factor. Education should be based on the goodness factor as well. Everything should depend on the goodness factor. Only this is the effective antidote for the virus called *chhaya vairi*."

CHAPTER 5

EXPENSIVE IGNORANCE

Greedy for more, I, Mahendra Manu, asked *Swamiji*, "Can you please reveal any story that *Gurudeva* shared with you?" Kripananda thought for a while and said, "He highlighted the perils of gossip and slander through the following story."

"It was a small, beautiful, serene village with about ninety dwellings. In the center of the village, there was a temple. A young, handsome priest lived there and maintained the temple. He was friendly with all the villagers who were very fond of him. He used to attend to the villagers' minor needs and gave help and advice whenever needed. Also, the villagers shared their food and other materials with him, for they considered him as family. Thus, all lived happily in that village.

There was a young, beautiful widowed woman, living in a house not too far from the temple. She kept herself aloof from most of the villagers. Everyone considered her unfriendly and did not bother to enquire about her well-being ever. Early one morning, the villagers saw the young priest coming out from the house of the young woman. This surprised them, but they ignored it. The same scene got repeated following day, and then every day. Some villagers ignored it, thinking it was not their business, but others started to gossip amongst themselves. Some people warned the priest about the alienation developing between him and the villagers, but he merely smiled.

Soon some of the villagers took it upon themselves to slander the young priest's reputation. Some people also directly addressed their concerns with him. The priest, however, did not change his ways. He continued to visit the young widow every night, without fail. Nobody knew what transpired there, but people started brewing a scandal. Soon, they labelled the priest as immoral, and stopped supporting him. The priest reciprocated to their indifference with silence. A few months went by. The gap between the priest and the villagers widened. The priest continued to visit the woman, often carrying household materials. People even decided that they were secretly married. Some branded her as an immoral woman who had lured the innocent priest.

One evening, the villagers saw the young priest taking a doctor to her house. They speculated that the woman could be pregnant, and experiencing labor pains. The doctor visited the woman daily for a few days. One morning, the villagers saw that a horse-drawn cart had stopped at the woman's house with a few workers in it. The doctor and the priest appeared at the door and behind them the helpers carried the lifeless body of the woman covered in a white cloth. The villagers were surprised at this sight. While the body was getting loaded in the cart, some villagers asked the doctor how she had died.

The doctor replied, "The woman was suffering from leukaemia and she was at the last stage. Out of compassion towards this lonely and ill woman, I informed the priest about her state. He volunteered to assist her. She made him promise that he would not let anyone know about her ailment. He kept his promise and tried his best to give her some solace during her last days on earth. He used to fulfil her smallest desires if he could afford it. He was with her until her last breath."

The villagers were sad to hear this. They regretted being judgmental. Guilt gnawed at them within. They spoke amongst themselves. "We suspected a good man. How frail and fragile are our minds! We are worse than devils to suspect a good man for being immoral. We have committed the worst possible sin by tarnishing the reputation of a noble man." All the villagers repented their behaviour.

One day, some of them went to meet the priest with their heads hanging in shame. They said, "Forgive us, O noble priest, we did not know you or your intentions well, let alone your nobility of mind. Pardon the error we made." The priest said, "Never mind. I do not keep any negative feelings in my mind. I believe in purity and peace of mind. So, there is nothing to forgive from my side. It is you who need to forgive yourselves. I would like to offer you some help in understanding existence and removing your ignorance, because everything you think, say, or do in life has a price, a karmic price."

The villagers were willing to do anything to get the priest's pardon and eliminate their guilt. They agreed. The priest gave each one of them a pillow stuffed with cottonwool and told them, "Take it to the top of the hill behind this temple. When you reach the top, tear open the pillow cover and spill out all the cottonwool. Bring me back the empty pillow covers." The villagers climbed the hill with happiness and relief. They did exactly what the priest had asked them to do. When they brought back the empty pillow covers, he gave them fresh pillow covers and said, "Now, I would like you to climb the hill once more. Take these pillow covers and fill them with all the cottonwool that you had earlier spilled on the hilltop."

The villagers thought for a while and said, "This is impossible. The cottonwool that was spilled from the pillows has already been carried by the wind in all directions. It is impossible to collect it back." The priest said, "Exactly. So are the words that you spoke about me and the ailing woman. Can you take back the words that you spoke against us? The wind has taken them to many ears. You can never repay the karmic debt of your ignorance. If you can repent, as well as reverse all that you said and did against us, you can expect some relief in the bad karma that you have earned.

There is a price for everything that you say and do. There is a heavy price to pay for your ignorance. When you talk badly about someone, understand that you are adding karmic debt on yourself and your family. Your children will unnecessarily have to bear the burden of your ignorance. No thought, expression, or action is ever wasted. Everything has a karmic price. I have unhooked myself from your actions which I had no control over, anyway. I will not suffer for it. You must compensate for all that you said and did, not only to me, but also to someone who is not even in her body to forgive you."

His words shook the villagers, and with the result the whole village soon became a haven of kindness and compassion where no one ever uttered anything against anybody ever after. If at all someone attempted to express something negative, the others stopped them, relating this incident.

CHAPTER 6

THE PEAK OF EMPTINESS

Kripananda related a final story recounted by *Gurudeva*, and its significance, which I, Mahendra Manu, describe below.

The Master sat on the rock. Five disciples sat on a cloth spread on the ground, expecting the profound transfer of knowledge from the Guru. *Gurudeva* said, "What I am going to tell you may sadden some of you. But inevitability cannot be changed."

The disciples reacted with silence or surprise.

The Master continued, "I am leaving my body. Before I leave, I shall give all of you the highest and the noblest gift any Guru could give to a disciple. I shall give that to you. I give you **emptiness**. Go. Go into this wide world. Use your knowledge to walk the path of mysteries. Use your acquired knowledge more for the benefit of others and less for yourself. If you use it for yourself, it may become your addiction. It may affect your naturalness. It may develop your ego. It may deviate you from your path. If you use it for the world and not for yourself, you will always remain in awareness of who you really are and what your purpose is in the world where all paths lead to Liberation. You may do any work to earn a living. But never sell God. God never asks for explanations. Hence, always remain in gratitude to God and never sell God."

With these words, the Master left his mortal abode.

Emptiness is the most sacred and the most divine state. It is difficult to achieve, and even more difficult to maintain. Life is a constant flow. Time never stands still. While we exist in this borrowed body which is glorified by our identifications, we float in delusions of doership. We own our thoughts, words and actions. When the results of all these are completely beyond our control, we suffer. Very few achieve realisation. For many, ignorance wraps them and takes them further into darkness. This is the state of our world, and especially in the time of Kali.

The peak of emptiness is realisation. At the peak of emptiness, all identities dissolve. All deities dissolve. All relationships dissolve. Guru and disciple become one in consciousness. Thus, we become one with the supreme consciousness. That state takes time and effort.

"Seek nothing. Ask nothing." That is the realisation. Do we know what to seek or ask? Everything is provided at the right time. It cannot come a day before or a day after. It will come only at the right time! Seek nothing. Everything is provided. Be available. Be empty so that nature can fill in. Silence. Silence. Silence. All you need to practice is silence. Look within and just stay in the state of silence.

An average seeker usually has no clue as to what exactly he is seeking to achieve. A true Master has full awareness. When liberation is the only aim and when that motive also dissolves, grace beckons. When the accumulated bags of karma are an impediment to clarity at every stage of life, ignorance has to be corrected with disciplined practices. When disciplined practices cleanse our inner space, liberation dawns on the horizon of our consciousness. The peak of emptiness becomes the refuge.

Before he left, Kripananda asked me, "Were you with him when he left the body?"

I said, "No. He sent all of us to different locations on different errands, and silently expanded beyond the body."

"I am not surprised," replied Kripananda.

"But *Gurudeva* is with me always," I replied. "There is not a single moment when I do not remember him. Distance between minds is the real distance. Distance between bodies is no distance at all."

CHAPTER 7

THE PATH OF THE PATHLESS

Kripananda ended his reminiscences with a spiritual discourse by *Gurudeva* which is outlined below.

A baby is born. A beautiful baby. Everyone is happy. Joyous atmosphere in the house. It overflows into the neighborhood. Visitors come to see the newborn. They congratulate its parents, bring them gifts. A new journey of a soul in a new body began there! A small body was carefully created inside the womb of the mother. All organs were assembled properly. Nerves, muscles and veins were attached properly. The spine was created first and then the other organs. Brain, heart, lungs and intestines were put in their proper place. The parents who took all the credit for the beautiful baby, had nothing to do with any of these. Divinity made everything. Divinity put everything in its place to accomplish a pre-determined journey and make sure it can withstand the wear and tear of the total journey till its karmic end. The product was also packaged well and everyone agreed that it is indeed attractive! What brilliant craftsmanship! Everything in proper order! This is human life. Extremely perishable, but brilliantly beautiful.

Each entity has its own beauty. Even a tiny ANT is specific. All are "hand-made", with extreme care. There are no two products alike! Every package comes with a specific duration or, in commercial terms - shelf-life. Birth and death are simultaneously decided. There are no surprises, no accidents. Karma is the contract, the shopping list. Body, mind and intellect must exist together as long as the specified karma is accomplished. When karma is finished, the body is terminated. There is no tragedy attached to it. There is no belongingness to earth. There is nothing to cry for. There is nothing we can own. We are just like tourists here.

The child's parents had nothing to do with the child's karma, or the shopping list. They had no clue. They never decided their child. Assuming ownership, they started taking decisions on the life of the child after it was born. They refused to accept that they have no role to play in the child's life, except to provide an environment for it to grow and express itself. That is it! Nothing more. They could not control its thought pattern or the usual minor illnesses that it contracted from time to time from the earth. They had no clue about its natural tastes and inclinations. They did not know anything about the child, even what it will become when he (or she) grows up. They did not even know if their pretty child will behave as per the standards of an angel or a devil, upon growing up. They tried their best to cram the child with various kinds of conditionings – social, family, community, religious, and so on. The child accepted some, discarded some. Sometimes it rebelled. Sometimes it surrendered. Thus, the child expressed its own conditionings that it brought forward from past lives and fine tuned them with some of the newly acquired ones. Parents foolishly attributed its qualities and characteristics to themselves and their ancestors. Nobody knew the real truth, the third dimension of the entity at hand!

Every soul that walks the earth must pay rent. Just as we pay rent when we rent any space. We are temporarily renting the space on earth, to exhaust our karmas. We must pay for the space that we use. This is the debt that we owe to the Mother Earth! We walk on the earth as if we own it. We do not. Nobody does. We are only temporary custodians. We will pass on and someone else will walk over the same space on earth. While living, we must pay the debt in order to exit smoothly. If we do not pay our house rent, the landlord will get us arrested. Likewise, we will keep coming back until we pay the rent that we owe to Mother Earth. Mother Earth will arrest you and bring you back. Debt usually breeds more debt, sometimes with compound interest. So, each visit will cost us more.

The only way to pay our debts towards Mother Earth is to serve its children selflessly. Social service or self-less action of any kind, will relieve you from the accumulating dues. We must remember this always. Hence, some religions insist on regular, compulsory social service and paying a portion of their followers' income for the welfare of the poor. Compassion and sincere expressions of kindness will help clear the dues for sure. Talking and sharing opinions do not help. This is also for sure. Hands that help unconditionally are much holier than the lips that pray.

God needs nothing from you. God is self-sufficient. Do not try to bribe God either. He needs none of your rituals too. You have formed the rituals only for yourself. This was your effort in identifying the God aspect within yourself. All the rituals and spiritual practices including yoga, *pranayam* and meditation are your attempt to reach God. He is not outside of you. God is within you. If your spiritual practices cannot take you inside yourself, discard them. They are just another burden for you. Remember the golden rule of travel – the less the baggage, the more the comfort in your journey.

Destiny is equal to the original shopping list, the agenda for existence. Time is precious. Time is specified. Agenda is specified.

Where is the time to rest and procrastinate? Karma is exhausted in three states – the waking, dream and deep sleep state. Where the waking state cannot reach, the dream state does. Deep sleep state reminds man of his real home, beyond his currently acquired identities. Every pain and pleasure is part of the shopping list. The list that we had carefully or absentmindedly prepared during our past lives. God never interfered, just as your soul never interferes in your current life. Your soul just provides the fuel. It is neutral and unconditional. Your soul and God are one. Both are unconditional. Body is like a rented house, rented for a period. Mind and Intellect are its operating tools, such as electricity and water. Time is precious. Postponement is a waste of time. Escapism is also a waste of time. Equanimity in pain and pleasure will ensure a smooth sailing. Acceptance and adaptability are the key. Non-resistance is the method, because the shopping list is yours. You made it. You own it. Hence, you enjoy it. It is your life.

The food of the mind are the sense objects. Mind's sensors or sensory buds are our five senses. Minus the sense objects, the mind dissolves. Without food, the food sheath or the body cannot exist. Without procreation, earthly species cannot exist. Likewise, when the senses are in control, when sense objects do not lure us anymore, the mind dissolves. A mindless state is also a karma-less state. Mind is the operating tool of karma. Our existence shifts to the dharmic mode, when mind dissolves and karmas vanish. We exist purely for the sake of *dharma*. Duty towards existence.

Liberation is a state. By liberation we mean the end to the birth-death cycle. Liberation is a process. Entanglement is easy. It needs no deliberation. It happens by itself. Staying liberated requires extreme awareness, caution and equanimity over pain and pleasure, which includes physical and mental diseases.

Liberation is the path of pathlessness. Anything regular binds us as the mind easily feeds on it. Any ritual is a binding. Any habit is a binding. Any relationship, with the associated expectations, is also a binding. Living it staying detached or unattached is the key. This means perfect witness-hood in all three states – waking, dream and deep sleep state. Detachment is not aversion. It is also not under-performance or escapism. It is a perfect action with 100% application without attachment to the results of the action. The essential agenda points for liberation are as follows:

A. Accept your life as it is, because you created it. Act out your karma, without resistance. Whatever you are experiencing now, was your choice, consciously or unconsciously, probably the same way you are handling your life now. That means, a life of partial consciousness and partial unconsciousness. Luckily, all our vital functions are handled by our active sub-conscious mind. Otherwise, we will forget to breathe or pump our heart; or will create a heart-attack out of stress due to these matters!

B. Karma is happening, whether you like it or not. Each situation, event and experience of your life is formed out of it. Every thought, word and action, along with the glue of emotion, created your life, and is continuously creating further lives, right now, while you are at it. You have only your present to handle your karma. You can only do something now – tomorrow never exists in the now, and past is history and non-existent in the present. So, karma will happen whether you like it or not, the way it will happen in your present life, as per your individual experience level. It is up to you to accept it gracefully as a child of your own, or resist it and suffer the pains of resistance. Resistance also leads to further involvement, postponement and maybe an intensified experience too. Thus, we might as well act it out now, in its intended intensity, without resisting. Who knows what is in store for us tomorrow, and who cares?

C. The Immediate *Dharma*. Along with your karma, which is the purpose of your existence, is the *dharma*, which are your inherent duties. They are often inter-linked and difficult to segregate. *Dharma* of a mother is to take care of the children that are born through her. The first is the *dharma* towards own family members, such as a husband towards his wife and the wife towards her husband. Likewise, father, mother, husband, wife, children, brother, sister, grandparents, so on and so forth. One should handle one's *dharma* with utmost care and application. When each operates with kindness and compassion, we see happy families and happy families make happy society. For this, we should completely discard pretension and our expressions should become sincere and honest. When we do something, it should be with 100% application, devotion and sincerity. *Dharma* liberates man. Performing *dharma* to the best of one's capacity certainly liberates the man and makes his life worthwhile. Regrets will vanish and guilt will not bind his feet like chains tied to the earth. Performing *dharma* in the unit level is essential for liberation.

D. *Dharma* towards the society. This is the third and final. When we also take care of the social needs within the best of our ability, we become completely liberated. This means, taking care of the poor and the needy, birds and animals, and the old and sick. Protecting the environment around our house, our street, the way we can. We are only temporary custodians of our property. We will leave it all here and go. We will carry nothing abroad, when we die. So, handle them carefully and return it to the landlord in good condition, so that your dues are in control. You will have to pay for all your indiscriminate thoughts, words and action. Remember this well.

When we are comfortable with our own existence and when we operate comfortably in all the three capacities, such as individual karma, individual *dharma* and the social *dharma*, without expectations or emotions of ownership, we will stay liberated while living.

The simplest operating levels are purity and faith. Purity in thoughts, words and actions. This also means self-less-ness in thoughts, words and actions. Faith in oneself and existence, and non-resistance, irrespective of our existing realities. This will make your mind like a shining mirror, without any dust or finger prints. The more shining the mirror is, the better is the image. No image stays in a mirror permenantly. It vanishes when the object departs. Mirror remains objective always. Mirror never follows the object, nor does it capture and store an image, even if the image in front is celestial. It stays neutral all the time. Likewise, if our mind stays completely unattached to any sense object, it stays liberated all the time. Senses will not be bound to any sense object either. They will enjoy and detach, continuously and consistently. Images will come and go, people and situations will come and go. We will be firmly rooted in our own existence and liberation.

All are individuals, sometimes operating on a collective level. This is situational. People come together for a purpose and depart when the project is completed. Emotions based on relationships make it painful to part. They also chain the feet of the being to the realms of earth and similar situations eternally. We keep coming back. Emotions are anti-liberation. We should feel, because we have the faculties to feel. We should act dutifully, but, we should never be "emotional" in a way that leads to procrastination and eventual depression.

Be aware of a fundamental truth. When a soul assumes a body, it operates within the characteristics of the body that it has assumed. When a soul operates in a lion's body, it operates or behaves as a lion, fully. Every entity in the whole universe expresses such characteristics. A man is a man. An angel is an angel. None comparable to another. Within the commonness, there is diversity. There is unity as well as diversity. So, when an entity expresses itself in a human body, it expresses the general nature of humans including decay and death. It will express all the strengths and weaknesses of humans. None can be immune to the basic nature attached to a particular specie. When an entity, using the assumed body, evolves beyond the needs of the assumed body, it liberates itself. Still, it is a continuous process of constant vigilant attention, rooting firmly in one's soul.

The mind-intellect-body will always lure the consciousness. When a man shifts from mind, intellect and body to his consciousness, depending on his levels of consistency, liberation happens. So, each entity has a common behavioral pattern of its own. Its needs or requirements are also the same. A cow needs grass. It does not need meat. A tiger needs meat to survive. Grass will not suit its need. An angel operates in a plane in which it is supposed to operate. Its powers of operation are purpose-bound. Everyone's operating levels are purpose bound. So, let us shed the idea that some humans of higher evolution are immune to the nature of humans. There could be a degree of variation. Basic nature of species cannot be changed. If nature need to be changed, the body and species should be changed too. When a tiger takes birth as a man, it will look and feel like a man, even though it may behave like a tiger at times. Yet, all the attached strengths and weaknesses attached to humans will be definitely displayed. Assuming any body will also mean assuming its nature and characteristics. Every body is bound by the usual processes of Mother Nature, such as wear and tear and eventual annihilation.

A Few Roadsigns on the Path of Pathlessness
- There are no do's or don'ts. Just live a selfless life, without resisting, judging or criticising oneself and others.
- There are no binding expectations, including expectation for a specific result for one's word or action.
- Always operate rooted in the spine. Do not sway with fleeting emotions.
- Complete non-violence – in thought, word, action, food, as well as in all your other expressions.
- Respect and perform the individual karma as well as *dharma* towards own family and *dharma* towards the society, with perfect equanimity and zero expectation.
- Purity in thought, word and action. This also means perfect self-less-ness and equanimity in pleasure and pain. Serve selflessly. No discrimination at all, on any basis.
- Divinity is Simplicity. Lead a simple life full of love and benevolence. Always feed the hungry with what you have. Always protect the helpless, old and abandoned with what you have. See the spark of God in every being.
- Do not flaunt anything, be it your wealth, possessions, power, money, achievements, relations, relationships, contacts, or even *siddhis*. Lead a simple and unassuming life.

Remain grounded and simple in outlook and existence. Be benevolent to all and care for all. There is nothing to prove on earth. All that we earn here needs to be spent (left behind) here too.

- Do not worry about what you do not have. Rejoice at what you have. Never compare yourself with another.
- Avoid anything that binds you, irrespective of whether the habit is positive or negative. If you cannot live without something, it is definitely a binding for you. This could be even a bed tea or a particular person. It could even be your Guru. It could be an alcohol addiction or even meditation.
- Live in the present. Act in the present. Keep time. Do not waste even a moment, because, time in existence is specified, measured and un-extendable. Do what ever your current tasks are – right now – never postpone or procrastinate.
- Understand all individuals as karmic beings. Everyone lives their karma. Each pattern is unique. Respect it.
- Never censor your thoughts. You are what you are. Accept yourself with all your strengths, weaknesses or "imperfections" that you think you have. In absolute sense, there are no imperfections.
- Observe. Be a witness to your own thoughts, words and actions at all times. You will stay liberated from all of it. Objective observation is liberating. Involvement is binding. Remember this always.
- Every being on earth has a definite purpose. No creation is by accident. Respect every being, animate and inanimate. Never disturb or destroy. Live and let live.
- Emotions, guilt and regrets are ropes that bind us to earth. Have nothing to do with it.
- Love is the most beautiful of all feelings. Express it unconditionally.

- Do everything with full application, sincerity and objective commitment. Never do anything absent mindedly or half-heartedly. Avoid all such actions. You will always be true to yourself and life will be regret free, ego free and fulfilling.
- In our path, Gurus are just roadsigns. Gurus are perfectly unconditional. They never bind a seeker to themselves. They never interfere in your experience or your journey. They never criticise, judge or censor. They are objective and truthful. Gurus never display their powers to attract and control. Gurus never demand anything from any seeker. Gurus lead a liberated existence and they lead the seeker to liberation as well.

CHAPTER 8

RULES OF THE TRADITION

The Do's
* All acts of kindness, compassion, unconditional love.
* Selfless service.
* Education for the sake of empowerment.
* Moderation in any kind of consumption, utilisation, and saving for future.
* Help the helpless without discrimination.
* Respect oneself and others.
* Respect *karma* and *karmic* beings of earth. Do not disrupt life in any way.
* Share without discrimination.
* Sharing food and knowledge should be considered as highest priority.
* Less luggage, easier travel.
* Truthful testimonials, no propaganda.
* No *Gurus* are higher than the tradition; Tradition is the highest.
* *Parabrahma* is our Supreme Guru. All Gods and Gurus are its representations. It is formless. Worship the formless that lives in all forms.
* Highlight the goodness in all, all have goodness in them.
* Always be grateful. Be grateful about all experiences of life. Everything is completion in some way.

* Inner space should always remain clean. The mind should be clean of vile thoughts, words, and memories of actions.

Don'ts

* Never abandon a friend or relative in distress.
* Never hurt any being.
* Never scandalise or talk badly even about your enemies. You attract their *karma* on yourself by doing so.
* Do not highlight your or another's imperfections.
* Never compromise on *sadhana* and surrender. They are both significant at each level of stability.
* No violence in thoughts, words, and actions. We do not know their *karmic* configuration.
* Never criticise, condemn, or judge. They will all happen to you, too.
* Do not kill any being, except in self-protection, while evolving. At a later stage, divinity will guard your body. Character assassination is equal to murder. Karmic effect is the the same.

CHAPTER 9

QUOTES FROM ATMANANDA

One-word answers from Atmananda

1. What is the reason for poverty? –**"Inner Poverty."**

2. What is the reason for ailments? –**"Suppression."**

3. What hinders liberation? –**"Ignorance."**

4. What causes sorrows? –**"Inner darkness."**

5. What is success? –**"Contentment."**

6. What is the highest human expression? –**"Compassion."**

7. What is the sign of a true seeker? –**"Patience."**

8. What is downfall in spiritual journey? –**"Desires."**

9. What is being absolute? –**"No Mind."**

10. What is the ultimate? –**"Nir Beeja - No Seed state."**

Short quotes of Atmananda

* "Experiences die when the experiencer dissolves."
* "Those who invoke and maintain emotions are the enemies of Liberation."
* "Friends who put prejudices into your mind should be considered as enemies."
* "Those who stay with you against all odds should never be abandoned."
* "Greed breeds crime."
* "Understand you are a unique expression of the divine and you need to do nothing about it."
* "Just like fire uses materials to express itself, the Source uses matter (bodies) to express itself."
* "Tradition sometimes seems to be cruel, only out of kindness and compassion for the seeker."
* "In the lap of a Grand Tradition, life eternally flows."
* "Gratitude and surrender get expressed as temples. Deities happen."
* "The only path possible is the path ahead of us."
* "True spirituality is obvious to the inner eye, but always invisible to the mind."
* "When the mind is conquered, all fears disappear."
* "Every communion is important, every meeting has meaning."
* "When faith nullifies the suffering of pains, man takes another step towards Liberation."
* "As long as thoughts exist, you exist; only if thoughts exist, you exist."

Long Quotes of Atmananda

* "I am not here to experience anything. I am here to prove that experience is nothing but a projection of the experiencer; just like the waking state reality is a projection of consciousness which has nothing to do with any of the three states."

* "Desires maintain thoughts. Thoughts maintain mind. Liberation is a state of no thoughts and hence no mind, let alone desires."

* "Prejudices make the good look bad while love makes the bad look good. Our world is as we are, and not what it is."

* "Acceptance is the first step towards Liberation. The seed of Liberation starts sprouting only from the *nirvikalpa samadhi* state. Yet, states are not stable unless carefully nurtured."

* "You are a complete incarnation like any other. You are not creating or uncreating anybody's destiny. All are complete incarnations that came here for experiences and expressions. Their only bonding and binding factor would be emotions."

* "Life is all flavors. Life must be taken in its totality. Nothing is absolutely right or absolutely wrong. Karma dwells on relative truth, experiences, and expressions. Karma carves destiny from nothingness."

* "If you consider consciousness as spirit, it is beyond mind and emotions. Soul is beyond consciousness too."

* "You as consciousness are neither the doer nor the

experiencer. Unattached, you are witnessing both. The soul is witnessing the witness."

* "Expectations maintain the mind. Expectations distort the truth."

* "Doubts, like gossip, is deadly poison. Even a drop of it can kill faith and push the seeker backwards in evolution of awareness. Doubts reverse spiritual progress."

* "Do not be afraid of friends becoming enemies, and enemies becoming friends. Both are bound by illusions of mind. The truth is that everyone is oneself."

* "Those who pretend, criticise, judge, malign, and condemn others are usually hypocrites. They are either afraid to be authentic, or are jealous of authentic people. They are even afraid or ignorant about their originality or the law of karma. Deficiency creates anger, jealousy, and prejudices. Society is full of such hypocrites. They only see what they are programmed to see. Absolute truth is not accessible to them. They cling on to relative truth and form their opinions. Do not waste your time on them. They keep you prejudiced and bound with their ignorance of reality."

* "If you fear criticism, you will be a compromiser. You will not have growth and evolution. If you have no fears, you will have growth in awareness. Those with firm conviction on eternal truth will never revert to hypocrisy. They will not fear enemies."

* "There are no children or adults. There are no men or women.

All are incarnations and its stages. Categorisation is in the mind, so is separation and alienation. When man begins to see Chaitanya of every being, there is only the light. There are no divisions. Chaitanya appears through forms and stages of forms. Hence there are no children or adults, men or women. There is only the eternal brightness."

* "We need nothing from the earth. We already have whatever we need. We are the earth and we will one day return back to the earth."

* "Vision has more value than sight. The right vision is only through the inner eyes. What eyes can see is relative truth bound by time, space, and various factors. What the inner eye sees is absolute, undistorted truth beyond time and space."

* "I shall talk to the world through the positive transformation and metamorphosis of my consistent companions."

* "Fire symbolises heat and light. Fire symbolises life."

* "Soul is one. Manifestations are many. When the soul manifests into many, normal eyes will see it as many. This is the illusion that binds us and makes us suffer. This is the ignorance that stands as a wall between us and the Supreme Brahma. One soul manifests through all beings because each body helps a different experience."

* For every mother, her child is the most precious. Not only for humans. It is the same for all beings. Before killing the child of any being – humans, animals or birds – please remember the unforgivable agony of its loving mother."

* "Take care of the sick, the old, the abused, and the abandoned of all species. This will elevate your awareness. Let there be no gender and species differentiation in your mind. Lack of differentiation means freedom."

* "Desires are traps, one spontaneously leads to the other. They also change forms and nature. Desires cause illusions and hallucinations. They takes us further and further away from Liberation."

* "No words are wasted. No actions are wasted. Everything bears fruit at some point in time. The Tradition takes care of it."

* "Love and respect all beings. Every being feels, just like we do. Sensitiveness is a real virtue. Have plenty of it. Have plenty of Love within. Let love overflow from you all the time. Love all and serve all – your life will become total and complete. Remain blessed."

* "There is nothing to 'gain'. Empty-handed we came, empty handed we leave. We cannot 'own' anything. All the competition of this world is a product of ignorance, total ignorance."

* "Love eternally flows as Guru Tattwa. We need eyes to see its eternal splendor."

* "The journey from being mankind to the state of a kind man is not difficult. Awareness is the key."

* "Himalayas – the abode of everything precious. Destination

to many. Life to a lot."

* "Time is unstoppable. Life is transitory. The gush of the river reminds us of the eternal flow of transitory time."

* "Love is the food of life. Nothing can substitute this food. Our world is starving – for love."

* "The mind poses conflicts. Conflicts create stress. Ego reins. Liberation slips past."

* "Who knows who comes to you with a begging bowl? It could be God."

* "For the poor and the hungry, food is God. There is nothing more noble and holy than giving food to the hungry."

* "What is life without kindness? What is life without compassion? We are all just visitors here."

* "The mind races after changes and speed in spirituality. True spirituality is elusive."

* "More luggage is more discomfort. Less luggage makes the transit easier."

* "Tolerance and co-existence make life worthwhile. Love transcends everything."

* "Tradition never leaves the hand of the true seeker. Gurus transcend oceans of existence to be with a true seeker. This is the promise of the Tradition where eligibility is the only factor."

* "You gave me this life. You gave me this breath. This life belongs to You. I do not exist. Only You exist, my Supreme Lord."

* "Tradition brought systems for Liberation. Systems often bound ignorant humans."

* "Every bit of darkness is afraid of brightness. Even a tiny spark of light means death for darkness. Hence, darkness will try its best to avoid light. Extreme conviction and focus are required to bring light to life and to keep it alive always."

* "Greed breeds corruption. It contaminates the entire society, shakes its integrity, and leads it to its doom."

GLOSSARY

acharya - teacher
adharma - unrighteousness
aghori - an intense and radical form of spiritual practice
ahankara - pride
ahimsa - non-violence
akshaya patra - inexhaustible vessel
amrit - the celestial nectar
ananda - happiness
asooya - jealousy
atma - soul
Baba - Fatherly figure. Used as a mark of respect.
Bharat - ancient India
bhiksha - alms
Brahma muhurta - The time between 3 a.m. and 6 a.m. (the time of Brahma heavenly time) – considered ideal time for spiritual practices
brahmachari - celibate
brahmacharya - bachelor student
brahmins - Hindu priestly class
chakras - energy centers
charpoy - A light bedstead made of wood and coir rope
chhaya - relative truth or even illusion
chhaya vairi - shadow enemy
dakshina - donation or offering
danda - staff
darshan - divine sighting of a saint or a deity
deeksha - initiation
dharma - righteousness or one's righteous duty
dharmic - based on dharma
dharmo rakshati rakshitaha - Dharma protects those who protect dharma
dhoti - A garment consisting of a piece of cloth tied around the waist, andand extends to cover the legs.
dhuni - An ever-burning sacred fire
dhyana - meditation
ghat - A flight of steps leading down to a river
ghee - clarified butter
grihastha - householder
gurudakshina - the tradition of repaying one's teacher or guru after a period of study or the completion of formal education, or an acknowledgment to a spiritual guide
Gurudeva - Revered Master

gurukul - A residential school system where students live as part of the Master's family and serve and learn under him

himsa - violence

homa, havan - fire ceremony

jatadhaari - person with long braids of matted hair

kaala sarpa dosha - severe curse of the snake gods

kaama - terrestrial ambition

kamandalu - pot

krodha - anger

Kundalini shakti - divine feminine energy

linga - A divine symbol of Lord Shiva

lobha - greed

loka - realm or sphere of existence

mada - lust

Maharishi - a great sage

manana - contemplation

matsarya - competition

Maya - the grand illusion

mind-matter - mind, intellect and ego, the processors of our system

moha - attachment

naadis - meridians

Nava, Nav - The number nine

Navnath, Navnaths, Nava Naths - the nine Nath saints

paduka - sacred footprints of the Master

Parabrahma - supreme unmanifested consciousness

param buddhu - most ignorant

parivrajaka - spiritual wanderer

prana - life force

prana pratishtha - a ritual where the energies of the presiding deity are induced into the idol

pranayama - regulate the life force

rajas - passion, active, confused

rasta - road

saboori - patience

sadhaka - spiritual practitioner

sadhana - spiritual practices

sadhus - renunciate monks

sahasraara - the crown chakra – the energy center at the crown of the head

samadhi - conscious exit of the soul from the physical body accomplished by yogis to merge with the supreme Consciousness when their time has come

samhara - dissolution

samsara - mundane existence

samskaaras - inclinations

Sanatana Dharma - The eternal religion

sannyasa - renunciation

Sapta Rishis - the seven illustrious sages

sari - Long traditional garment worn by Hindu women

sattva - goodness, constructive, harmonious

shanta - peaceful

Shweta Rishis - the council of the pure white sages who are considered the twenty-one pillars of Earth

Shyambavi mudra - eyebrow center gazing

Siddhartha - Gautama Buddha

siddhi, siddhis - spiritual powers

sookshma - subtle

srishti - creation

stithi - preservation

swadharma - one's dharma by birth

Swamiji - a respectable address for an ordained monk

tamas - darkness, destructive, chaotic

tamasic - inertial

Tapt Kund - hot water spring

tulsi - holy basil

Uttarayana - The day after the winter solstice when the sun starts on its course towards the northern hemisphere

vanaprastha - seclusion

yoga bhrashta - fall from grace

yoga siddhi - power of yoga

Printed in Poland
by Amazon Fulfillment
Poland Sp. z o.o., Wrocław